We dedicate this book to Anita Lyons Gage, Maryellen Montgomery-Freeman, and to the late Fr Eric Freed.

Biblical Time Out of Mind

Biblical Time Out of Mind
Maps, Myths & Memories

Tom Gage &
James A. Freeman

Biblical Time Out of Mind:
Myths, Maps & Memories
by Tom Gage and James A. Freeman
© 2016 Tom Gage and James A. Freeman
Cune Press, Seattle 2016
First Edition
2 4 6 8 9 7 5 3

Hardback	ISBN 9781614571346	$34.95
Paperback	ISBN 9781614571353	$21.95
eBook	ISBN 9781614571360	$ 9.99
Kindle	ISBN 9781614571377	$ 9.99

Library of Congress Cataloging-in-Publication Data

Names: Gage, Tom. | Freeman, James A.
Title: Biblical time out of mind : myths, maps, and memories / Tom Gage and James A. Freeman.
Description: Seattle : Cune Press, LCC, 2015. | Includes bibliographical references and index.
Identifiers: LCCN 2015006497| ISBN 9781614571346 (hardback) | ISBN 9781614571353 (pbk.) | ISBN 9781614571360 (ebook) | ISBN 9781614571377 (kindle)
Subjects: LCSH: Bible—Controversial literature. | Mythology. | Bible—Evidences, authority, etc.
Classification: LCC BS533 .G27 2015 | DDC 221.6/7—dc23
LC record available at http://lccn.loc.gov/2015006497

Other Books in the Bridge Between the Cultures Series from Cune Press:
Gulen's Dialogue on Education by Tom Gage

East of the Grand Umayyad	by Sami Moubayed
The Plain of Dead Cities	by Bruce McLaren
Steel & Silk	by Sami Moubayed
Syria - A Decade of Lost Chances	by Carsten Wieland
The Road from Damascus	by Scott C. Davis
A Pen of Damascus Steel	by Ali Ferzat

Coming Soon:
Leaving Syria	by Bassam S. Rifai
Art in Exile	by Natasha Hamarneh Hall
Gate of Peace, Gate of Wind	by Patrick Hilsman
Quwatli	by Sami Moubayed

 Cune Press: www.cunepress.com | www.cunepress.info

Table of Contents

Introduction
Table of Illustrations   9
Maps of the Ancient Mediterranean   10
A Note:
What's the Caliphate to California?   17

Chapters
1 Biblical Time out of Mind   18
2 Historicizing the Past:
   Directionality, Westward the Hyksos   41
3 Appropriation of History   56
4 Narratization of Society   72
5 Narratological History -
   Historical Narratology   91
6 Sociality of Knowledge   113
7 Maps & Territory   135

Resources
Timeline   166
Appendix   172
Notes   175
Acknowledgements   195
Index   196
Authors   200

Table of Illustrations

Maps of the Eastern Mediterranean Sea
A From Rome to Babylon   10
B From Macedonia to Krete   12
C Showing MISR / Egypt   13
D From Aleppo to Jerusalem   15

Photographs
1 "Herodotus of Halicarnassus"   33
   Public statue, Bodrum Castle. Present day Turkey.

2 "Temple of Saturn/Baal in Rome."   66
   Roman Forum, Rome, Italy.

3 "Canaanite/Phoenician Temple."   130
   Kommos, Krete. Circa 1150 BCE. Present day Greece.
   Excavated by Dr J. Shaw.

Note
Photograph #3: In Rome, Saturn was worshipped as
Baal by Phoenician / Punic citizens.

Credits
Maps were composed by Dr Matthew Derrick, cartographer.
Photos were taken by Tom Gage.

Eastern Mediterranean
From Rome to Babylon

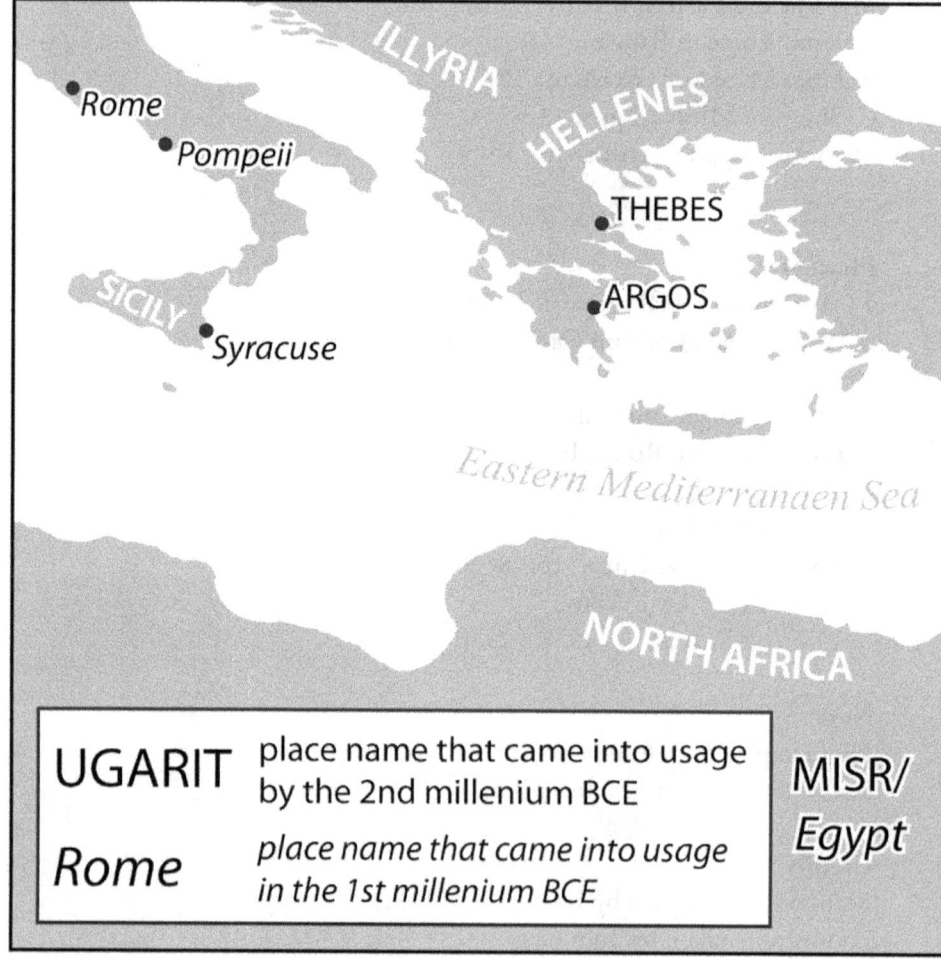

(2nd Millennium featured in upper case. 1st Millennium in italics.)

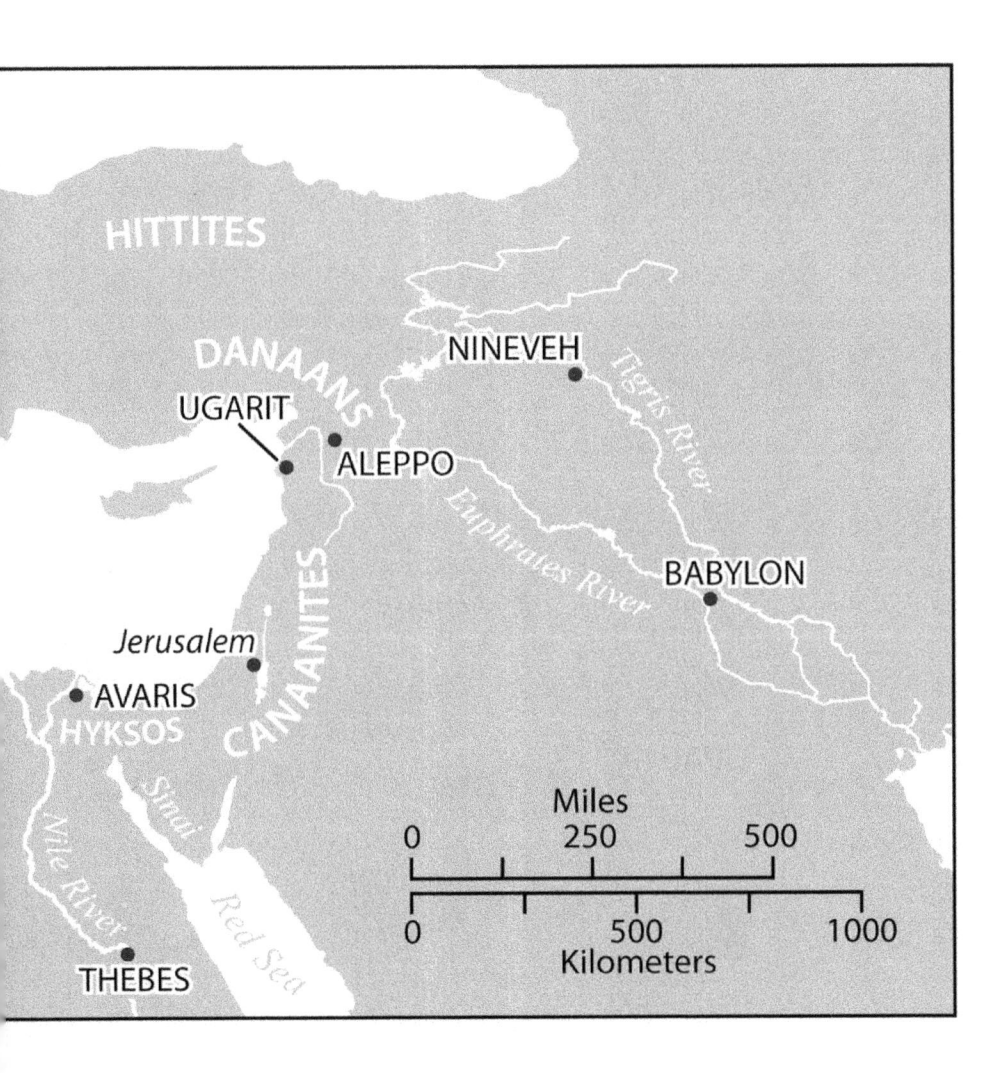

Eastern Mediterranean
From Macedonia to Krete

(2nd Millennium featured in upper case. 1st Millennium in italics.)

Eastern Mediterranean
Showing MISR / Egypt

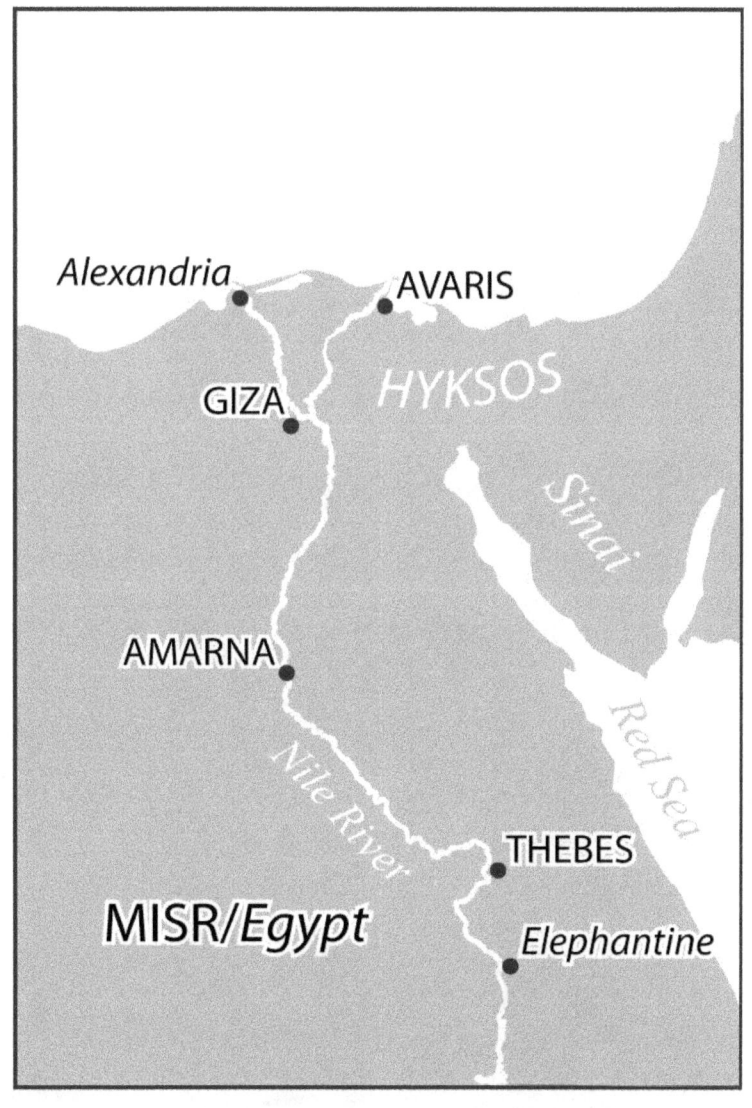

(2nd Millennium featured in upper case. 1st Millennium in italics.)

Eastern Mediterranean
From Aleppo to Jerusalem

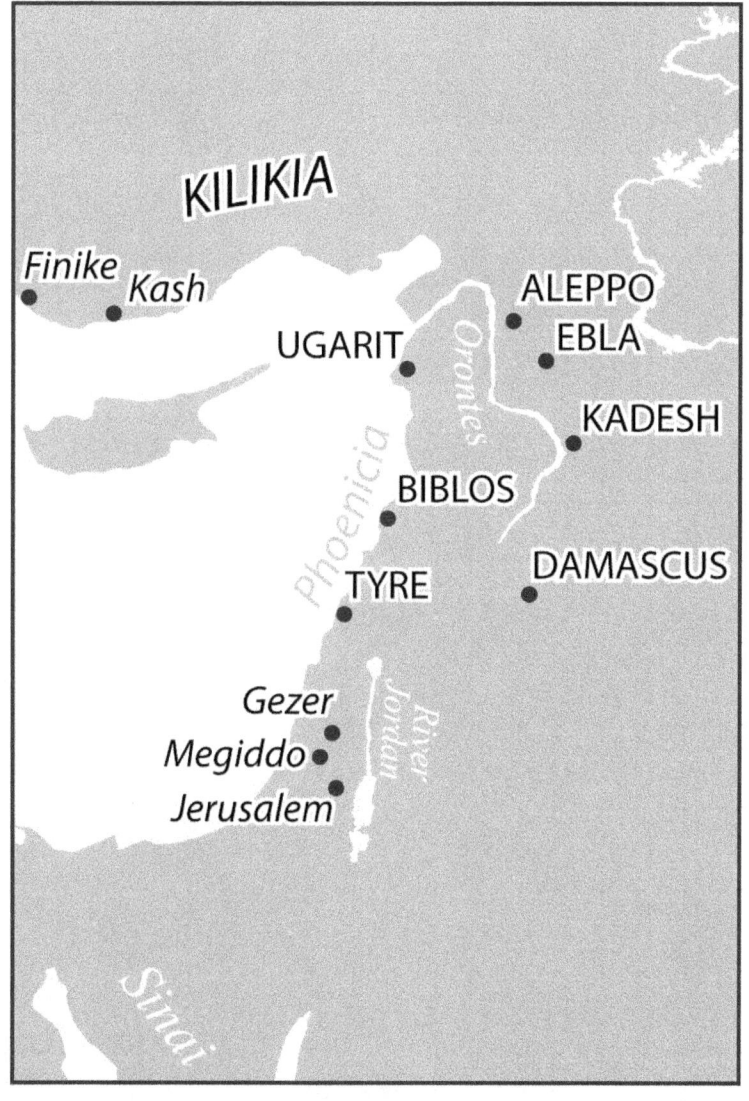

(2nd Millennium featured in upper case. 1st Millennium in italics.)

A Note
What's the Caliphate to California?

Northwestern Semitic languages have several features distinctly different from English. This makes difficult spelling English words translated from Hebrew, Aramaic, and Arabic. Words generally include three consonants that form a root, a feature hence referred to as triconsonantalism. A reader of a long passage who encounters "m-l-k," devoid of vowels, will recognize a concept of relating to kingdom or monarchy. Both authors come from California. The word "California" is a portmanteau, composed two Arabic roots, the first "Kh-l-f," the general idea of a successor, a title of a religious leader. The second part of the State name derives from "f-r-n," an Arabic noun denoting "oven" or "hearth." California means "the hearth of the Caliph," accordingly named by Cortes, or his followers, when sighting a landmass across the gulf that bears his name today. Cortes came from al-Andalusia, the region of Spain that was heavily populated by Muslims, whose remaining kingdom had been defeated the year Columbus set sail for the New World.

Spelling Semitic in English words requires the translator to add optional vowels or of diphthongs to benefit readers. The English alphabet was inherited from Rome, which was heavily influenced by the Etruscan and the Greeks, who got it from the Phoenicians. Each advance caused problems. For example the letters "C," "K," and "Q" actually come from Etruscan, whose people before the "Grandeur that was Rome" spoke each letter distinctly, though once inherited by Latins was expressed in a single phoneme such as the "C" in California.

Authors of many of our sources represented principal characters with several different spellings. We decided to spell the mythic heroes as Cadmus and Danaus, along with their tribal associations, yet at times readers will encounter variants on the same page. Among the sources cited in the Notes, many options confronted us: "Cadmus," "Cadmos," "Kadmus," "Kadmos," "Qadmus," and "Quadmus." The children of Cadmus appear in the *Bible* as "beneqadminites," and the excavated fortress in Greek Thebes is Cadmeia. A similar array occurs for Phoenix and for Danaus, the protagonist of Aeschylus' drama *The Suppliants*.

1
Biblical Time Out of Mind

Hands
Inside a cave in a narrow canyon near Tassajara
The vault of rock is painted with hands,
A multitude of hands in the twilight, a cloud of men's palms, no more,
No other picture. There's no one to say
Whether the brown shy quiet people who are dead intended
Religion or magic, or made their tracings
In the idleness of art; but over the division of years these careful
Signs-manual are now like a sealed message
Saying: "Look: we also were human; we had hands, not paws.
All hail
You people with the cleverer hands, our supplanters
In the beautiful country; enjoy her a season, her beauty, and come down
And be supplanted; for you also are human."
Robinson Jeffers [1]

WHOSE HANDS? WE ARE DESCENDED FROM PILGRIMS, immigrants, those from exoduses, and likely so are you. Thus, questions abound. From whence, from whom have we come? And which cultures and histories come closest to our ancestral truth? Are those truths objective, timeless? Are these sojourners' commandments relative to time and place?

These two pilgrims, authors here, seek to answer these large questions, with your help. Professor Tom Gage is a descendant of John Gage who landed at Plymouth in 1630: Fra Tomas Gage, John's cousin, landed in Vera Cruz in 1625. Prof. Gage's great grandfather was Civil War and Braddock/Carnegie Steel hero Captain Bill Jones.[2] James Freeman's ancestors, John Howland and others, likewise landed at the Plymouth, Massachusetts colony, arriving on the storied Mayflower in 1620, blown off their compass course for

Virginia, landing far to the north in the new world. This picaresque human theme unites us with every clan which has migrated for complex and sometimes simple motivations, such as historian Frederick Turner's famous immigration theory points: free land, escaping both religious persecution and criminal prosecution; economic opportunity, a fresh start. Like other pilgrims and even many indigenous folk who never left their home places, the Gages and the Freemans were weaned on treating the mythology of the three great Abrahamic religions as historical fact, just like many of you. Yet three other equally valid sources, Egyptian, Ugaritian and Greek, don't purport to impose God into their narratological histories.

We seek here to examine how congruent these cultures are with our own American ones. We sail into common waters where the Jewish faith is an important amalgam of a generating, ancient Hyksos source, adapted generously like Israeli couscous or Italian poi as food for thought. Migrating and non-migrating cultures have to eat as well as think, after all. The greatest mythographer of all, Joseph Campbell, sang a beautiful, common theme song of "mono-myth." When we crack the shell of any myth, any explanation of our creation, migration or exile, "it will always be the one, shape-shifting yet marvelously constant story that we find."[3] In these pilgrims' words, all myths tell the same kinds of stories, the one story really, the human story of our movements across the land, the rich and immortal legacies left behind, important and potentially uniting stories that have sometimes been forgotten.

We pilgrims have found abundant evidence of that which Bakhtin called the "unfinalized continuance of heteroglossia," a fluid language cacophony of speech and text, or "utterance" that continues unabated through the literature of real history cum literature, that literary manifestos, even the Old and New *Bibles*, historicize from fictions that are based on historical events like the real Hyksos exodus from Egypt in the 16th Century BCE. Such amalgams are many: from a "60-Minutes" television episode, chronicling a story of the Marsh Arabs of Iraq, Scott Pelly referenced an original Akkadian flood story, one a millennia before Noah and his famous Ark.[4]

Analysis of neo-myths like modern Mickey and Mighty Mouses, or Maxine Hong Kington's novel *Tripmaster Monkey*,[5] provide a narrative that reveals examples of an unfinalizable utterance. Yet, Maxine Hong Kingston's narrative is only a latter work of Chinese heteroglossia derived from Wu Ch'Eng-en's 16th Century novel *Journey to the West*,[6] which originated from the ur-myth of Tripitaka (CE 602-664), a Tang monk who journeyed to India for three baskets of Buddhist texts, which he brought home to spawn the new religion in his homeland.[7] We see that texts, even those purporting to be a record of objective history, are unfinalizable and that they grow, mutate and morph, as Bakhtin defined. Hence it is that Theodore Gastor in *Thespis*[8] holds that the four famous poems found at Ugarit, excavated in the 1920's, "The Poem of Aquat," "The Poem of King Krete," "The Poem of "Dawn and Dusk," and the bull god's "The Poem of "Baal," are written in Canaanite, a Northwestern Semitic dialect much older than Hebrew.[9] Passages from these four taproot poems stem directly into the Psalms of David.[10] The "Land of Milk and Honey" phrases have the same kind of second life as any myth narrative lacking an Ur-version. This regeneration evidences Milman Perry's thesis that fixed texts, like Homer's *Iliad*, derived first from fluid songs before scribes decoded the songs into epics.[11]

Generations of *rhapsodos* performed their repertory morphing lyrics until their songs were found and recorded by a Hesiod or Homer or an anonymous Hebrew author after returning from an eastern Exile. Likewise, Cyrus Gordon has shown, too, that Canaan songs echo throughout the *Pentateuch*.[12] We feel these echoes resonating their archaic way into at least five books of *The Old Testament*. It is a wonderfully rich but humanly-flawed subjective game of literary and historical "whisper down the lane" that we play here with you. Please come along with us, we scribes, and add your human, common-culture voice to the diverse discussion.

Our present thesis is that some anonymous scribe portrayed a lawgiver, Moses, who historicized a divine plan by spinning a Hebrew palimpsest upon a nearly half-millennium older Hyksos people's exodus. This earlier escape, well known to Egyptians and remembered darkly by mythologizing Greeks, occurred sometime after 1565 BCE. For the newly enfranchised and now imperial Egyptians, continually nudged northward their foreign oppressors, the pre-Hebrew Semites, eventually nudging westward along the coast of Anatolia until sometime between 1600s and 1300s when Hyksos Cadmus and his clan arrived in Greece with his alphabet, the earliest and seminal event recorded in the Parian Calendar.

These vengeful Egyptian nudgings of the Hyksos occupiers patterned a geographically reversed frog jumping, resulting from multiple surges commencing with Pharaoh Nebpehrire Ahmose I, 1550-1525 BCE, the name Ahmose itself a cognate echoing the Hebrew Lawgiver himself. We find that Hebrews progressively and extensively historicized earlier Canaanite myths. The ancient myth battle between the Sea, Yam of Ugarit, with the god Baal, was embedded directly as the story of Leviathan and Yahweh of the Psalms. This episode became a historical narrative with Yahweh opening the sea to allow a warrior king to escape Egypt. Drawing from Donald B. Redford's

Egypt, Canaan, and Israel in Ancient Times, four biblical traditions associate Hebrews with Egypt: Genesis 1 and 2; The Family of Nations in Genesis 10; Joseph; and Moses.[13]

We will follow, like an embittered Egyptian, the paths of these Hyksos people to wherever they lead, unflinchingly, creating what we already see as clear plausibility, asking the tough questions, like Socrates, who refused his forced exodus, drinking the hemlock instead, rather than recanting our proposed Hyksos genesis of much of what we mistakenly now take to be Hebrew, asking why, what if, and why not? We are driven, likewise, to answer the poet Jeffers' implicit question about whose hands have touched those metaphoric and literal cave walls, here in an ancient narrative far from extinct Esselen, California.

We'll trace the hands and artifacts of those who left indelible human imprints on Egypt and on Greece that need to be appreciated for what they were and for how they richly fund our histories, myth and literature to this day. We ask you to join us on this journey culminating at a common supper table. Our overarching thesis is that Egypt and Greek texts rival the primacy of Hebraic ones and that the earlier Hyksos exodus, a historical fact 300-400 years earlier than the myth of Moses and the Red Sea, provides the grounding for Hebrews historicizing the Hyksos myth. The secular author Josephus (37-100 CE) writing for his Jewish emigrant community to his new Roman audience buttressed Biblical lore by citing one of few Egyptian sources knowledgeable of the Hyksos. In Chapter 3, we explicate the social context of his dialogic rhetoric that conveyed his heritage, ignored by Greek and defamed by Roman historians in a culture of defied Caesars.[14]

Ironically, all the well-intended excavating by today's Israelis and Christians to validate these modifications and elaborations putting the Hebrews deep into the 2nd Millennium BCE have not turned up a single Troy, a Tiryns, a Pylos, or a Knossos that might have corroborated myth as historical fact. This does not diminish the heteroglossic reach of Joseph Campbell's "one human story," from the Hyksos people through the Egyptian to the Greek and Hebrew; in fact, the authors see this common history morphing into common literature, art, commerce, and ritual as an important thread of common modern heritage and culture.

A post-modern analogy might be a large group of strangers attracted to a fashionable club in New York City for a party honoring a celebrity. Initially, some of the strangers arriving early seek out commonalities or the familiar among the mixed culture while late comers, marking each other and sensitive to differences among the guests at the world table; until finding sameness join in the US, a uniting thread. But what if the honoree suffered individuation too, like any human of the earliest times, according to the Leaky family's compelling research, out of Africa, or from Mesopotamia, the golden cradle, where some other anthropologists believe that humanity prevailed? What if it could be demonstrated (and really has been) that one or both or any of many places from China to First Nations of the Americas inspired the prism of hues called civilization? What would the difference seekers, those bent on Othering, have to say? And what new celebration among those who had already once celebrated the common human bond of sameness, outweighing differences, would occur?

The Hyksos people were early at the Egyptian party, although not first, and have informed it since subsequently: while those bent on political territory and religious dogma might be shaken by this, we see the potential to unite, to find despite petty and not-so-petty differences, that common cultural thread that might help us all get along much better in the world. Peace is our transparent motivation here, that and human stewardship of the sustainable earth.

We know that myth, history, literature and religion blend to ground a significant proportion of the identity of not only collective cultures but also of the personal. This fusion often results in a psychology that unifies one culture against the Other to inspire patriotism, identity, and unintentionally to warp reality, an *espirit*, neuroses, and a socioses that leads to cultural triumphs but also to historic distractions such as war. A Golden Age thus glimmers from the past to galvanize clan, tribe, race, team, or nation. The authors here have seen this psychological, human trend in their personal lives in every endeavor from editing numerous anthologies to motivating the beer league softball team to repeat as four-time champions.

Sacred narratives entertain, inspire, ignite, unite, legitimize, and rationalize. The Alamo, Ali, and Arthur rally followers regardless of how many eons have passed since the precedent provided warrants for cause and action. This discussion delves to demythologize and to hypothesize alternative foundation stories, creating plausibility for another way of looking at those interrelated genres of myth cum history cum myth that leave footprints of these peoples' tracks, detritus of shipwrecks that reveal clues, archeological digs uncovering olive oil jars with seal imprints and evidence infrequently of even biblical literature on the skin of this common earth, left by human hands.

"Choose your century to plant your flag," remarked one medieval specialist who argued that studied knowledge rather than rant can count as a paid-up insurance policy against the xenophobic bandwagons of nations. From Israel itself, scholar Smolo Sand has followed this line of reasoning with his seminal *The Invention of the Jewish People*,[15] of how, in the 19th Century, European Jews answered Christian nationalists who racialized myth to fashion Jews as false monsters. Likewise, Christopher B. Krebs documents exactly how one Roman author's text in the 1st Century CE led later to the abomination of the Third Reich. In *A Most Dangerous Book: Tacitus' Germania from Rome to the Third Reich*,[16] the author elaborates how Himmler, Hitler's architect for the final solution, amplified Tacitus's "Germania" as the foundational text that led to Camus' famous Nazi revulsion and shock:

> A result of a peculiarly modern penchant for thinking: "In more ingenuous times, when the tyrant razed cities for this own greater glory, when the slave chained to the conqueror's chariot was dragged through the rejoicing streets, when enemies were thrown to the wild beasts in front of the assembled peoples, the mind did not reel before such unabashed crimes, and judgment remained unclouded. But slave camps under the flag of freedom, massacres justified by philanthropy or by a taste for the superhuman, these in one sense cripple judgment. On the day when crime dons the apparel of innocence through a curious transposition peculiar to our times it is innocence that is called upon to justify itself.[17]

Camus understood literary, historic, and political distortion and the creation of false monsters.

In this essay, we are neither grounding nor creating another foundational myth but advancing the plausibility that narratology often is founded on earlier fact, by advancing the proposition that narratives are often then misappropriated as second facts to galvanize national and racial identity. We want to advance the theory that identity under threat often dons the apparel of the innocent or the victim, and we believe that second millennial Hebrew narratives likely and naturally appropriated Egyptian facts. History teaches us that it doesn't take much fact to culturally galvanize, as the famous case of King Arthur proves. With only a scrap of text citing that Arthur and Morgana died in battle, heteroglossia and the passage of time and authors from Mallory, to Caxton, to Tennyson provide from this ambiguity a present day cottage entertainment industry with engaging media.[18]

Time out of Mind fashions many narratives. Here we ask readers, how long can cultural memories endure and morph? Could an Egyptian event of mid-16th Century BCE reverberate down eleven centuries to the Greek tragedians? What are the limits of institutional memories? When do concrete events metamorphize as eponymic genesis? Is Cadmus a Hyksos or perhaps a third generational Hyksos? Is Danaus a first generation refugee of civil strife like Heinrich Schliemann fleeing the 1848 troubles in Europe all the way to California to garner his wealth to afford spending it on digs in Anatolia? A Muslim invasion of Spain in 711 CE provided Elizabethan England with morris dancing and provided playwrights with a trove of plots that secured Tudor England with an identity that led to a world-wide empire where a sun never set.

The elasticity of mythic utterances provides both great fantasy and real monsters. We wish to examine deeply the human impulses behind these morphing narratives, in literary, historic, religious but most of all in cultural terms, seeking a common-culture remedy for such present day Othering horrors as those occurring in the Middle East but also over all our shared planet.

Factual events have often visited a span of centuries, perhaps a millennium, so long as some community lingers to rely upon the narrative to be a resonant source of identity. We argue that this measure of second culture, "Time out of Mind," approximates the span from the Hyksos peoples' legacy to the time of Aeschylus, Greek narratology fleshing out Egyptian documentation. The Delphic Oracle, though fixed in marble and written texts, sustained from the 7th Century BCE to the 5th Century CE, an incredible span. We can provide a more fluid example in the long span of time beginning with the leaf of a page documenting the subject of Arthur and Morgana dying in battle, but lacking predication of cause or objective knowledge of whether one killed the other or whether both died alongside while fighting. The question arises of whom was the scribe that imprinted this extant parchment during the same century as the Pythia's drying up at Delphi? Each new manifestation occurred during attempts to reinvigorate Catholicism or to ramp up English identity. Arthur has to do with nationalism and hegemony, just as Wilfred Owen blamed Tennyson's chauvinistic verse for many deaths in World War I, including what would poetically become his own. Today's "Merlin" series on TV is the less tumescent entertainment that helps prop up fading identity with the simultaneous influx of multiculturalism, with an African-British cast as Genevieve.

The resulting embodiment provides a stronger case than what too many people accept as fact when truly it is often *faith* that binds identity against the Other. Our identity as researchers here isn't cultural or racial, only as seekers and as objective inquirers, *sans* ideology. We wish here to do what Descartes promised and did do for sense data and the physical world in his "Cartesian Meditations," to strip away all the assumed and here to start from European historical and literary scratch. Recently, one of us came across an autobiography of a Syrian general in Saladin's time, 1170 CE, who is associated with the Syrian town of Shayzer on the Orontes.[19] This same setting was cited as Senzar and Sezar in inscriptions to glorify Menkheperre Thutmose III (1479-1425 BCE), a pursuer of Egypt-fleeing Hyksos descendants and also of his successor, Askheperrune Amenhotep II.[20] These citings of the same *topos* bookend temporal frames of some 2,600 years! Importantly, Shayzer/Senzar/Sezar, a fortified bottleneck, leads north into Ugarit territory, very close to the mythic setting of Cadmus, who in one myth assisted Zeus himself in His struggling with Typhon.

More importantly is that the Pharaoh likely overcame those defending this natural fortification in pursuit of the Hyksos, warranting inclusion on a celebratory stele. However, among all the hundreds of thousands of inscriptions or papyrus texts from tombs valorizing Egyptian hegemons, there is little to no citing of cities occupied by those in the Hebrew Pentateuch. Even more important is the fact that the biblical cities cited in the *Torah* identify locations in Egypt that only emerged during the first millennium, not earlier during the second millennium BCE.[21]

The point here is that citings date the source: say, a pharaonic text alluding to Hyksos as "Phoenicians" reveals an audience of Hellenistic ears, or of the First Millennium; but another pharaonic text referring to the Hyksos as Hyksos or *retenu* reveals an author composing for a Second Millennium audience.[22] The anachronistic geography and onomastic mismatches cry out for updating historical facts by separating them out from Hebrew myth.[23] Perusing written texts from oral renditions beginning around the mid-6th Century, and reading the Prophets of the First Millennium BCE, there are plausible grounds for some Hebrew-reported events occurring. Those writing these texts had returned from Babylon, prisoners of the New York City of that millennium. To approximate the dates, those authoring these accounts wrote around 550 BCE, some four hundred years after Solomon's rule of 940. This can be likened to today's Francophobic hagiographer writing about the Sun King, Louis XIV, and his ostentatious palace of Versailles with its over-the-top courtly Hall of Mirrors and its vast gilded gates that failed to keep out in the long run the *bourgeoisie* and the peasants.

One of us just visited the Place of the Sun King and marveled at how insular and cloistered the royals were, how understandably righteous the rabble marching over twenty five miles from rioting Paris and quickly overcoming the Swiss guard to imprison his sleeping successor, Louis XVI, he of the famous portrait in red shoes and bewigged, along with the oft-quoted "let them eat cake" Queen Marie Antoinette; then their holding the two royals imprisoned for two years before their "heads rolled" in the Concord Square in Paris, where now a genuine, gold-capped Egyptian obelisk stands guard and reflects the Franconian sun, sometimes glinting over more modern protests, a "modern antiquity" brought up the Seine River on Pharonic-like Cedar boats, not up the Nile.

At the risk of digression, the French democratic middle class quickly proved unable to govern as well as even the corrupt, deposed monarchy; Napoleon, a militarist from Corsica, rose quickly in France and then appointed himself Emperor in the then not yet 850-year-old Catholic Cathedral of Notre Dame on the left bank of the Seine. The message here emerges: be careful what you wish for, whether Corsican, French, English, Hyksos, Egyptian, Greek or Hebrew. The histories we inherit, those histories we topple, and those histories that we appropriate become a very large part who we are; our amalgamating culture results in the essence of who we become, the very ontology of what defines that new culture. This is a central reason why peace solutions to clashing cultures today must come from common cultural understanding, if not ideally from common cultural ground.

More to the current point, like Mosaic and Deuteronomic laws, the descriptions of King Solomon's building program from this late period attune more with the Assyrian socio-archeological Chain of Being, hierarchically dominated by a wrathful deity that anticipates earthly kings to fulfill a providential contract.[24] This relationship is so unlike Ugarit theology, a heteroarchical, or horizontal and filial, community of mortal kings chatting up gods over dinner, a communal discourse closer to the Greeks with heroes like Achilles, born of an immortal and mortal, to whom his mother provides with free choice. For that matter, the Hittites' communal socio-theology at Hattusha shared that of those from Ugarit to the Danaans, Argives and Achaeans, of Argos and Krete.[25]

This Hebrew conceit is more Assyrian, in fact, than the Egyptian Chain of Being with the Pharaoh as God overseeing a land with predictable natural disasters, such as floods, which, though destroying property markers and some folks, do *recede*, leaving richer soil for abundant crops. Should the flood be tepid, the resulting soil augured famine: disaster was greeted with stoic enthusiasm and a big-picture understanding of how the present catapults into the future. Their theology accommodated bad times not as manifestations of some evil Satan out of a Manichaean tradition but rather as a worldly acceptance that bad times happen and a long view of the cycles of time. That was the Egyptian cosmology, until a crowd of Hyksos established a precedent that was—for Hebrews, Assyrians, and Hittites—more ambiguous and less time-bound than that of floods and natural cycles, a bit like what Montezuma faced on Cortes' arrival.

The myths from the Syrian port of Ugarit date back into the shadows of early second millennium BCE and survived until its fall to the Sea Peoples in 1200: this is around the real time of mythic Troy, which has been well excavated since Schliemann in the 1880s, bearing vast evidence of Mycenae and Cretan civilizations. Until around 1050 BCE, with the waning of the devastation of the Sea Peoples that bleached for two centuries nearly all records of civilized interactions and cultural trade, the only earlier mention of the Hebrews being present in Egypt are very questionable ones, made by those who have stakes in that interpretation of history and who also thrive on wishful thinking. *Perhaps* a vestige identifies the Tetragrammatons[26] and/or the Merneptah stele (1213-1203) may be a signifier for a specific group among the *shasu*,[27] or perhaps the nomadic wayfarers, the *'abiru,'* who had been around for a millennium, are Hebrews, though Redford convincingly discounts this.

But these dates and suppositions are just that, supposings, not findings, not supported by any evidence like those of findings elsewhere. Our thoughts that follow have been fired by many authorities, cited below, and by podcasts available that convey utterances or oral critical thinking only now available. For example, consider the work of Melvin Bragg, anchoring the BBC's *In Our Time* series, particularly the consortium on Solomon featuring Martin Palmer, Director of the International Consultancy on Religion, Education, and Culture; Philip Alexander, Emeritus Professor of Jewish Studies at the University of Manchester; and Katharine Dell, Senior Lecturer in Old Testament Studies at the University of Cambridge, and Fellow of St. Catherine's College, Cambridge.[28]

After his father David unified the Hebrews in Jerusalem, Solomon built the First Temple to house the Mosaic Covenant.[29] This construction enslaved fellow Hebrews but relied upon King Hiram for Philistine architects and upon their craftsman to build it.[30] This new setting and building program unified centrifugally an emerging nation during a crucial time or even a bit earlier when, among the Greek poleis around the Aegean, people suffered as a result of competing cities claiming the authority of the same deity. Before Solomon, Hebrews suffered contentious and competing claims of a Yahweh of Bethel and Yahweh of Samaria, whose people linger still today, though fewer than three hundred and fifty.[31] It isn't until around the time of Alexander in 330 BCE that we see the resolution of these contentious Hebrew claims. Such claims of legitimacy remind us of those in competing states of America, like in Alabama and in Maine, who both assert knowledge of the true intentions of the Founding Fathers.

Kings 1-10 and II Chronicles 1-9 identify four Solomonic cities during the 10th Century BCE, which have given rise of late to archeological activity seeking proof of Solomon's touch: Jerusalem, Gezer, Megiddo, and Hatzor.[32] No excavation has revealed evidence of any Versailles-like splendor in Jerusalem. Though Jerusalem had long been occupied by humans, there is no material proof of Hebrews occupying the city until approximately 1000 BCE (see maps beginning on page 10 above).

We read of lavish features in building the Temple,[33] but of even greater grandeur was Solomon's own Palace,[34] a project that took close to twice the time to build than the temple itself and a project which required enslaving his people to complete.[35] The domicile did have to house his 300 concubines and 700 wives, one of those, the daughter of Pharaoh. Yet, no name of the Egyptian is mentioned, nor do these accounts synchronize with the copious information available from the Nile. There is *no citing* of possible Pharaohs such as Aakheperre Setepenre Osorkon, Netjerikheperresetpenamun Siamunmeryamun, or Hedjkheperre-setepenre Shoshenq I of the coterminous 21st Dynasty with the David and Solomon era. It seems likely that the wife is a trophy wife, a point of grievance that angers Yahweh in the biblical account.[36] Unfortunately for those who insist that myth legitimizes, the evidence here for early Hebrew presence in Egypt is thin at its best and non-existent in archeology.

During infrequent periods when both Egyptian and Assyrian dynastic powers waned, Israel and Phoenicia thrived economically from 1000 to 800, the period being during Solomon's reign. Like in the time shortly after the death of the Prophet Mohamed, when Islamic armies conquered both war-exhausted Byzantine and Persian empires, Solomon's inland Israel thrived. It dominated the southern spice route but had to supplicate coastal Phoenicia for maritime access and for their sailors to conduct commerce west into the Mediterranean.[37] Its only maritime port was near modern Elat, a western limb of the "Y" entering the Red Sea.[38] Close reading of biblical texts reveals that Solomon's imbalance of payments with Phoenicia indebted him to Hiram, balanced by ceding a twenty-villages repayment deal.[39] This overspending accounts for the taxing and enslaving of Jews, very unlike David's reign.[40] It is only during the rule of Solomon's son that the first specific, factual historical foreign ruler is identified in *The Bible*.[41]

Looking back for external verification of the presence of Moses uncovers very little if anything. The *Bible* is one of history's greatest anthologies, much of which was assembled between the Greek Aeschylus around 480 BCE, and the time of Christ.[42] Ruminating like an anthologizer, one might liken Abraham's experiences as legends, and the story of Joseph,[43] as a Horatio Alger novella, which Redford argues convincingly is a narrative filler linking patriarch myths to the time of Moses. Moses' Red Sea exodus was but one utterance among multilingual tongues of the heteroglossic Mediterranean, of Greeks, Cretans, Egyptians, Hittites, Nubians, and those of Ugarit, many of which echo simulacrum of a Hyksos overthrow very long before. Some may see the potential to divide in this argument, but we see the potential to unite over common cultural experiences and narratives, no matter how real, how fictional.

In this language stew of oral utterances, each was appropriated from the earlier horse-drawn chariot-riding Hyksos Mediterranean exodus wedge of civilization that fled the revenge-seeking, vengeful Egyptians after suffering more than a century of Hyksos hegemony. Among the many loan words in Egyptian, one-eighth are Semitic, and half of these relate to chariots and technological gear that reveal Hyksos military influence from the 17th and 16th Centuries, yet chariots are missing in Biblical history down until Solomon, for David never had any such innovation.[44] Much of Icelandic diction appears in Cumbrian agriculture of early English; Arabic ranks third as source of English vocabulary behind Roman and then Greek. Both signify evidence of earlier heteroglossic influences and of earlier technological innovations that map and make cultures and, in turn, worlds.

Biblical texts lack evidence of David having had chariots. If we are correct in this line of reasoning, and in the surprising suppositions to follow below, the Abraham stories are later fabrications and composites, along with genealogies, to extend back from the mid-first millennium to early second millennium BCE. Let's likewise consider the Greek analogue. Literate chroniclers from the Aegean wrote of their oral history only about seventy-years after the Hebrew scribes of Judges, Kings, Chronicles, and Deuteronomy composed after exile, but the Greeks composed in greater varieties of genres: in dramas, in odes celebrating athletic victory, in panegyrics, and in histories. Hebrew scribes wrote to standardize what for the past had been the polytheism of Canaanite gods (Isaiah's Tamuz) with competing Yahwehs of both Bethel and of Megiddo, as mentioned above. Astour and Bernal enlighten us that Greek culture dates back to the 15th Century BCE.[45] Thutmoses III's portrayal of his conquered islanders dates back to the early Greeks of that same century. External validation of mutual sources are not found in the *Bible* until the 9th Century. After analyzing ten cartouche inscriptions of Thutmoses on a Karnak temple carved next to those of enchained figures, Robert Aubreton's investigation determined that the temple inscriptions reveal the origins of prisoners from Krete and the Greek Argolid soon after the time of the Hyksos expulsion from Egypt, from 1450-1380 BCE.[46] "Daanoi" and "Nauplia" link the tribe of Hellenes to the Argolid port and congruently what the Greek tragedian Aeschylus later wrote about his play *The Suppliants* in 480 BCE.

This corroboration is important for several reasons: 1) It provides proof of an institutional memory of historical fact, thus extending information beyond the millennia from Thutumoses to Aeschylus; 2) It warrants textual evidence of heteroglossia of the Greeks, shared with the Hebrews, both as runes and song, and suggests an Exodus of Canaanites but not one of Hebrews; 3) It advances that, from this time, no parallel exists for verifying Moses or the culturally famous Hebrew Exodus. It casts in glaring contrast and in having spent millions if not billions, with great advances in archaeology, with aerial photography, and with metal detector searches, etc, the fact that essentially not much evidence has been found since the 1967 Six Day War to legitimize these huge expenditures and efforts.

Findings from excavations and ancient texts bear evidence. Although the tragedy, *The Suppliants*, reports the sacking and raping of women of a Greek polis, Aeschylus wrote for Pericles' contemporaries at mid-5th Century, certainly not for moderns. The Egyptians who composed their glyphs continually document conquests; we scribes are saying that Egyptian pursuit in revenge for 150 years of Hyksos subjugation was akin to our cultural memories of tragedy, like of Pearl Harbor or of 9/11, etched on the vengeful psyche of Americans. Such cultural traumas of 9/11 and of the Hyksos-Egyptian hegemony imprint on the psyche of any community as that community conceptually records a semiotics of the Other, of Tiananmen Square, of the Kremlin, or of the Pyramids. As Redford says, "in origin, form, and ethos, Israel owes nothing to the Egyptian cults."[47] The Greek pantheon derives from Egypt,[48] and the Hebrews acquired their sociological epistemology from Assyrians[49] along with some of their theology from the Ugarit.[50]

We *are* arguing that this conquest came following a 16th Century BCE chase of Canaanites in a route following geographically counterclockwise, eventually leading to Greece, a trek documented as a common trade route as early as mid-3rd Millennium.[51] We know that Canaanites landed in Thebes, north of Argos, discussed soon below when reviewing Platon's excavation findings now housed in the Thebes Museum, Greece.

The BBC's well known 2010 series *A History of the World in a 100 Objects*, based on artifacts from the British Museum, features the "Rhind Math Papyrus," composed in the time of the Hyksos.[52] The Rhind was composed up river at Thebes on the Nile, during the reign of Apophis, at the end of the Hyksos occupation ending the Egyptian Second Intermediate Period. This last Hyksos king ushered in the 17th dynasty of those Pharaohs who commenced the New Kingdom of subsequently Imperial Egypt. In approximately 1550 BCE, the Rhind was a school primer, which included eighty-four mathematical exercises dealing with measuring pyramids and answering other concerns like how many bottles of beer were needed. Plato, presuming mathematics but the games of idle priests, cites Egypt as the main source of computation,[53] as does Herodotus, who more correctly infers its use in pyramid building.

The Father of History also cites Egypt as the source of the Greek gods. Later, Strabo, at the time of Jesus' birth and a citizen of Rome, like Josephus, credited Egyptians for creating geometry to solve land disputes among farmers about annual flood disruptions of land markers, and Herodotus further credits, in parallel reasoning, the Phoenicians with originating arithmetic and accounting skills needed in their commercial enterprises.[54] We advance as *plausible* that these and others from the ancient world convey a common notion that Egyptians and Phoenicians (their ancestor Hyksos) entailed a rich common and contentious history from sharing the Nile, which included a tsunami exodus. The violent overthrow and pursuit of the Hyksos (four centuries before Moses) seemingly plots a path east along the Mediterranean across the Sinai north past Gaza to Biblos, then on to Ugarit, across Cilicia (in myth the name of Cadmus' brother) to Karia and across to the Peloponnese of Europe (in myth the name of Cadmus' sister). During the next four centuries, Mycenaean texts in linear B accounted, rather than narrated, records of the results of similar computations as found on the Rhind, which evidenced sophisticated numeracy skills of arithmetic, subtraction, multiplication and division as the means to solve problems like how many cats pursuing the rats pursuing mice that consumed the grain are needed to save the wheat in the house that Danaus built.

We find here that *any Exodus is by its very nature an Immigration,* and we close the loop from the classical Hyksos culture of Cadmus and Europa from Egyptainized Tyre to Greece and the Krete, then back to Avaris in the Nile Delta, evidenced in the bull leaping frescos that also appear in Alalak between Aleppo and the coast of Syria, a trek that drafts a historicized palimpsest upon which the important Hebrew culture layered its more well-known, but likely plagiarized text.

Permit us to draw an analogy here.

Modern evolutionist Darwin's huge impact from 1859 onward launched a reactionary response among those holding fast to prior creation dogma. We can here explain much of modern archeology as attempts to validate and prove, with archaeological material finds, attempting to validate that the world was created in about 4004 BCE, only to more recently discover real time reaching back to far beyond, in astronomical inferences today, to 14.5 billion years past. The idea that Ilium must exist materially is simply and foremost an analogic refutation of Darwin's evolutionary theory sending profound ripples that became reactionary waves of social and scientific investigations seeking Ilium and cosmology to explain what Darwin has already explained.[55]

As stated, our thesis is that Egyptian texts document happenings, which later Greek texts remembered, texts that rival the primacy of Hebraic ones and likewise that which the earlier Hyksos *exodus/immigration* (when these Canaanites in their escape nearly closed a geographically counter-clockwise loop) laid out in the later-Hebrew-appropriated Ur-template of Exodus. This thesis could explain what moved Sigmund Freud to discourse with deliberation on Moses and Monotheism. Freud delved into the subject of Moses with the attentive stance of an analyst. He concluded that the legendary eponym of Judaic law came in fact from two sources, a non-Hebraic Egyptian and a priestly Hebraic hero, similar to Cadmus, but who never strayed much from the region beyond the coast of the present day hill country and the Dead Sea. The non-Jewish Egyptian had been a devotee/follower of the monotheistic Akhenaton 1352-1334, whose remnant of pious adherents fled East upon the Pharaoh's death and who converted Semite tribes in the post-Amarna Age, around 1375 BCE (Amenhote III). Freud shared the critical exegesis, commonly accepted since the 18th Century CE, that identifies sources «P,» or Priestly, and «J,» or Jehovah that also conflated to form sequences of the Pentateuch.[56] Freud envisioned locatively that two figures, the Yahweh proclaimer of the volcanic Petra region in Jordan, whose deity so contrasted with the other, the Elohim, the desert aristocrat, who maintained the vestiges of

Herodotus of Halicarnassus" public statue, Bodrum Castle, Turkey.

the Pharaonic milieu of Nefertiti and her curious husband, the sun worshiper.

This Moses bore the Egyptian suffix evidenced in Ahmoses, he of the earlier dynasty who expunged the Land of the Nile of the Hyksos people two centuries earlier. Freud's Moses, escaping east, retreated in exodus like that of Caliph al-Hakim bi-Amr Allah (985-1021), who two millennia later in the early 11th Century CE escaped east to found the religion that bears the name of his general Drusus, (Mauhammad al-Dar), the Druze of the Levant, a truly curious example of repetitive and amalgamated history. Cultural threads sometimes form time out of mind mosaics of surprising color patterns, but hands on walls, steles, alphabets and inventions, like the chariot and the loom, help us see those patterns emerge.

Our thesis is very like that of Freud's, excluding the role of Akhenaton, but one rejecting Freud's early dating. Freud evidenced his case on circumcision, a clearly Egyptian and, according to Freud, also a Semitic practice. Freud finds evidence in Herodotus, who reports that circumcision was a Nilotic and Levantine practice, but the Father of History who travelled these regions never even once cites in his 450 BCE writings the presence of Hebrews, though Freud asserts, as if obvious for today's readers, that the Greek's Syrians were post-exilic Jews. Freud claims circumcision was non-Semitic, but the ritual may well have been a regional, maybe chthonian practice of the speakers of Aramaic. Most interpreters cite Genesis 34 as a historical fact that the Canaanites did not practice circumcision, but that the Hebrews did so when Dinah's brothers convinced Sheckem and his kin of Canaanites to suffer the agony of this intrusive surgery, only to slaughter the ailing afterwards.

However, this folklore from the legendary time of Abraham and his grandchildren was written *after* the exile from Persia and during the 5th Century, the period that Herodotus reported on, *a thousand years after* the purported fact. The *Bible* in *Exodus* differentiates the Hebrews of Moses' time from the legendary patriarchs of Jacob and Joseph and their fore-bearer Abraham, whom God graced when He interrupted the foretold father of the race from sacrificing Abraham's first born, a paradox bordering on contradiction. The biblical language sharply reveals our present thesis that the Hebrews of Moses' time were late, only emerging as an autonomous culture slightly before King David, as according to Exodus (6:2-4):

2 And God spake unto Moses, and said unto him, I am the LORD:
3 And I appeared unto Abraham, unto Isaac, and unto Jacob, by the name of God Almighty, but by my name JEHOVAH was I not known to them.
4 *And I have also established my covenant with them, to give them the land of Canaan, the land of their pilgrimage, wherein they were strangers.*

The yeasty period of our inquiry extends from 500 BCE to 700 CE, once alphabetic writing extends beyond the priest cults in Egypt or Assyrian administrative chores and accompanies commerce throughout the eastern Mediterranean; however, the oral historic citing of Abraham and the patriarchs using myth could stretch back a millennium. The Babylonian captivity is well documented in inter-textual Biblical citings, in Hosea and other

Prophets. From Amos and Isaiah, one infers historical events of David and Moses the lawgiver, but these mythic extenuations have become unchallenged dogma. The two fields, theology and classics, are famously separate and supposedly exclusive, yet the motive driving each is the same: the quest to discover truth in reaction to Darwin's cosmic unsettling theories that dislodged faith foundations, identity grounding, and sometimes political hegemony. Proving the historical validity of Troy is analogous to finding evidence of racial distinction from other Semites before the Sea Peoples incursion of 1200 BCE. Among all that rich 5th Century Greek literature in a variety of genres, we find no mention of the existence of Hebrews then or earlier, though Hebrews may have had in mind the Greeks when citing a grapheme approximating *Yovan*, which might refer to "Ionian" in the *Old Testament*.

We find the same compelling absence of evidence regarding the presence of earlier Hebrews in Egyptian lore; and the same lack of allusions to Hebrews in the Hittites' archives, though Sarah was buried on a Hittite's property; and the absence of Hebrews among the texts of Ugarit, although their voices were accepted by Hebrews in several psalms and in other works citing "the land of milk and honey." Naming foreign lands proves little. Proper nouns to evidence external politic are missing until the 1st millennium. Therefore, we must conclude that extenuations of what we know to be earlier history into historicized Hebrew myth are yet to be proved.

One would naturally assume that if Egyptian texts a millennium earlier than any Biblical allusion to Egypt were to cite externally verifiable locations of Israel or Hebrews in or beyond Egypt, then there would exist in the *Bible* some factual evidence. But in the *Bible* no specific name of historical Pharaohs of the second millennium validate its Kingdom's international intercourse, other than the general title, Pharaoh, until in the late 900s BCE when Biblical text documented Pharaoh Shoshenq I, known as Shishak. And cities cited in the *Bible* were not around in the earlier period. In contrast, as early as 14th Century Ugarit and Greek cultures identify Pharaohs and Egyptian cities whose names only persisted during the second millennium. Egypt was the breadbasket of the region, a magnet for the starving during drought years. Egypt is cited in the *Bible* some 600 times, but what during the second millennium evidences Hebrews cognizance of everyday life in Egypt?

The referent of these citations, we argue, is all uttered during the first millennium. Dating before the arrival of the Sea Peoples (1250), Egypt's awareness of Hebrews, according to wishful thinkers, is limited to *one very questionable telephonic morpheme and an inference that foreign wayfarers who run and kick up dust in retreat are called 'abiru,' a general appellation used as far back as the 1800s BCE.* Not until sometime after King David is there a biblical citation of an actual person of non-Jewish identity at the head of state. In contrast, evidence from Ugarit (1375) documents the name of the 12th Dynasty Pharaoh Senwosret I with association with Hathor, who often fused with the Canaanite goddess Anat. Further, a statuette at Ras Shamra celebrates by name a hometown girl as Pharaoh's wife, as does a sphinx that celebrates another hometown girl from Qatna, just south of Ugarit, as Pharaoh's wife, with dating between Senwosret II and Amenenhet II.[57]

Egypt in the early days was more geographically remote than one might suspect. Even earlier in the third millennium BCE site at Ebla, excavated in the 1960s just south of Aleppo, there are vast findings that document abundant interaction at the heart of the Fertile Crescent, with little awareness of Egypt but clearly actively engaged with the East. Cyrus Gordon's landmark *Forgotten Script* cites Eblaic texts from 2500 BCE, contemporary with Egypt's Fourth and Sixth Dynasties, that discuss relations with Akkad (1968). We are compelled to ask, why don't *Bible* allusions to Hebrews pre-date 1000 BCE? Only after the year 1000, does the *Bible* reveal familiarity of Egypt or Assyria, familiarity substantiated by onomasticons and toponyms cited by either of these kingdoms. And only much later in the earlier CE millennium does anyone, Roman, Greek, or Jew, attempt to address what we are raising— but of Josephus, later discussed at length below.

In order to conclude this beginning, to migrate where we scribes would lead you, we must go backward further, then forward. In fact we ask readers not to abandon notions of time nor shred them, as the chronology of Hyksos culture is a *key* to understanding our case to consider Hyksos-truth plausibility, even to some of their descendants back in Canaan having formulated some of the sacred *Ten Commandments* much earlier than in the Biblical version. But we ask readers instead to also consider the mutations of history into the ebb and flow of literature and myth time, more like the layers of a shiny pearl, forming around the germ of truth in the luminescent oyster of the world. Let us go then you and I, together . . . Let us go questing after peace. . . .

At the end of Professor Gage's Fulbright Award in Syria in 1984, he had the opportunity to come across the Texas A&M aqua-archeological investigation of the Uluburun ship wreck off the coast of Kash.[58] This obscure 14th Century BCE wreck, a commercial ship, yielded artifacts and materials that wrote on the map of the Eastern Mediterranean to identify for us today many geographic references of the earlier sagas of the Hyksos people. Findings included a gold inlaid iron figurine of a Canaanite goddess, likely an avatar of

Anat; an Egyptian gold piece bearing Nefertiti's cartouche; a volcanic scepter that could only have come from Bulgaria;[59] raw ingots of both copper from Cyrus and glass from Canaan, indicating not only material utility but domestic use; and a diptych with missing inlaid wax. Wax provided the material for imprinted messages like those Homer reported in the episode in the myth of Bellerophon.[60]

The hero, named in the *Iliad,* attunes with the Hyksos/Ugarit bull-god Ba'al. The wreck's hoard punctuates Cadmus and his brothers' epic search for their sister Europa, and it also evidences support for hypotheses about 2nd Millennium commerce. Treasure troves and myths support Bernal's thesis of Egyptian diffusion progressing counterclockwise east to Levant and north and finally west to Krete and Greece.[61] The momentous, mid-16th Century exodus of the Hyksos, and subsequent thriving sea-borne commerce connected Egypt with Northern Syria, Krete, and possibly to the Black Sea.[62] Consider both the Uluburun and another ship, the Cape Gelidonya, both shipwrecks with evidentially-accepted material testimonials of transactions between Egypt, Canaan, and Greece, both wrecks yielding ample evidence of literate cultures whose documentation failed to allude to a single hint of the presence of Israel but which remembered later from the 6th Century the family members of Cadmus peppering the Eastern Mediterranean map: brother Phineas, who ends his days on the Black Sea, location of the Bulgarian volcanic scepter. Kash is a bit west of Kylix's Cilicia, where this brother landed after his short trip away from his angry father. This is just north from Phoenix's Phoenicia, for later Phoenix had reached the Gates of Heracles, Gibraltar, where he learned of the death of his father Agenor whose curse could no longer harm him, and he could now return home, though without his sister Europa. Perhaps, the Uluburun ship was headed for brother Thasos' Thasos, the island in the north Aegean. Cadmus and his siblings of Tyre surely didn't exist in individual ontological status,[63] but the proper noun denoting their tribe undoubtedly signifies the eponym for some group of Hyksos, or their descendants whose presence were collectively remembered from Homer's 8th Century reworking of 13th Century Mycenaean lore to the Hellenistic Parian Marble and Hecataeus of Abdera, who in reporting of Sparta mention the Hyksos people repeatedly.[64]

More recently, after 2000, Professor Gage visited Bodrum's Uluburun lab to discuss with the Texas A&M investigators further findings, including the earlier specimen of tin aboard the vessel that sunk around 1374 BCE. From what limited supply did this required amalgam for bronze derive?

Six centuries after the sinking of this northbound ship, Greek culture initiated the Olympic Games and Homeric *rhapsodes* chanted of ancestors battling to retrieve and return another abducted girl, like Europa, while simultaneously overpopulated poleis commenced colonizing territories previously colonized by earlier Semites from the coastal areas of Palestine. Greeks over-laid Cumae and Neopolis in today's Italy, Marseilles in France, but not as far as Spain's Cadiz, these later palimpsests now Greek. Carthage and Neo Polis both mean the same in each language: new town in English, ironically now the home town for Freeman in Newtown, PA. But excuse us for our language inquisition, for language proposes, and now there is a need for apposition. Semites, Canaanite Hyksos, whose venturing into Greece occurred as early as the 15th Century, already influenced those singing, competing, exploring Greeks, and Plato's racial memory had not forgotten this fact.[65]

From the 8th Century on, bards like Pindar of Thebes celebrated the earliest Hyskos visitors in his language, transmitting mytho-poetic versions of likely historical records of the tumultuous Canaanite Exodus from Egypt of their first and long-term conquerors. The wrecks of the Uluburun and that of Cape Gelidonya, sunk two centuries later, are layers of commerce and exodus, appropriation to the pearl necklace of amalgamated history.

The Hittite sculptor/scribe representing the storm god Teshub is recognized by Delta Canaanites as Seth; in Ugarit he is referred to as Saphon.[66] The New Kingdom mythological battle of Seth over Yam has as its genesis the Hyksos Ba'al's fratricidal struggle with Yam, and this older proto-narrative finds enhanced incarnation in Moses' parting-of-the-Red-Sea, another variation, though even more enhanced myth than that of Yahweh and Leviathan. Egyptian Seth and Nephthys narratology equals Ugarit's Baal and Anat, who morphed into Astarte.[67] For example, in one version it is not Ra as protagonist but El, flaccid like the El of Ugarit. But who were these Hyksos people who formed the Ubermensch of Egypt for so long, and where did they come from, from whom did they descend? There are, at present, varying theories of the genealogy of the Hyksos, but we favor the Canaanite discrepancy. Here's why.

The Scholar Bernal, like Jewish scholar Porten and many other colleagues and recent historians of Israel like Smolo Sand, excepting the Israeli Zionists and fundamentalists, finds little or no *historical* evidence for a *Zion* legitimization of the new State of Israel. Bernal's Volumes I-III of *Black Athena* and *Black Athena Responds* make a case for another genesis of much Biblical literature, as does Bernal's book *Cadmean Letters*.[68] Bernal argues that the horse was unknown during the Old and Middle Egyptian Kingdoms. The Hyksos mention horses first, in art, artifacts and literature.

The Egyptian word for horse has a Semitic root. Bernal's Volume II of *Black Athena* spends an entire section on the Hyksos' inventions and importations to Egypt,[69] key among them the importation of the horse and the horse-drawn, single-person chariot, instruments of both rapid transportation, and of war and of hegemony.

Bernal's motive for his extensive investigation is to refute the racist model, which he calls Aryan, by returning to the ancient, classical model of history of this period. Many pre-World War II historians felt that the equine-culture linked not the Hyksos but the ancient Hurrians, the Mitanni, who were unquestionably great horsemen and not too far away geographically for consideration for introducing into Egypt this military weapon. As our readers know, a period's sociology of knowledge conforms to its zeitgeist; scholars construct theories and hypotheses that fit that zeitgeist. There was a recent time in English pedagogy and grant-writing when any grant proposal mentioning transformational grammar would likely get funding. Thus from the time of Carter's finding Tutankhamen to the time of Hitler's bunker, the Aryan Hurrians were considered to be the source of this weaponry, not the earlier Hyksos invaders who had occupied the Delta for over a century groveling to the people of Pharaoh. We, like Bernal, do not agree.

After World War II, a new *zeitgeist* emerged, especially after 1967 and the Six Day Day war, a big-picture view that favors the *antithesis* of the older interpretation, not Teutonic racism but perhaps Hebrew racism. Despite Bernal's Jewish heritage, and having as an ancestor the great Egyptologist Alan Gardiner, his fairness and analytic acumen lead him to not buy into Zion legitimization of the new Israeli State with its "new" finding of the too-recently-established-to-debunk-the-Hyksos-legacy.

Bernal, like us, finds not one iota of evidence that supports Hebrews being in Egypt in the 2nd Millennium. Instead, he uses the volcanic eruption of Thera to *refute* the dating that lets the Aryan model posit that the Hurrians were the Hyksos. For Bernal and others document that the Hurrians came at the end of the 12th Dynasty. In 1802 BCE Bernal, with us, finds that the Canaanites of Biblical reference were the Hyksos, not the Hurrians, and he agrees with the chronology for their dominating Egypt and then fleeing to Greece as we have been outlining thus far. Bernal likewise notes that long after the Canaanite Hyksos (following the last Pharaoh of the 12th Dynasty) took advantage of the chaos of the 2nd Intermediate Period to occupy much of Egypt, an Egypt that was in a state of chaotic civil war coinciding with the downfall of a hierarchal centralized state. What followed was a variety of feudalisms, some Semitic and some Egyptian, headed in each case with pharaohs fighting one another for rule; hence, the lists of pharaohs and place names scrambles a lot during this break-down period of internal war. The six Dynasties of Hyksos rule end in Egypt with Pharaoh Ahmose who chased the Semites out of Egypt in 1550 BCE.[70]

Bernal does admit that there may be some small chance that the Hurrians as Johnny-come-latelies joined in with the Canaanite Hyksos as the dominant culture, but the evidence for this possibility is thin, and the dates are a stretch. The preponderance of evidence *does* show that Hyksos were Canaanites and that they substantially drove the cultural engines of both Egypt and in time Greece. Even admitting that the Hyksos genealogy is not an exact science still allows them their considerable influence on all culture that came after and on the most famous record of our common history that we call the *Bible*.

These Canaanite/Hyksos occupiers, riding the innovations of horses, horse-drawn conveyances of weaponry, with metal of bronze and with glass, and with their invention of the loom, reigned most powerfully from the Mediterranean coast south to Memphis, leaving their storied imprints in and out of time. With this clearing away of distractions, let us turn toward the importance of understanding how much more we humans are alike than we are different and toward how our common culture threads, even if amalgamated, can serve to unite us as well as divide. Human hands, as Jeffers wrote, are human hands, "not paws," and we should seek to join those hands whenever and wherever we can. Eric Cline's important new book *1177 BC: The Year Civilisation Collapsed* about the remarkable multi-cultural artifact finds aboard the excavated Uluburun shipwreck shows compelling evidence of cross-cultural trade among disparate, sometimes warring peoples, finding peace and stability in common-ground trade. The rest of Cline's pithy title is a warning: we marginalize and wall out competing cultures at our own human peril and loss.

2
Historicizing the Past
Directionality, Westward the Hyksos

To satisfy my wish to get the best information I possibly could on the subject, I made a voyage to Tyre in Phoenicia because I had heard that there was a temple there of great sanctuary, dedicated to Heracles. I visited the temple and found that the offerings which adorn it were numerous and valuable. . . In the course of the conversation with the priests I ask how long ago the temple had been built, and found by their answer they, too, did not share the Greek view; for they said that the temple was as ancient as Tyre. . . . I also saw another temple there, dedicated to the Thasians and Heracles; so I went on to Thasos, where I found a temple of Heracles built by the Phoenicians who settled there after they had sailed in search of Europa. Even this was five generations before Heracles the son of Amphitryon made his appearance in Greece. The result of these researches is plain proof that the worship of Heracles is very ancient; and I think that the wisest course is taken by those Greeks who maintain a double cult of this deity, with two temples, one in which they worship him as Olympian and devine, and in the other pay him such honour as due to a demigod, or hero.[1]

TIME & HABIT OUT OF MIND, Inquiry into Cultural Assumptions: Ancient Mesopotamia provides an analogous template for political/religious hegemony and geographic succession of rulers, cities, lands and mythology that mirror the rise, partial fall and exodus of the Hyksos people, sometimes indirectly touching that very history. Mesopotamia, roughly marked by the Euphrates in present day Iraq, has always marked the confluence of cultures, as long as there have been *Homo sapiens*. These lands and peoples, reverberating currently and awkwardly, atonally, like a recently and violently struck bell hit by a clanging American-led strike force, provide a Persian-Gulf area metaphor for Heraclitus' mandate that change and chance are constants in the region and on all of planet earth. It was here, somewhere between 3500-2400 BCE, that Sumerian city-states flourished between the Tigris and Euphrates rivers. It was here that the Sumerians invented the Cuneiform writing that took time out of minds from an oral tradition to put into historic record that survives today. By 2300, the Akkadians invaded Sumer, moving down the Tigris below present day Baghdad toward An Nasiriya. Somewhere around 1750 BCE, the early written stele record registered that the ruler Hammurabi (1792-1750) built the first Babylonian empire in the region, one that was to last a millennia until the emergence of the Assyrians in about 710 BCE, when the mighty Sargon II began to rule over a massive Assyrian fiefdom, covering modern-day Iraq, *Israel*, Syria and *Egypt* itself.

The "Richelieu wing" in Paris' Louvre Museum holds 2,000 years of Near Eastern Antiquities from excavations between the Tigris and Euphrates Rivers, dating back to the beginning of civilization 6,000 year ago. During recent visits, the authors were especially interested in the largest and oldest artifacts in the entire Louvre, those of statues and steles of Near Eastern rule and succession, ironically housed under the Louvre's outdoor 1989 I.M. Pei Pyramid addition entrance.

To see these ancient holdings firsthand is to marvel at progress, yes, especially in warfare, empire-building, architecture and art, but the overwhelming lesson is of man's desire to dominate others, to subjugate, limbic drives that might also defeat our race. These achievements are a paradox. There in the Louvre, one finds relics attesting to the sweep of civilizations toppling previous ones, tearing down its statutes, destroying its palaces, looting and absorbing its cultural heritage, amalgamating, replacing monuments and steles with victory and law-giving monuments of its own, appropriating the literature and making history into myth, each only to be toppled again by the next wave of history breaking on the sands of time.

There are the vestiges of once-powerful rulers and peoples, reminding the visitor of the Shelley poem "Ozymandias," of how "Time and Chance Happeneth to us all," no matter how once mighty. The Stele of the Vultures (2600-2330 BCE), as old as the Pyramids, makes this point as the world's oldest surviving historical document, its images and words recording the great battle between the city of Lagash and its rival Umma. Bearded King Eannatum waves to the crowd from his chariot in a victory parade while a priest gives thanks to the gods and while, in the lower panel, a mass grave is dug for the 36,000 dead enemy and a huge, tethered ox, his head tied to a stake, is about to be a burnt sacrifice.[2] Always seeking peace, we scribes want to study our ancient human motivations, using the Hyksos as our model of a war-like people, culturally like so many of history's citizens, unflinchingly searching for remedies to blood lusts, power, and old aggressions that become those of the present if we are not vigilant and nimble with new ethical thinking. Empires rise and fall only years and yards apart in this section of the Louvre. The Statue of Ebih-il, Superintendent of Mari (2400 BCE), his eyes made of seashells and lapis lazuli, stares widely into space in the goddess Ishtar's Temple where he has planted himself to declare his devotion to "the virile goddess." The statue goddess of both love and war, who no doubt spurred many a soldier's fantasies, miraculously remained a virgin, "her lips sweet, her figure beautiful, her eyes brilliant, women and men adore her."[3] Ebih-il seems to be in the after-effects of sexual rapture, if not provided by the goddess Ishtar herself (does making love with a King count as losing one's virginity?), than perhaps from having been serviced well by one of the sacred prostitutes who graced Ishtar's temple.

There is, in the Louvre's Richelieu Wing, a fine statue of Gudea, Prince of Lagash, "the Destined" (circa 2120 BCE), one of Sumer's last rulers who, history records, was the rare pacifist, who actually *rebuilt* previous temples to thank the gods for their help in establishing his new rule.[4] We find a rare model for peace in the Prince of Lagash, Gudea, one worthy of the best contemporary ethics in and out of mind. Likewise, a rose colored stele of King Naram-Sin of the city-state of Akkad, the new top dog, commemorates the Akkadian conquest and plundering of Sumer in 2250 after a millennium of Sumerian prosperity and rule. The vertical rune statue, or stele, is aggression personified, a time-stamp of screaming (but temporary and temporal) victory: in it and on it, King Naram-Sin climbs up to the heavens wearing the horned helmet of a god, a cod-piece like protector of his loins hanging down like a bull's testicles, his many soldiers looking up the precipice at Him, admiring as he is frozen in time trampling his Sumerian enemies.

One victim is prone and attempting to remove the King's spear from his unfortunate neck, another also prostrate and cowering, begging the King for the mercy that never comes from war.[5] The message from all acts and artifacts in the Louvre is clear in the vision of Joseph Campbell's "one story:" in the human pageant of history and myth, it is *all* reproduced to ensure genetic survival, killing game or harvesting foodstuffs to eat, waging war to expand, gain resources and land, political hegemony, killing or being killed, and, sometimes, the best of us peeking out from behind the chaotic curtains of killing sprees that we call history, seeking peace, conciliation, common humanity, even rebirth. *Common culture* and not genetics, *created in time out of mind*, may be the *key to peace*, we argue when we study the Louvre's frozen moments of where man has been and what has been memorialized. Even in the ancient world, as with the Prince of Lagash, there are models for a new kind of sociology, well before the time of Jesus, of Mohammed, of Gandhi, of Mother Teresa, and of Martin Luther King, Jr.

In a classic back-and-forth struggle for hegemony, the kind that the Father of History, Herodotus, would later describe with intellectual rigor and a scientific mind, the ancient Assyrians and Babylonians traded dominance and revolution, with the Babylonians revolting against the oppressive Sargon II and his Assyrian armies, destroying the Assyrian capital of Nineveh (250 miles north of Baghdad) by 612 BCE. The successful revolutionaries eventually built their own *Torah*-recorded capital, eventually rife with metaphor and resonance itself: Babylon. While we find no previous evidence of Hebrews in Egypt, either in the *Torah* or extra-*Bible*, the *Torah* historically reports some of these events through the reverse mirror of history: heteroglossia of myth and texts. Asks a Hebrew scribe: "Nineveh is in ruins—who will mourn for her? Everyone who hears the news claps his hands at your fall, for who has not felt your endless cruelty?"[6]

King Hammurabi (1792 BCE), centuries before the Ten Commandments were purportedly issued, proclaimed 282 laws of behavior for his vast empire, which joined Sumer and Akkad. His surviving eight foot tall, black basaltic rock stele, now located in Susa, Iran, likely is typical of many Hammurabian law-giving stele(s) that dotted the King's empire, proclaiming not only his rule but the coda of ethics that stitched his empire together in divine-issued consensus, the breaking of any one of which could have severe or fatal consequences. The 282 laws of Hammurabi, carved autocratically into this basaltic pinnacle, in effect a giant phallus with writing, mark one of *Homo sapiens*' oldest legal documents. At the stele's top, King Hammurabi stands, wearing one of Gudea's—Prince of Lagash c. 2120 BCE— ostentatious hats of Kingship. Properly royally be-hatted, King Hammurabi is frozen forever receiving the scepter of judgment from the gods of justice and the sun, who radiate flames of light from the King's broad shoulders. Proceeding down from the top, the inscription begins, "When Anu the Sublime . . . called me, Hammurabi, by name . . . I did right, and brought about the well-being of the oppressed."[7] The laws follow, all 282 of them, scratched down the considerable length and girth of the phallus-like stele, 3,500 lines reading right to left, covering every transgression and consequence from lying, theft, trade and marriage, even medical malpractice, perhaps pleasing later Sophists and extending across the millennia to modern lawyers. King Hammurabi's innovation appears to be the swift administration of "justice," immediate punishment and retribution for wrongdoing, with no modern trial nor due process necessary, often executed with poetic justice. Here follow some translated samples of the laws in chronological order:

If any man ensnares another falsely, he shall be put to death.

57) If your sheep graze another man's land, you must pay 20 gur of grain.

129) If a couple is caught in adultery, they shall both be tied up and thrown in the water.

137) If you divorce your wife, you must pay alimony and child support

218) A surgeon who bungles an operation shall have his hands cut off.

282) If a slave shall say, "You are not my master," the master can cut off the slave's ear.[8]

One quickly sees how much ancient Near Eastern concepts of justice and fairness influence modern theology and law, perhaps even more so than western British and inherited North American law notions that came much later. Even more relevant to our thesis of the important reverberations of Hyksos culture and myth on the Greeks, Egyptians, and Hebrews is the fact that *Torah*-an law and the Ten Commandments are centuries later than to the original concept of written law. The most quoted Code de Hammurabian laws make this transparent and are familiar chestnuts, scratched upon a black rock spire of "truth and consequences," as a series of absolutist ethics nearly two millennia before the time of Christ. These two laws are Near Eastern justice personified, a distant yesterday dawning again and again identically until today, Absolutism in a pithy nutshell:

196) If a man put out the eye of another man, his eye shall be put out.

200) A tooth for a tooth . . .[9]

King Hammurabi, the Babylonian law-giver, preceded both the Egyptian Ahmoses and the Moses of the later Hebrews, also law-givers. We of the contemporary cultures live in a world where nuclear "justice" and bio-terrorism might happen in nanoseconds of time, even swifter and more deadly punishments for "sins," potentially causing planet-wide tsunamis of change and extinction that we must avoid, using new and more nimble thinking in *time out of mind.*

On those two cheery but oddly reassuring notes of codification of surviving ancient beliefs, we proceed to pick up the human drama of our present Hyksos thesis. But first we would like to allow ourselves, briefly, our own shape-shifting leap of political perspective and judgment here, to reserve our right to do so again until our end. A little later, we hope also to try to help answer the eight-year-old daughter's question of *Bible* scholar S. David Sperling, who wrote *The Original Torah: the Political Intent of the Bible Writers*. Sperling's young, prescient daughter asked of the Torah's narratology, "Since no one could have known what really happened, why were these stories made up?"[10]

We warn here that we find, along with the fine Israeli scholar Sperling, expert on the 5th Century BCE Elephantine Jews, that it was a Hebrew *Bible* anthologizer's *zeitgeist*, the social context including the political and cultural agenda of Identity that goes far beyond enhanced fact and history. Even beyond the accepted Biblical muses who mythologized earlier cultures and events, it was designed to create one culture from the others and to ensure lasting identity, beyond appropriation deep into the realms of political and artfully morally didactic *fiction*. While one can easily relate to these very human identity motivations, it is incumbent on all who take the *Torah* as fact to wake up and smell the now dusty heteroglossia of texts and cultures. Dr. Sperling's now-adult daughter, living the life of a modern Israeli, warrants appreciation on the asking of the question behind her then question: "Why?.." Identity and distinction from those earlier, foundational cultures are two large parts of that answer. Now the post-modern political comment we mentioned, again seeking peace…

If our recent tours of one wing of the Louvre has taught us anything, it is that nothing last forever, that human life is corporal, that even monuments to power and identity crumble and are supplanted. This supports both Jeffers' and Shelley's poetic warning to those who come after, to not be guilty of hubris, unbridled ambition, avarice. The lucky among the temporarily powerful end up with handprints traced in museums, a kind of cruel joke of immortality. On a recent trip to the south of France, to Nice, Cannes, Antibes, Monaco and Monte Carlo, Freeman saw a contemporary middle-eastern billionaire's yacht docked, costing $1.2 billion. The big boat sits idle, sometimes for years, fortified with both a submarine to explore undersea to escape from enemies, as well as missiles for defense against the unseen enemy, the most expensive private yacht in the world. Flying in to Charles DeGaulle airport outside of Paris, Freeman saw a Concorde SST with gossamer wings, set atop a display pole like a fragile late 19th Century CE sparkler never to fly again. Later from nuclear powered TGV electric bullet train at 225 mph, he viewed from its windows wisping by horizontally nature and history as usual: blurred sheep, cows, green field, vineyards, watering ponds, agriculture performed just as in ancient times by human hands, but now unclear and blurred by technology, speed and time-warp interlarded by 13th Century hilltop cities, including the medieval walled Palace of the Popes in Avignon with its vertical 25-foot-high solid gold Virgin Mary atop the highest 1308 CE tower.

Some progress is folly, distraction, although convenient; misuse of technology for possible Armageddon, to steal identity, secrets, to foster passive, digital play of the mind separated from bodies are all examples of this entropy. Aristotle's theory of virtue correctly argued that his lists of virtues and vices could be bent by excess, that too much of anything, even a virtue, would be a vice and that conventional vices, if well intended, could become virtuous.[11] Surely the world does not need a 1.2 billion dollar yacht with a submarine and a missile that stays in port and benefits no one, rich or poor. Shelley had his invented King Ozymandias call out in hubris, "Behold my works, all ye mighty" in his monument's inscription, the stone desert visage tweaked a little bit by its sculptor just enough to ironically please the temporary king in time but with an artist's added bonus of a mocking sneer on his visage's lips that passed divine muster and then lived on to mock the King in time out of mind.[12]

Readers will recall that the statue is broken and crumbled in the desert sands in Shelley's famous poem, its inscription ironic and archaic, rendered futile by time, erosion, chance, the big sweep of real time. Put simply, there are no works of empire left to admire: only an empire of sand. The above brief review of near eastern rulers leads us right to the excess of the present. Examples from this part of the world and from all over the planet abound. Saddam Hussein was not the first iron-fisted, palace building conqueror to fall in the long history of failure to cheat the "one-story" mono-myth that tells the truth, the cycle of birth, living, eating, reproducing, killing or being killed, living and dying, hoping for an after-life of any satisfactory sort. He was just the latest Fertile Crescent would-be divine poser to fall. There will likely be other empire builders who fall.

Sargon II (721-705 BCE), as noted, attempted the same folly to cheat death as the sweep of time accelerated. His Assyrian rule made the palace of the king—not the temple of gods—the locus of life, building a whole new city, Dur Sharrukin, near Nineveh or modern-day Mosul: 4,000 cubits or a 150 football fields to feature the twenty-five acre palace of excess, its center, in turn, a wedding-cake shaped temple, the ziggurat, dedicated ironically to the god Sin. Two thirty-ton, fourteen-foot-high alabaster bulls with human faces guarded the entrance to Sargon II's throne room, guardian spirits warding off demons. Visitors who penetrated the artificial mound of a city then could have looked over the twin bull's heads and seen the fifteen-story ziggurat towering overhead, a pyramid temple not to gods but to a king. Today, bending time again, the bulls stand in the Louvre, inscriptions between their legs. The emperor/king Sargon II's city and palace are long supplanted by their Babylonian supplanters who are likewise gone. One of the guarding bull's inscriptions mocks divine rule and immortality: "I, Sargon, King of the Universe, built palaces for my royal residence... I had winged bulls with human heads carved from great blocks of mountain stone, and I placed them at the doors facing the four winds as powerful divine guardians. . . My creation amazed all who gazed upon it."[13]

As poets, Jeffers and Shelley persist as conveyers of what Joseph Campbell called the "one true" story of literature, without irony or hubris or self-interest, just the desire to truth-tell the one real theme: that we cannot cheat death; therefore that we should live as if each ethical, in-time moment might be our last and that, in choosing one momentous decision, one life, we chose all.

The conquering pre-historic peoples abandoned agriculture in the northern Mesopotamia to trade and pillage, using an aggressive and innovative army with chariots, mounted cavalry, siege engines, and policies of ethnic cleansings, mass deportations of the vanquished, efficiency of logistics like roads and postal service, and most of all a policy of absolute terrorism against all enemies, the Other-ed, the "Romans of the east." We contend that in the west the Hyksos people and their metallurgy earlier laid the foundations for these innovations in warfare that likewise became so important in the Egyptian overthrow and forced exodus of their occupiers and ancestors, the Hyksos people, not far from where the Semitic people ruled by force. A royal palace inscription, by a Semitic king, says it all, speaks the blood lust that we have not learned, then or now, to avoid: "I tied their heads to tree trunks all around the city."[14]

The Richelieu wing of the Louvre tells this sad story in three-dimensions, out-of-time. Sargon II, at the height of his "power," invaded what is now Israel, and, after a three-year siege, took Jerusalem, deporting most of its population, creating 7th Century legends of the Lost 12 Tribes.[15] The prophet Isaiah saw Sargon II as God's weapon to punish sinful Israelites, "to seize loot and snatch plunder, and to trample them down like mud in the streets."[16] The prophet himself seems guilty of the vice of revenge, blood lust. The wonderful innovations of culture and civilization, driven too often by ambition and decree, are like boats of gorgeous Lebanese cedar created to carry the very wood products they were made of, depicted on relief panels in the

Louvre. Literally and in metaphor, they take the finest cedar logs to kings like Sargon for his palace of empire, across "a wavy sea with fish, turtles, crabs and mermen." They bespeak the best and worst of us all in one, yin and yang. The *Bible* reports "My men will haul them down from Lebanon to the sea, and I will float them in rafts to the place you specify."[17] Next to this elegant accomplishment, put to greedy royal use, are more relief panels, brown eroded gypsum once painted and varnished against time, of big, winged animals, scenes of the ostentation and humiliation of subjects in the courtly life of stratified wealth, that human theme, one of the huge hero, Gilgamesh, crushing a lion as if it were a mouse. How many of our family crests, our narratives and our genealogies are those of violence to establish identity?

Brian Boru, the Irish warlord, runs in Freeman's blood imported to the former Presidio in San Francisco by way of the Mayflower on the Massachusetts coastline. In Gage's, courses the blood of a Civil War hero and a history of Welsh struggle imported to Oakland, California. Perhaps that's why Gage cut loose in 1958 and hitch-hiked to Syria. We find ourselves as scribes now to do our best to mutually record. When some of Freud's last words were "the struggle is not yet over," he may not have been alluding wholly to psychology but referred holistically to the human struggle to improve our natures as a species by questing for the one and many truths, discovered or invented. We need more nimble, collective thinking if humans are to not only persist but to flourish via a common-culture higher ground.

Sargon to Saddam Hussein happened faster than the centuries' durations might indicate. King Nebuchadnezzar moved the capital of conquest to Babylon near modern Baghdad, then moved quickly to conquer Judea in 586 BCE; recorded in *The Bible's* many references to "Babylonian Captivity." He built a palace with "Hanging Gardens." That the Hanging Gardens are one of the Seven Wonders of the World says a lot about our collective wisdom and about us. The centuries seem to speed up as we approach the present turmoil of conquest with war that was just waged in Iraq and is now ongoing in Afghanistan, with other hot spots like Iran and North Korea looming, and ISIL now sadly importing the old blood lust into the present.

Babylon/Baghdad fell quickly to the Persians (539 BCE); to the Greeks under Alexander the Great (331 BCE); to the Persians again who held it for in redux (2nd circa BCE to 5th Century CE, bridging the time of Christ); to Islam, CE 634); to the Mongol hordes (Genghis Kahn's grandson, 1258); to Iranians (1502); to Ottoman Turks (1535 - 1918); to British-controlled kings (1921); to a military coup in Iraq (1959) when wounded Saddam Hussein passed on the highway west co-author Gage heading east; to the installation of Hussein in 1979.[18] But let us not quibble about our nature. Let us just say here that five thousand years of invasions, violence, genocide, displacement, exodus and regime change, as well as current events bursting around us as we scribes write, in hot-spots like Syria, suggest that it is unlikely that the second cradle of civilization, the Fertile Crescent, will see permanent peace anytime soon, nor will Africa, the first cradle of life, nor any continent anywhere. For that, we need altered fundamental human motivations and beyond-limbic thinking. The history of history, biblical literature, extra biblical texts, genres of literature, common myths, creation stories and religions seem to suggest that we can do better and should do so as soon as possible in this nuclear age, seeking and celebrating commonality rather than obsessing over difference. We should listen to our few remaining WW II veterans, both those who defended the Allies and France by landing at Normandy Beach and those who saw colleagues carrying their eyeballs in their charred hands after the bombings at Hiroshima and Nagasaki.[19]

We must learn from our successes and our mistakes, clearly defining which acts and artifacts are in fact those successes, which are the mistakes. Hiroshima and Nagasaki were pragmatic successes and ethical mistakes. Pearl Harbor's still-rising oil droplets from the USS Arizona underwater tomb/museum testify to Japan's temporary pragmatic success and moral failure in World War II. To fail to use the perspective of all that has come before, to fail to chip away at the long, dark dross of history searching for the pressurized carbon we call absolute diamonds, is more than absolute folly.

The ancient Hyksos, Egyptian, Greek, and Hebrew nexus of warfare should, by now, have taught us this objective truth. During their long occupation, the ruling Hyksos innovated in Egypt horse-based warfare, forged metals, enabling chariots, and these then new-age weaponry. Once the Egyptians no longer feared dying in foreign lands that vetoed chance for individual immortality, they eventually used these weapons on fleeing Hyksos, to end their near-200 year domination of the Canaanites. The television show NOVA's episode "Pharaoh's Chariots" valorizes the technological achievement of chariot building in warfare.[20] It correctly cites Ahmose, the first Pharaoh of the New Kingdom, as expelling the Hyksos occupiers, but the documentary fails to credit the Hyksos for having introduced both the horse and the chariot in the region. It was this innovation that enabled the first foreign armies to overrun Egypt in the Second intermediate period (the First period suffered a cultural breakdown and implosion, not an invasion). The documentary, while interesting and well made, is essentially an Orientalist report. Our thesis, that these innovations and the Canaanite culture that produced them are four centuries earlier, is more of a bombshell. After the five generations of documented Hyksos governance, the outnumbering Egyptians eventually turned their own Hyksos-invented weapons upon their occupiers. The NOVA documentary mistakenly attributes the invention to the Egyptians and their eventual match, the Hittites at Kadesh, who genuinely did further innovate a *3-person* chariot.

We know that Hyksos introduced the chariot; hence, the Semitic and Hatay worlds were always technologically ahead of the Egyptians, from bronze and iron forging to chariot production, as Egypt was never a cross-roads but rather a cul de sac geographically and commercially. It acquired this new weapon from the Hyksos, and in time, with its increasing population and further chariot modifications, the army of Pharaoh Ahmoses (1570-1544) was finally a match for those Hyksos, who'd antagonized them for decades. Egyptian incursions to the north, with its revengeful memories of Semitic occupation, came to a stop with the standoff. The Egyptians from 1550 until 1240 had been quite troublesome to Syria and Anatolia and Greece, as viewed darkly through the aging windows of Cadmus and Danaus stories.

Here is our uber-*Exodus* in a nutshell, the might of the south in manpower with the new weapons marched north to drive the Hyksos east, north, and, according to our argument, west to the Aegean. The New-Age Egyptian no longer appeared as concerned with the afterlife; hence, the soldiers of armies dying outside of Egypt were no longer as worried as those of the Old and Middle kingdoms had been, of needing to die in Egypt in order to warrant eternal life. The Hyksos foreign occupation taught the Egyptians the nomadic need for *offense* as the greatest *defense*, so those Pharaonic armies extended their conquests of any hated Hyksos ancestors all the way counterclockwise to Greece.

The vestiges of Hyksos culture became naturally appropriated in the narratologies of those overrun by Egyptian armies. One can easily see how expected distortions occur in the adaptations of fact to myth or myth to fact, our implicit premise or heteroglossia of texts and artifacts, Bakhtin's brilliant term for the children of all nations' ongoing game, "whisper down the lane."[21] It is no accident that the last person at the dinner table of history inherits an often vastly different narrative than the one who organized the narrative. In our zeal to both *preserve* and *add to* the objective truth, we naturally add our relative point-of-view in time and place, even during a few minutes' duration. Just imagine the distortions inherited by the Hebrew authors of the *Torah* from two millennia time of historical truths. Imagine, too, their understandable agendas of identity and culture building, as layers of that historical and luminescent pearl that was to become the anthology we now call *The Old Testament Bible.* If we are to have peace, we need both an accurate understanding of the past's distortions and its truths *and* a plan for the future, both in and out of time. We need too, to study the very language and literature of our common and different cultures for what they reveal about *us*.

For instance, consider the fact that epochal references to *both locations* and *language* date *both* the rhetor and the audience. That said, we will deal briefly first with location references, then deal with the very word Cadmus, the enthonym, for what we associate with the Hyksos, cultural amalgam credited with dispersing Canaanite culture from Thebes of Egypt to Thebes of Greece, its own origins, addressed a little bit later. We should note, however, that place names and locations are themselves examples of language. All narratives carry this double-bladed chronological dating possibility for speaker/ scribe and for intended audience. With language considered, the knife's or sword's edge becomes triple-edged. *The Torah* is no exception. Neither is the Elizabethan cannon of Shakespeare's literature.

The audience of *Loves Labours Lost* may be confused by the reference to Navarre and may not know that Navarre and its hegemonic neighbor, Aragon, dominated the Mediterranean from Iberia to Sicily to Greece to Hungry for close to half of a millennium a century and bit more before Shakespeare. Norman Davies in *Vanished Kingdoms,* cites Alt Clud of 800 CE when no one knew of Scotland; of Rosenau rather than Germany; of Galacia in Russia not Spain: those kingdoms and nation states whose lights have gone out in the dark rooms of history and in parallel have gone out in the room of our minds today.[22]

Such lacunae of knowledge parallels the authors of the early books of the *Pentateuch,* for their appellations of Egyptian territories, cultural habits and geopolitics date them from between 900 and 500 BCE, certainly not further back in the early and mid-Second Millennium about which they purport to be accounting,[23] but we feel here, based on reasoned, dispassionate, Cartesian-style analysis, that the *Pentateuch* reports these earlier histories and myths fallaciously as factual history. This premise allies us with the Biblical "Minimalists," to be elucidated soon, but we share some empathy for the Biblical "Maximalists" as well. We are insisting on a further historical reach backward to earlier Hyksos real history and to collectivized myth as the genesis for Egyptian, Greek and Hebrew cultures that followed. We are drawing our line in the sand earlier than the later lines sketched by Hebrew scribes who drew theirs by amalgamating and inventing a past pushed forward into heteroglossia. Perhaps we can soon find the Greeks' golden mean in this line of reasoning, a kind of Biblical "Moderatism." Perhaps. But we scribes cannot ignore the tracks of Hyksos history—revealed in maps of Canaanite historical and mythological genealogy from mid-16th BCE century down to the period of Solomon—some eight hundred years in the midst of the void caused by the invasions of the Sea Peoples.

Solomon lived from around 970 to 920 BCE. The only cities cited during his Alt Clud-like Kingdom were four, Megiddo, Jerusalem, Hatzor, and Gezer (see Maps). Solomon's father King David never had chariots, and only Solomon had a maritime presence, largely thanks to Philistine Hiram, who towards the end of Solomon's reign repossessed twenty Hebrew unnamed towns, 1 Kings 9. This was to cover costs incurred for Philistine support of the wise King's massive building projects. Remember, Solomon enslaved Hebrews, not Philistines, to do the work.[24] Modern cartography from Egyptian stele depicts escaping Hyksos. Modern cartography from carved stones (dated from 1500 to 1200) appear to cite only a single allusion to any Hebrew presence, that being their occupation of territory, not in Egypt, but near the Jordan River in Canaan. And the Egyptian history does not note any exodus of such ecological violence as reported in the *Bible*.

This is where Cadmus comes into sharp focus. His five siblings map the eastern Mediterranean: a brother whose name persists as the island of Thasos; a brother Kylix, or of the soft "s" in the days of St. Paul of Tarsus "that is in Cilicia"; brother Phineas who got to Bulgaria; brother Phoenix who reached the Pillars of Heracles and returned to labeled the Levant with his name; and then there was sister Europa. Brother Phineas, though leaving no named landmass, his name does appear curiously, as Moses was buried on the property of a man named Phineas. Cadmus himself founded Greek Thebes but along with his wife, the daughter of gods, Beauty and War, find gerontological haven to age in up the Adriatic in Illyria. No one has been able to explain the identical names of Thebes, in Egypt and in Boeotia: clearly the Greeks named the Egyptian site, but why Thebes? Likely, for the same reason founders called New York after the English York. These Hyksos siblings and archetypes likely never existed as individuals shaking the tail of history, but rather the eponyms are likely Hyksos tribes. Regardless, the place names stuck, and, with the monikers, came the narratives of each, told and retold down to Plato, via Bakhtin's heteroglossia, the unfinalizability of texts defined. Let's give the fleeing Hyksos a century to reach Greece. Please note the cognates of "Danuna." This is one of the three names Homer gave Troy's enemy and also denotes the northernmost tribe of the 12 Hebrew clans. The Hyksos went west...

Consider, too, how historically Egyptians had to be buried on the West side of the Nile to achieve immortality, for dynasties until the New Kingdom, few Egyptians would engage in Imperial war for fear that they would be killed outside Egypt as noted earlier and thus not achieve desired immortality. Only sometime before the pre-Armana age did Egyptians get so angered at invaders that they did begin to fight foreign wars, but, mostly, they had proxy kingdoms do their other-side-of-the-Sea-and-river fighting. One pre-Bernal scholar, in challenging the longevity of Cadmus, summed up others from the previous century and cites the Hellenistic Parian Chronicle at 1516 BCE, a date which would be just the mark, or a 4th Century Church Father who estimated dates as Cadmus' presences, between 1455 to 1285 BCE, as dealt with in Chapter 4 below.[25] This tradition and history explains why it took tribal Cadmus or the Hyksos to get to Greek Thebes after a long exodus of between one to two hundred years. However, consider that people fleeing tend to victimize those in their paths as obstructions, which may have entailed the Hyksos pausing for periods long enough for locals in their path to get their fill and join the Egyptians in their pursuit of deracinating Hyksos by allying as mercenaries for the Egyptians, who *had been* for a long time mortally afraid to die in foreign lands.

This logic is supported by the Bass aqua-archeology excavation of the Uluburun wreck, a ship sunk around 1375 BCE.[26] So far, the path of the Hyksos' exodus is land, but how about the sea? Among its finds deep underwater were a gold cartouche of Nefertiti, crumpled, signifying that Akhenaton and Nefertiti were already dead, the cartouche of crumpled gold likely destined for re-smelting. Also found deep underwater were 149 Canaanite jars, some with resin of Pistacia, an ancient source of turpentine. This type of jar, assessed to have come from what is today Northern Israel, is commonly found in Egypt, Syria-Palestine, Cyprus, and Greece. Analysis of the clay jars found near Tell el-Amarna from the 18th Dynasty is quite similar to that from the Kash wreck.[27] Clearly, there were maritime linkages between Avaris and Tanis and Krete: please note the bull-dancing motif imported here.

Some Hyksos likely arrived in Krete, as clearly later Phoenicians, but the sea and the required sophistication of ship building in the Second Millennium made this kind of over-water passage dangerous and likely limited to a small number of refugees, likely the ones with the biggest funding.[28] Now, following their path, we get to deduce the compelling archeological evidence from the Hyksos olive oil jar cylinder seals. These are seals from Knossos in Krete linking the bull dancing icon with Tanis/Avaris, finds of Bietak's excavation in the Delta to cylinder seals in Thebes, Greece. Professor Gage took pictures in the Thebes Museum in Greece of the forty-two cylinder seals found at digs at the Old and the New Cadmeia, the levels of the palace, excavated by Nicholas

Plankton in the 1960's. Here we find a Cretan-like goddess and here an ivory throne; here are material finds of artistic expression linking from the Nile to the Cadmeia, whose Theben onomasticon cry out Hyksos.

Here, too, is a strong argument for the plausibility of the Hyksos *Exodus* and *Immigration*, a case for the *real* history of a pre-Moses exodus and expansion, a picaresque journey of fleeing and conquering. In this case, history derived from facts transmogrified into myths stands solid compared to the shallow, popularly embraced whimsies of those buying into Arthurians' and Hebrews' reconstructions to establish nationalisms, except that they have media infotainment and armies with technological warfare to erase an archaic past. As cited, evidence of Arthur's historical presence is but a page of musty velum. More likely the case is that in the time of King Henry II (1170 CE), when England needed some Charlemagne-like hero to warrant this vassal lord Plantagenet who owned half of France to invent mythic status as propaganda against his liege king.[29]

If the past teaches us anything, it is the lesson that empire-builders and those who support them will bend real history to fit their present purposes, using time of the past to augur present, often selfish goals. Artistic expressions in stone, in song and in edifice beacon toward futures, and the futures often attune according to novel genres, material plasticity, and geopolitical realities. We scribes suggest attuning in particular to the late Edward Said, to avoid selectively erasing the important past.

In looking at the grave markers circa 2490-2472 BCE of the Pharaoh Menkaure and his Queen Khamerer, housed in the Graywacke Museum in Boston, the giant nudes, fourth dynasty couple are advanced stone carvings, tall Khamerer resting her immortal arm on equal heighten Pharaoh Menkaure in a forever stilled embrace, their impressive and life-sized expressionless faces.[30]

We in the west and east have been long married to the idea that Moses parted the Red Sea, that the books of the *Bible* are literally true, that the multiple scribes recording were faithfully rendering what they knew in ignorance of a history already forgotten though traces of which lingered in Greek song. Listen to the Hyksos mistress. Let her have her *real Exodus* song. The Hyskos came to Egypt after the Pharaoh Menkaure's reign, an added Hyskos onion layer of foundational history, informing so much of what we take to be the culture and innovations of later Others who in turn followed them. Both Menkaure's descendants and their occupiers sang the Hyskos song of conquest and flight and had multi-centuried moments in the 1700 to 1560 sun, strongly influencing the history of History.

3
Appropriation of History

When Kadmus marched in [Boeotia] with a Phoenician army and [the Hyantes and Aones] lost the battle, the Hyantes ran away during the very next night, but the Aones made a ritual supplication so Kadmus let them stay and intermarry with his Phoenicians. The Aones were still living in villages, but Kadmos [Kadmus] built the city which we still call Kadmeia [Cadmeia]. Afterwards as the city grew, Kadmeia became the acropolis for Thebes down below.... In Kadmos' time the greatest power after his own was that of the Spartoi ... but the outstanding one for many quality was Echion, and Kadmos decided to make him a son-in-law."[1]

HISTORIC & LITERARY ACTS AND ARTIFACTS OF COURAGE: The very act of collaborating on this inquiry is a two-part act of courage, one we make seeking peace in the Middle East and around our shared planet, through common culture. Our subject matter is potentially controversial, as we are objectively comparing and shifting emphasis away from long held assumptions about the interplay of the Hyksos, Egyptian, Greek and Hebrew cultures. We seek here to re-examine canonical *Biblical* literature with fresh eyes, insisting not on absolute historical truths but rather concentrating on an objective and fair *comparison* of the true original conceits of chapters 1-11 of the "Book of Genesis," Chapters 1-6. This includes the canonical *Flood* story, as well as the stories of Noah's Ark and the Tower of Babel, the latter about the failed human / tribal attempt to merge among the ancients one common language culture. The impetus of the central passages of *Exodus* examines the very history of *Biblical History.*

For another reason, our collaboration is a Hegelian dialectic, plus one: the tria-lectic of two thinkers, each with his own social and cultural assumptions, undergirded by the habitual memories, likely non-conscious influences of a heritage from Western Europe. And for each exists his accidental impressions qua-memories resulting from personal history further abused or massaged each day by the media's breaking news about what is happening. Even

Intra Time and Culture, the radical ambiguity of a shared language reverberates with resonances and cacophonies, the heteroglossia of connotations, the language stew accreted in *Time Out of Mind.* Just consider the ironic title of a recent popular 21ˢᵗ Century CE English composition handbook, *Eats, Shoots and Leaves: A Zero Tolerance Approach to Punctuation* distributed in a time of school-shooting tragedies ranging from Connecticut's elementary horror to the latest breaking campus mayhem.[2] (Truss 2004). That title already resonated with connotations beyond its Panda-bear-munching-bamboo denotations with, sadly, more broadcasted layers of school shootings *In Our Time.* Out of *Place and Mind, Out of Time,* the way grows wider, and the potential for radical ambiguities of rhetorical interpretations becomes even more likely with its passage. Our subject of time reaches back epochs to the migration of cultures in the eras of BCE. With fortitude, we attempt to attune when supersonic and electron Internet migrations occur every nanosecond in the post-modern 21ˢᵗ Century era, to the blur when even the beautiful symbol of the late 20ᵗʰ Century, the Concorde supersonic jet, is now housed a museum.

Additionally, beyond the troubles and joys of shape-shifting accounts of both historic and mythopoetic retold events, there is also the problem and joy of cultural-literary-cum-history spin, that of heteroglossia of not only texts and events, but also of the identity of whose hands painted the California cave walls and from where they descended. Seeking peace for us requires not only a common understanding but at least some common interpretations of past events. You see, we have here called the hand tracings text "of Jeffers,'" as he wrote a powerful poem of the western tradition about native Americans gone extinct, knowing that in the early1800s approximately 300,000 native peoples thrived in California before and during the Spanish mission systemization; that approximately 30,000 survived the gold-rush into the19ᵗʰ Century before a 20ᵗʰ Century rebound.[3]

The results of shapeless heteroglossia and shifting cultural perception remains a problem, as it did for Jeffers in his fine poem, heteroglossia-cizing, as Jeffers' *hand* and *mind* composed art in language, ποιέω—*the Greek meaning of poem.*[4] Yet, of the important association of the ancient Middle Eastern with the Native Americans, who left their tracings thus *wrote* the poem as well, we scribes, *here* and in the *now, are* documenting a literary artifact of the 1930's, which in turn looks back recursively at a 5,000-year old archeological artifact of pre-European and Asian history immigration. We are putting a Hyksos to Hebrew "spin" on California cave walls at least twice denoted and multiply connoted.

We do this for good reason: to understand the sins of the past, hoping we humans might do better than war and school shootings as we propel into the future. We scribes do not seek here, as mentioned earlier, to find one history as *exclusively historic*, certainly not just our own western history, as we do find Hyksos and Egyptian histories to be seminal, as Greek and Hebrew histories are certainly seminal as well. We just do not want to ignore the fluid permutations of history undeniably becoming the literature, often mythic, of earlier acts and artifacts, which ought to be interpreted as such and not as *the one* history. Consider the Tassajara cave walls, an act and an artifact become literature, a poem. The potential for ambiguity abounds. The anthropologists of the 20th Century wondered out loud, and we scribes with them, the question, did "these shy, brown people" Jeffers writes of result via Spanish immigration and intermingling with southwestern Native Americans (producing a Mexican variant as well)? Or did these "shy, brown people" walk across the land bridge from Mongolia via Russia to Alaska and down from the Pacific Northwest? Add to this literary question "what did they mean/intend by deliberately leaving tracings of their 'cloud of palms'"? Why did they choose their hands as symbol of who they were? As one answer, Jeffers implies a quest for an immortality and a warning for these shy people's "supplanters," and one could fairly say that the supplanters, followers of manifest destiny, are *us*, but the poet is Robinson Jeffers.

We scribes ground our history of the history of literature argument in the nature of the sociology of knowledge, how we know what we *know* of our past, our cultural assumptions both in and out of *time* and *place*. Despite taking pains to seek absolutism in epistemology and ethics, we personally come into other civilizations "full of ideas," specifically Western ideas, as relativists. We are so steeped in Western thought and culture that, if one of us visited Istanbul, seeking to go to the Egyptian spice Bazaar, we might leap to the assumption that overhead plaque bearing the name "Mısr çarşı" is a Turkish cut-rate clothing label product name. In fact, the very word is a Cartesian thing-in-itself, a place name, the very word that the Hebrew authors of *The Bible* used for what we know of as the land of Egypt. "Egypt" is a Greek name that derives its etymology from the same source the playwright Aeschylus used, the scholarly diction here and elsewhere providing us with a biblical epistemology as a truth or myth. Here is the market (çarşı) of what those of the Nile and Bible called Pharaoh's land.

We find that the oldest Hebrew script, the Gezer Calendar, dates to about 900's BCE,[5] and Hebrew authors anthologizing the *Bible* dated approximately 250 BCE, creating the reasonable assumption that these authors, often writing in the langue Franca of time, Greek and Aramaic, were rendering oral texts from earlier times. Hebrew writing came relatively late, composed post-Exile, 6th Century BCE, and fixed more copiously in Hellenistic times, its grammar codified following Arab grammar during the Al Andalusia hegemony period prior to the Christian Reconquista.[6]

Music and poetry, most commonly songs, amalgamated with voices speaking historical fact through oral-tradition communal memory. This is the "X" on our treasure map of evidence, but is can be a map-chimera, sometimes clear and two-dimensional, at other times gossamer with ill-defined edges. Why this fluidity? We find ourselves sometimes up against the limits of understanding our own cultural palimpsests, our pasts, our very language. We are often shut-in with only what we know intimately as our tent, sleeping bag and pillow, and that cloistered situation is our shared conceptual memory of *our* cultural nomenclature, and that is highly biblically funded. Here we attempt to get out from underneath the tent of this collective memory, to temporarily push aside both our sleeping bags and pillows, to clearly view the 2nd and 1st millennia BCE through focused eyes in search of sources of habitual memories of daylight, to see at night the stars without any cloth or canvas filter of distortion.

Richard Jude Thompson's Harvard dissertation on the governance and sociology of the Hebrew people finds that it has an Assyrian conceit, not that of Canaan, Hittite, or Egyptian—that it is Assyria that grounds Hebrew epistemology, its sociology of knowledge.[7] Thompson says: "This study thus hypothesizes that the Deuteronomic history depicts an imperial, military covenant. After a survey of the inscriptions of the second-millennium BCE Levant, the Hittite empire, the Neo-Assyrian empire, and the first-millennium BCE Levant, the study concludes with an hypothesis that the evidence points to the ideology of the Neo-Assyrian empire as the historical precedent for the Deuteronomic covenant. The study challenges two suppositions, both the Deuteronomic history and its scholarship: that of the *Torah* as law and that of YHWH as a unique god."[8] We infer from Thompson and others that the Deuteronomic history of the Second Millennium obviates much if any Egyptian influence, that the 9th and 8th Century Hebrews cast an Assyrian model as their covenant, one not very much influenced by the Ugarit or Hittite cultures. We likewise infer that Hebrew strictures of obedience, fear, and punishment derive from Assyrian hierarchical theology, whereas the Ugarit system was heterarchical, as their gods even dined with the Ugarit King Krete, and, according to legend, Greek mortals married the offspring of deities.[9]

This Assyrian cum Hebrew model for divine obedience is oddly like the "miracle, mystery and authority" theory that Dostoevsky, execution reprieved and subsequently newly-Christian, warned of in his "Grand Inquisitor" chapter in the 1880's. The Grand Inquisitor demands marvels of the returned Jesus (in Seville, Spain), now ironically imprisoned by the Inquisitor for not enslaving men by providing those very same "miracles, mysteries and authorities." This refusal of "enslaving them to faith" and their willingly giving up their freedom has implications here in the search for common cultural understanding.

Such relinquishing rids humans of troublesome volition which implies existential ethical responsibility.[10] In this famous scene, one of Fyodor Dostoevsky's best, readers may recall that Jesus does not answer the Inquisitor's strident question of why not enslave man with the religious striking of fear? Instead, He offers the Inquisitor a meek kiss on the lips and no rhetoric at all, seemingly an unconditional act of forgiveness. Would that we all could have that kind of faith which provides such deep funding/grounding that the reality of the world in extremis (the setting and plot qualify as extreme duress as the Inquisitor is about to burn Jesus in an auto de fey if He won't recant his pacifism and actively enslave all men who cry out to be led). For Christ, a second mortal death might mean something else entirely. Even more to the point here, consider also the Hammurabi Code. Editor J. Pritchard, in his reproduced English version, lists seventeen passages that are borrowed from the Code of Hammurabi (1750) and appropriated in the *Bible*; ten more of these passages are embedded in *Exodus*; and a few more during the first millennium edited into *Leviticus, Numbers* and in *Samuel*.[11]

The operative question then becomes, where are the examples of Egyptian epistemology in *The Bible*? In spite of 600 referents, there are precious few citations, except the *Exodus* palimpsest, of accidental memories recalled in eidetic images. This lack of biblical evidence of 2nd Millennial Egyptian influence on the writers of those various biblical books cited above suggests at least two things. One, there was not any 2nd millennium BCE exposure of Egyptian Pharaonic culture on its Hebrew authors, for what there is derives from the First Millennium. There are no *Bible* records of 2nd millennium BCE gold-tipped obelisks to reflect the Sun God's light; no Great House of Amen Rah Temple where the Karnak Pharaoh, a God, supposedly lived 3,500 years ago. There are no examples of the granite quarries of Aswan, south of Thebes, that produced up to one-hundred-foot-tall, 500 ton granite monuments shipped on boats from 2000 BCE on, shipped from the south past Queen Hatshepsut who once ruled on the Nile River. There are no allusions to the

Sphinx upward toward the Delta, nor landings to the great Pyramids, nor citings of huge granite carvings, any of which are incredible feats of ancient engineering, likely to have left traces upon Hebrew social, personal, or habitual memories. History also tells us that an excavation of a large sand mound finally cleared during King Faizel's visit to the Great Pyramids in 1954 literally called up the turgid, pungent smell of 4,000-year-old cedar planks excavated from a millennial storage compartment below, a jigsaw puzzle of cedar wooden strips and planks from far to the northwest, not out of desert climate. When reassembled, these fragments yielded the discovery of Pharaoh Kufu's death boat.[12]

Why, then, did these literally monumental cultural monuments and icons, obelisks of granite employed as ways to convince ancient Egypt's people of Pharaoh's divine power, not make their way into the Israelites' record? We conclude that there was no nexus of cultural exposure between the two peoples in the 2nd millennium.

Secondly, this lack of biblical evidence of Egypt, which in the 1st Millennium strongly suggests trade, intercourse between Israel and Misr (Egypt), argues that such started only later, after 1000 BCE. Then, created stories were told, retold, and probably sung as well as believed history, until the anthologizers of the *Bible* began to make the record that frames one of the major religions of the world, starting about 250 BCE, but had no referent to the earlier historical Egypt.

The aforementioned scholar Redford floored us when he pointed out the Shishak and Rehoboam sites in *Kings 14:25* as the earliest citation of sites referenced in *The Bible* that are validated elsewhere, outside biblical reference. And even the *Jewish Encyclopedia* states: "There was no Egyptian Goshen."[13] A text from Mari likewise identifies the site of Hatzor of the 1750's BCE,[14] which was likely the largest Canaanite city, but only a third the size of Avaris.[15] These extra-biblical findings and corroborations provide external verification of the Hyksos occupation in Egypt first, but there is no such secondary proof of the biblical site reference "Goshen" forthcoming from Egyptian texts or any other source. To be accurate, though, "The Merneptah" (1205 BCE) does introduce the term "Israel." Mernepath was a Pharaoh in waiting who eventually took over for his long-reigning father Ramses II, not unlike impatient Prince Charles awaiting Queen Elizabeth II's passing. History is vague about whether it was Ramses II himself or son Mernepath who invaded Palestine, but that mystery is not salient in this discussion. What is clear is that the Egyptian army first encountered Israeli's not in Egypt at all but rather in the foothills of Palestine, east of the Jordan River. Hence, we discount the notion of the "apiru," a word some project as Hebrew; our operant point here being that there is little to no evidence, other than wishful thinking, of Jews in Egypt in the second millennium. Snell[16] plots the location of Israel in 1205 BCE as being east of Jordon, where Freud[17] locates his Yahweh Moses there as well.[18] Also quite pertinent here is that Redford corroborates Snell's dating and geography.[19]

We know of the Hyksos people's presence from the early 20th Century discovery of the Rind Papyrus composed during the 33rd year of Apophis.[20] And we know from the *Bibliotheca* of Pseudo Apollodorus, a first or second century CE author, of the mythical son of Io, Epaphos, a Hyksos pharaoh. The Greek maiden Io who bewitched Zeus, causing Hera to morph her into a cow, driven to Egypt where Io births Epaphos.[21] We know that the Hyksos likely introduced their inventions and discoveries of the horse, the chariot, and glass, only once cited as Zekukith in Hebrew, which appears in the late book of *Job 28:17*. We know from excavations in the Delta of dual burial of donkeys, brought from Canaan to Egypt,[22] and with them the introduction of bronze metallurgy, the military strategy and tactics, such as the establishment of a fluvial war fleet . . . a typical aspect of their 'Knightly' culture.[23] Redford's refutation of the "apiru" as Hebrew and the citations of others who find the same provides weight to the present debate about what is history and what is literary invention.

Daniel Snell asserts, "there is no self-conscious identity among these 'apiru,'" and he argues that the earliest usage of the word is 1900 BCE, long before any presence of Hebrews in Egypt or any inchoate state of Israel claiming as a concept for fundamentalist and nation-building appropriations.[24] Somewhere around 1700, the Hittite king Mursilish conquered Aleppo, now known by those in the Middle East as Halab, a Hittite root derivation.[25] Today's visitor will be told that Halab is from Western Semitic verb "to milk" and that it comes from Abraham milking his cow on the citadel mount during the Third Millennium, which might be grist for the fundamentalist's mill. Yet, this once again reveals the epistemology we are discussing, where the real history morphs and shape-shifts out of *time* and sometimes out of *place* or into *mind* in amalgamated appropriation, the "one story." Even more telling, Halab in its Hittite verb form denoted metals, perhaps copper or even iron.[26] Consider the purported fact that Abraham "milked his cow on the citadel," and readers, the third essential factor in this tria-lectic synthesis, will likely find with us this as compelling evidence of our present thesis of how heteroglossia is rendered differently in genres of history, song, and poetry, as defined earlier, and that these utterances are fixed in texts extended beyond the past into our day of cinema, opera, and political propaganda offered to buttress nationalism. Snell and Redford further agrees with other scholars that the purportedly Hebrew term "apiru" is in fact Egyptian and that it denotes the concept "dusty" as in Egyptian and as in other surrounding-area desert nomads. Just as Heracles literally means the screaming of Hera, our thesis' material evidence screams out in answer to Egypt's thundering silence about Hebrews there, as in Bill Hotchkiss' haunting poem lines: "these mountains do not cry for tragedy/ nor pray for peace/ they laugh at us with lightning/ will applaud with claps of thunder/when the human race is gone."[27]

We scribes do not know fully what we think, for, as Soren Kierkegaard said in his lovely book on faith and ethics *Purity of Heart*, "faith is a leap away from reason to belief," but we intuit that the answer to the peace question in the Middle East and elsewhere must be found in a common and honest understanding of who we are and where we come from. That understanding is what we seek here. When we discern among the heteroglossia of voices a discontinuity in undeniable registers, we scribes are compelled, like Josephus, who corrected some distortions yet created others, to call foul, in the interests of peace and common understanding. That is and has been our primary goal in writing this book, along with peace-building, a goal that is heartfelt and as necessary in the *now* as ever.

To comprehend the sociology of knowledge as it pertains to how information about the Hyksos reaches us today, we will conclude this chapter with a review of transmission of information, as influenced first, by who is conveying knowledge, second, by how his social and habitual memories affect his retelling, and third, by how the setting—not of birth and rearing—but the setting where the author wrote and how this sociology may or may not shade his utterances. Utterance is a Bakhtinian technical term that provides generality for both that which is written and is spoken but also includes how the shape, or genre, of language is informed. Oral speech is fleeting but none-the-less important and proven to be fluid, thanks to Milman Perry's remarkable contribution to rhetorical scholarship. Without attended to orality, nearly any discussion of text is only partial. Recently, Lawrence Kim, who followed in Perry's tradition, opened inquiry into what we are investigating, discourse of Greece and Rome and the East.[28] "Orality, Folktales, and the Cross-cultural Transmission of Texts" Kim/Perry allow us to speculate reasonably among the echoes of 1st Century Rome after the time of Christ.

Parenthetically, Milman Perry, in early 20th Century, warrants our attention about how the Aryan Model prominent at the time blinded objective investigation. A master's candidate in classics at the University of California, Berkeley, Perry was advised not to pursue the doctorate should he wish to parlay what he was working on, the importance of oral transmission of texts, or he'd not be granted the MA. Hence, Perry went to the Sorbonne in Paris to write one of the most important dissertations in the field of classics in the last century. The academic and historic privileging of only fixed texts rather than spoken or sung ones, though convenient, had limited the pursuit of knowledge. Perry's research led him to study reciters in the Balkans. Perry's finding related to Homer, the rhapsode, and how formulaic phrases found fixedness in subsequent texts. Young Perry died tragically from a bullet, but his work is being carried out by others, including Albert Lord, author of *The Singer of Tales*, by Eric Havelock, *Preface to Plato*, and by Lawrence Kim. Extant texts are nearly always the result of a continuum through time of voice that includes layers of human spin, or palimpsests. Modern troubadours and Arab hakawatis reciting in the Syrian bars of Aleppo and Damascus promise how to value text generation. It is said that the death of one hakawati is equivalent to the death of a dozen libraries.

Perry's arguments that oral texts warrant academic investigation, based upon his recordings of strolling Balkan bards, like Homeric rhapsodes of yore, provide deep insights into how legend and myth inform subsequent texts. He provides a most important case for valorizing orality and not limiting inquiry only to that which was fixed in texts. In the case of the *Bible*, the Perry argument allows for reaching further back in Time. Perry proposed not just limiting study only to when Hebrew pen met papyrus or parchment coterminous with Herodotus or to later, just about the time of Josephus, writing when Jewish scholars on the coast of Palestine held the Council of Jamnia to decide further on the final canon, called the *Bible*, which also had Roman writers. Then again, just how far back into Time, when orality reigned, can Hebrews legitimately imply their presence against finds from excavations or literal utterances about history empty of Hebrew presence?

This record is just what Josephus sought to provide. He was a refugee from Judea, a land recently ethically cleansed of his people and culture by his new un-friendly host, Rome. Josephus is our primary source of Manetho's chronicle of Egyptian pharaohs, which includes information about the Hyksos—whom Josephus claimed were Hebrews. Manetho, an Egyptian, wrote in Greek, and he took issue with what Herodotus reported about his culture. Writing in mid-5th Century BCE, Herodotus never cited the Hebrews. However, between Herodotus' time and Josephus' time, around 90 CE, several authors had cited Jewish presence, both favorably and unfavorably. To fill in lacunae and to refute, Josephus wrote respectively two works, *The Antiquities* and *Against Apion*.

Josephus' new setting warrants closer inspection. Today, you can dine on Jewish cuisine, including delicious fried artichokes in restaurants along via Catalonia that parallels, only a block away, the Tiber and the tiny island Tiberina. Here, nearly two millennia ago, Josephus, a score of decades after Jesus' crucifixion, would have heard a far different heteroglossia from that of today. The setting hasn't changed much. From the Temple of Apollo on via Catalonia to Isola Tiberina, an arrow's flight is only blocked by the Theater of Marcellus. Today on Tiberina, the Rococo Church of St. Bartolomeo, patron Saint of Medicine, dominates the island. That later palimpsest sits atop an ancient Temple of Aesculapius, a healing God, whose prototype is possibly the Egyptian Imhotep, the architect of the Step Pyramid of Djoser of the Third Dynasty.[29]

At the end of the island, addicts shoot up and discard syringes into the river or litter the ground where parents warn children not to run and play. From this spot, Josephus would have seen what was left of the ruins even then of the ancient temple of Aesculapius, its base a marble replica of Aeneas' ship. Today's tourists can still see remnants of a snake, serpentine embossed on marble, which matches a stenciled caduceus on ambulance windows streaking down the frontage avenues shaded by massive trees. Josephus' gazed upon architecture associated with medicine which would recall mythically the serpent that signaled to the Trojan hero where to land to found the City of Rome by erecting a temple honoring the God of *pharmakon,* of drugs and pharmacy. From oral legends crafted by Virgil into an epic, to the medieval Church of St Bartolommeo and its Rococo palimpsest, and onto to scenes of ambulances rescuing the overdosed, a cult of continuity persists in *space* but out of *time*. In the space where Josephus strolled, today's tourists also stroll, where nearby oaks exist whose boles grew from acorns when Innocence III reigned in the 13th Century, then among trees matured from even earlier acorns released in Josephus' time.

But what can we surmise about what Josephus heard in Rome, and why is that speech utterance of importance? Why might multilingual Rome matter to a Jew, who spoke a Semitic language, and who wrote in the prestige register of Greek for a Latin audience? Lawrence Kim addresses these kinds of questions in "Orality, Folktales, and the Cross-cultural Transmission of Texts."[30]

Josephus's via Catalonia was alive with utterances in a variety of tongues and in silent forms with mimes and charades lost to the past. Rome was a cacophonous setting in which newly arrival Josephus wrote to his two audiences, kinsman warranting knowledge of their past and open minded infidels whose understanding of his people needed correcting. It was a setting made rich with the contributions of other minorities.

Here the ideational germ of the *pharmakon* had formed cultic space, now occupied by flora and fauna and by ruins, where echoes of myths reverberate

Temple of Saturn / Baal in Rome. (In Rome, Saturn was worshipped as Baal by Phoenician / Punic citizens. Roman Forum, Rome, Italy.)

two millennia back to and far beyond the time of Josephus. Virgil's protagonist of the *Aeneid* hovers among this island *temenos*, when the Jew had arrived driven by the Emperor Titus, who destroyed Jerusalem. Rome vibrated and reverberated a heteroglossia of many tongues, Etruscan, Latin, Punic, Sabine, and Hebrew, with other vernaculars brought by slaves from the known and unknown worlds. Contrary to advocates of the Aryan Model of history, Rome had long been especially influenced by Semitic peoples, perhaps later offspring of the Hyksos, the Phoenician cultures, as evidenced by the three golden plates inscribed in Etruscan and Punic around 500 BCE. About sixty miles northwest from Rome and a half a millennium from Josephus' time, Phoenicians had thrived, had worshipped some avatar of Baal and Anat, as evidenced by the Pyrgi Tablets, three golden inscribed prayer sheets apostrophizing Astarte.[31]

Prominent, too, was Baal, for the Roman Saturn is Baal, and, associated by some with Kronos, the Greek Titan. In Nero's time, Punic utterances in Carthaginian vernaculars were also prominent, as indicated by Dictys's *Journal*, said to have been written when Troy fell. Not surprisingly, this novel, by a Semite of Krete, was added to Nero's library in the Domus Aurea just a few years before Josephus arrived in Rome and just over the Capitoline Hill from via Catalonia some six stadiums' lengths.

Dictys' *Journal*, contemporary with Troy, or novel, in the time of Nero, was translated into Greek from Punic, and was purported to be from a witness of the Trojan War, in which, according to Dictys, Aeneas's brothers won—one-upping Homer. Whether Dictys' work should be taken as an historical document and not as a novel is a subject pondered by Karen Ni Mheallaigh.[32] So whether it is on-site reportage or a historical novel that upstaged Homer's version, the ur-text derived from the same language family as Josephus' native tongue. Yet, another spoken Semitic vernacular had advanced to writing. Sanchuniathon reportedly had composed another history also before Troy, about Canaanite and Greek intercourse. This must have been translated into Greek, for Sanchuniathon likely wrote in Aramaic, but if it's true that he, like Dictys, wrote before Troy, he plausibly wrote in a Canaanite/Phoenician cuneiform script, similar to that of Ugarit, maybe only years after his Hyksos ancestors fled in the real historical Exodus. But like Josephus' filtering of Manetho's history, we only know of Sanchuniathon from a Christian father Eusebius (260—340 CE), who acquired Sancthuniaton from Phylo of Byblos (64—141 CE), younger than Josephus. But unlike Sanchuniathon, the Ur-text of Dictys' *Journal*, found by Nero's henchman, had been translated into Latin.[33] Non-Greeks and Non-Latins wrote too, but losers in war lose libraries. We are fortunate that the Hebrews' canon survived the fickle victors' spoilage.   In Rome, Josephus composed *The Antiquities* and *Against Apion* after arriving from war-torn Judea, in order to rectify misinformation to his hosts who prayed to deified Caesars, about his own people, without revealing the whole story that they were God's Chosen People. This was indeed a challenging rhetorical task! In certain books of the *Bible*, like "Esther," he had to adjust the narrative to Roman tastes. He both corrected the record and contributed to enhancing/exaggerating what pleased both his overlords, a non-Jewish audience, as well as his fellow Jewish emigrants in Rome. Josephus, additionally, is of great importance as he was the first to cite the existence of Christian followers of Jesus.

After arriving in Rome at the age of twenty-six, Josephus wrote *The Antiquities* to acquaint those presiding upon the Capitoline hill and beyond in the Forum about the history and culture of the Jews. Josephus wouldn't dare mention that his former land was the covenanted Holy Land assured by Moses. He sought to inform the Roman aristocracy of gaping lacunae neglected by Greeks like Herodotus and, in *Against Apion*, to rebut scurrilous claims against his people. In much of Josephus' work, written in Greek, he informed audiences in novel genres and motifs via the Hellenic belles-lettres favored in Rome, foreign to Hebrew or Aramaic.

The Hebrew text of "Esther" is not exactly how Josephus rendered the narrative. According to Emily Kneeborn, Josephus appropriated Greek tropes and conceits, even though, since after Alexander, written texts had been under Hellenic hegemony.[34] Literate Jews in their homeland under the Seleucids down to the time of Paul may have known some Hebrew, but intellectuals and royal administrators spoke the prestige language, while the populace spoke Aramaic, as did Jesus. Formulaic portraits in Josephus' versions reveal indebtedness to the Greek. Contrasting Hebrew versions of stories to the retelling of them by Josephus demonstrates Bakhtin's thesis of how versions accrete new meanings under the constraints of social contexts.[35]

In his *Antiquities*, Josephus extends beyond his Biblical sources the story of "Esther," a unique narrative as it never cites God nor has allusions to the covenant, "the sacred institutions of Israel or Jewish religious practice."[36] The plot deals with a Persian King and Esther, who has withheld her Jewish identity, in order to aid her uncle Mordecai against the plotting of evil Haman. Set in diaspora Persia, the paraphraser wrote to a Roman audience in the prestige language of Greek and attributes to Esther's husband, the King, novelistic overtones. *The Bible* portrays a cold autocrat demanding that his first wife parade before guests. Will the wife follow the law of her husband or abide her modesty? *The Bible* versions touches on nudity, circumcision, and Esther's voicing of objections to her husband's orders are not included in how Josephus renders the story. *The Bible* has Esther vogue before the King to allow Mordecai and her people to live in peace in Persia.[37] Josephus depicts the Queen having to choose between her husband's law or her own culture's law. Josephus' version of the wife's motive reveals *nomos*, a code of the Greek polis. The conceptual depth is Greek *nomos*, or "norm," and is not just Greek diction, for *nomos* isn't hovering earlier in *weltgeist* of Persia or of Israel.[38]

Another aspect of Josephus' history is his conflation of Greek, Egyptian, and Hebrew utterances in telescoping known persons of Egypt and Greece, such as Sesotros as Aegyptus and Amrais as Danaus. Is his fusion, in fact, congruent with our thesis?[39] As Kneebon opens her stunning account "Josephus' Ester and Diaspora Judaism," ". . . gone are the days when we could have been tempted to accept Josephus' claim at face value."[40] Within a century of the birth of Jesus, the Roman Jew contributed to the unfinalizable discourse, of which ours is among the latest palimpsest regarding the abundant records in Egypt of texts and images, though in ours with no reference to Jews in ancient antiquity. Writing in Greek, Josephus confronted the paradox ($\pi\alpha\rho\alpha\delta o\xi\omega\sigma$) of Rome, a yeasty symposium of intellectual debate ruled by a defied Emperor. Nowhere in Josephus is there covenanted land. Like Esther of *The Bible*, Josephus never refers to God's covenant with his Chosen. History is the product of peoples of every period finding identity in their *now* by adding the latest palimpsest.[41] Josephus, well versed in its formulation, described a *Bible* as a compendium of books of antiquity that chained back three thousand years to Creation. Facing the problem at the heart of our inquiry, Josephus buttresses his history with a number of other authors since

Alexander, like Manetho, who, according to Josephus, included Hebrews in the surveys of world history.

Between a century after Christ's birth, then back four hundred years to the Macedonian conquest, there are a number of historians Josephus registered who wrote about the Hebrews. Josephus' agenda was to integrate Jewish history with the commonly known history of Rome of his time, a history informed largely by Latin and Greek texts. In his diatribe "Against Apion," Josephus cites those non-Jewish writers Cheremon, Lysimachus, Apollonius Molo, and Hecataeus of Abdera and Cadmus of Miletus, Acusilaus of Argos, Hellnicus, and Apion.[42] Josephus links Jews with Aristotle, Hecataeus, and with Alexander. Unfortunately, nearly all traces are lost of this record. As mentioned, it is Josephus' agenda to establish his fictional integration as fact, though clearly he is often embarrassingly excessive as he claims Pythagoras was weaned on *The Bible*, from which the Greek acquired his laws,[43] Josephus' dilemma reminds us, today, when hearing of the Golden Age of Islam, with many of us attributing the lion's share of this history and culture as being accomplished by Jews, with an equivalent number in the Muslim world attributing the lion's share of these accomplishments to Persians.

In addition to arguing the impact of Jewish presence and influence, Josephus took umbrage with Apion, and others who misrepresent Hebrews, especially when portraying the Hyksos, whom Josephus claims to be ancestors of Hebrews, as "shepherd leper kings." An Egyptian writing during the reign of Greek pharaohs, Manetho documented a list of Pharaohs and reveals his familiarity with Herodotus' words about Egypt, of which Josephus reports the Egyptian disapproved. By 300 B.C., Manetho's Egypt had been overrun since the Sea Peoples, Libyans, Nubians, Assyrians, Babylonians, Persians, and, by Manetho's time, Greeks.[44] According to a recent scholar who appears to have relied upon genre theory to adjudicate the reliability of our only extant source of Manetho's king list:

> . . . it is crucial for Josephus' purposes that it be seen so, since the central point of the "Against Apion" is to set non-Greek text against Greek ones and show the latter wrong about the antiquity of the Jews.[45]

A host of historians, Greeks and Romans, included reports full of contradictions and lacunae. Since Josephus' Manetho rebutted what Herodotus had gotten wrong in his history of Egypt, Josephus' mission was to straighten out the record of the Father of History, which included equating the Hyksos with the Hebrews and updating Biblical reporting of Joseph and Moses in Egypt. Rhetorically, Josephus corrected Apion, a grammarian who had claimed that Jewish ritual included cannibalism. In his recent essay "Manetho," Dillery cites three Hyksos-related narratives that chain Manetho's enumeration of Pharaohs' reigns.[46] The heteroglossia in ancient Egypt lacked Greek genres of story and the discursive essay, rather offered texts propagandized in chronicles, not histories. Pharaoh's fates amidst the waxing and waning of the Nile's floods stabilized in Ma'at, eventual harmony or concord that yielded sustenance and a good life, so the lists lacked embedded elaboration, for their ultimate design voided any need for dramatization, narration, or inquiry, an epistemology that fostered quietude and fatalism. The three stories and Josephus' Greek diction and semantics clarify how Josephus' spin influenced subsequent history. Josephus or Josephus/Manetho reveals how Hebrew identity became integrated with the Egyptians' version of a king list, previously void of Hebrew presence.

> I observed a considerable number of people giving ear to the reproaches that are late against us by those who bear ill-will to us, and will not believe what I have written concerning the antiquity of our nation, while they take it for a plain sign that our nation is of a late date, because they are not so much vouchsafe a bear mention by the most famous historiographers among the Greeks.[47]

Josephus' epistemology, or that of Josephus/Manetho, include what other scholars describe as deuteromonic and Messianic discourse, utterances featuring essentially bad guys fulfilling a mission of vengeful God's or gods' rightful punishing a Chosen for their evil ways, a Chosen who must kick back idle to await a messiah to arrive who embodies a Devine Will for restoration. Although granted that the Egyptians had always been placid in accepting regularity like the predictability of the flooding Nile and the nature of Ma'ah, they were not manichaean as were the Semites reared in deserts and by earthquakes. However, with Manetho, whose culture under the Ptolemies and by Josephus' time with a Roman yoke, Egyptians had suffered occupation for a millennium. From the time of the Hyksos exodus down nineteen pharaohs to Rameses II (1560—1300 BCE), history of these imperial New Kingdom Egyptians had exuded anger and wrath and frequent vengeful pursuit of the Hyksos. That occupation of more than hundred and fifty-years and their exodus would not provide closure for Egyptians to settle for a quietude and impotence, which in the *Biblical* portrayal of resignation is more accurate of the period from David down to Cleopatra (1000-1048 BCE). Foreign violation would live in the memory, language, and textual manifestations of Nilotic heteroglossia as 9/11 will for Americans; they would gird their loins for another Hyksos, and then for years, until exhausted by the 1st Millennium, maintain a vigil for any recurrence of this foreign domination.

Fortunately in modern times, there are several king lists to complement Josephus' "Manetho," like the Turin scroll contemporary with Mycenaean Greece, which provides a cross-references to Manetho's pharaohs. It lacks what Josephus likely added, any suggestion of a connection of Hyksos with Hebrews (Berard 1952). Its composition was a millennium older than Manetho's and contiguous to the yawning void between the Hyksos exodus and the advent of the Sea Peoples of 1200 BCE and before another yawning void between the Sea Peoples to Solomon of the 10th Century, beyond whom biblical texts do first correctly cite a historic Pharaoh. Those Egyptians knew no Moses nor an Exodus that unnecessarily dodged an easy land bridge but preferred to have God separate the sea. This is another stunning example of the heteroglossia, one we must study to parse apart in order to understand the past for the sake of the future, one we must consider deeply if we genuinely seek common culture and peace.

This is what we scribes know now, one of us ensconced deep in the quarter moon night in southeastern Pennsylvania, wondering, almost ready for sleep, the other wide awake two times zones away, not yet in twilight, about to see the same quarter moon-rise out of eastern time, in Pacific, wondering too, not quite ready for dinner and the bread that will be an offering for loved and understood humans, at least on this approaching night, waves rolling softly against the northern California shoreline as the sun drops into the Pacific, blood-red and orange, about to mutually make both a water-tracked sunset and an Oriental sunrise. We scribes share a belief in the uniting power of humans who seek common ground in shared ideas, in shared world culture, and in the truths we forge together about the best ways to live respecting the dignity of all of our fellow men.

Cline's recent book on the collapse of ancient civilization teaches us that we are at our best when brought together by a common interest, even if purely economic. He argues that Egypt's empire might have survived declining trade, earthquakes, even man-made climate change had its will cooperated better with others. What empires cannot survive is xenophobia, prejudice and yielding to our basest instincts, especially in times of mutual crisis. The truth is, only cooperation will stop the dominos of civilization from falling harshly across borders and artificial lines of demarcation.

4
Narratization of Society

The Greeks, surpassing all men in their natural genius, first appropriated most of these tales, then dramatized them colorfully with additional ornaments, intending to beguile with the pleasures of myths, they embellished them in all sorts of ways. Thence Hesiod and the famous poets of the cyclic epics made their own versions and excerpts of the Theogonies and Gigantomachies and the Titanomachies, which they circulated and, thus, defeated the truth. Our ears have over the centuries have become accustomed to and prejudiced by their fabrications; they defend the mythology they receive as a sacred truth . . . which, having been having been wrought over time, has made its hold inescapable, so that the truth appears to be nonsense, and an illegitimate tale, truth.[1]

FURTHER HYKSOS FOUNDATIONS of the History of (Biblical) History: Inland to the northwest of Athens is Thebes of Boeotia, ancient cow country, where, in winter, snow impedes travel. Thebes straddles an intersection of where mythical Hermes once hovered as purveyor of boundaries and as lord of highway thieves. A Sphinx-shaped mountain overlooks the crossroads where young Oedipus was accosted by an arrogant Theban king and so killed the offender who chanced to be his father. Oedipus' stain of subsequent incest with his father's widow has left a black mark on this polis still exemplified in the city today where the contemporary tourist can't easily find souvenir tee-shirts or coffee mug memorabilia, for the city prefers to forget its tragic shame.

Yet Thebes of the ancient world was a center of cattle country until Argos interceded in its fratricidal war, an incursion that devastated the Thebes to impotence a time just before the Trojan War. Surveying the extant literary heritage of Greece, the three major tragedians of the Golden Age[2] set their dramas at Thebes—Aeschylus' *Seven Against Thebes*;[3] Sophocles' *Oedipus the King*,[4] and *Oedipus at Colonus*;[5] Euripides' *"Phoenician Woman"*;[6] and *Bacchae*.[7] Thebes was the site of the birth of the god Dionysus, of Heracles, and Leukothea, the "White Goddess" of Robert Graves' attention.[8] Cumulatively in literary heritage, Thebes vies with Troy to host nearly half the settings of classical Greek literature. However, in Homer's two epics, Thebes is a Boston-like polis of old money, a shade of its once-grand past—a city that sent no ships with Agamemnon to retrieve hopefully Helen to Mycenae. Thebes is a key to connecting the Hyksos' exodus with Greece through legends and myths.

From the scenarios of the plays, readers or audiences comprehend the generational disintegration of the House of Labdicus, the offspring of Cadmus the Phoenician who wed the daughter of the goddess of beauty and the god of war, and whose marriage was attended by all the Olympians. The signifier Cadmus was a fleeing Hyksos and heir of those who several generations earlier were driven out of Egypt. Cadmus founded Thebes when he obeyed the Delphic oracle to follow a divine-marked heifer to the pear-shaped *huyuk* of his future citadel.

Some Greek legends of these scenarios, like versions or conflations remembered of Phoenician, or Canaanites, specifically tell of the denouement of Hyksian exodus. Fiction and the nonfiction from Herodotus to Pausanias record that the Semites established Thebes along with founding coastal cities and impregnating their women, like the mother of Thales (624—546), the first philosopher.[9] Material evidence from digs and from Herodotus himself offers first-hand testimony of seeing Cadmean letters on ceramics.[10] Thus, complementing a Cadmean chronicle supported by the Hellenistic calendar found on the island of Paros, referred to above.[11] Fleeing aristocrats and former pharaonic administrators brought with them to Thebes those artifacts, if not too burdensome, that furnished tastes to which they were accustomed in Egypt or the Levant; its art revealing a cosmopolitan grace only found north of the Peloponnese. For example, a fourteen-meter wall fresco representation of women bearing gifts in procession,[12] though of Minoan style, represents Minoan fashion present also in the Delta, Krete, and Alalakh in Syria, found by Woolsey.[13] Here at Thebes was the only examples of Linear B script in mainland Greece, suggesting a center of erudition that faded terribly by the 1184 BCE, of the Trojan War.

Clearly, the Cretan style painting appears along the same geographic track as our fleeing Hyksos, at Avaris in Egypt, the Levant, Thebes, and the island of Thera before the volcanic explosion.[14]

This Theban fresco is among the earliest of Minoan influence, though from some 200 years after the Hyksos escape from the Delta.[15] And furnishings found in deep basements on Oedipou Street reveal a penchant for thrones with ivory supports that place the source of the materials from Africa.[16] From an adjacent ancient shop, glass paste jewelry and gold, granulated and in sheet, expose a technology for creation from a Levant source rather than from Krete.[17]

The visitor of nearly any museum or student of academic study readily encounters the nod to Egypt as precedent for what subsequently developed in the Eastern Mediterranean. But the motives of most of those bifurcated towards specializations extending to secular and scientific study of Greece or towards faiths of Judaism, Christianity, or Islam. Our present thesis narrows the gap by identifying the Hyksos people specifically as those who bridged Nilotic and Aegean cultures to catalyze and germinate later a multicultural Greek splendor, not that envisioned in the last century of a pureblooded Aryan inspiration of near-fascism stemming from the 1930s. Today's Thebes museum holdings, in five exhibition rooms, display dramatic evidence of a Hyksos presence. One case in particular, No. 15, displays the essence of our argument.[18] Theban shared tastes for Cretan painting suggest these originated from Phoenician, or Canaanite aristocracy, plausibly of Hyksos traces, after maintaining hegemony for two hundred years, or nine generations, subsequently distilled into myths and in the above theater scenarios. From the new and old Kadmenia of Thebes, in the 14th to the 12th Century BCE, heirlooms once displayed opulence and honor like those of American families tracing their roots back to Plymouth.

Consider what was found beneath the town of Thebes since the 1960s. (The undergound of Thebes is like the living room of a Massachusetts home with an *etagere* full of familial memorabilia). The shelves of this Theban *etagere* are full of these treasures: carved legs of elephant ivory once supporting a throne with Eastern motifs;[19] four ivory plaques, one featuring a desert ibex, another a charging charioteer; a family treasury of 42-cylinder seals of rare stone, and seven unidentified acorns in ivory too, begging for any salient explanation of function—items only similar to those curious acorns exhibited at Cairo's museum off Tahrir Square, which have befuddled scholars for over a century.[20]

The items in the collection spanned generations, and all reveal Eastern provenance, with some bearing the most exquisite artistry of any now in the Middle Eastern collections at the Louvre or at the British Museum on Russell Square. Nowhere in the world is there such a collection of seals—some of lapis lazuli—more seals found at Thebes than half of all ever found anywhere in Greece.[21] Nowhere has there been found their equal, even in Iraq, the origin of the stone material and home land of Nebuchadnezzar.[22] The public display at the Thebes museum includes agate of Cassite origin; gold-plated faience; one only with cuneiform text; another representing the Baal-like thunder god clutching lightening shafts, framed between two mountain peaks; and a Heracles-like hero holding off battering rams, though likely known to Kadmanian Thebans as Melicertes, his Semite moniker.[23] It should be noted that in myth Melicertes was the son of Ino, the daughter of Thebes' founder Cadmus.[24]

This mythos, what Graves calls "a medley of early cult elements," harbors many proto-scenarios of motifs found later in the *Bible:* an aborted sacrifice of beloved son like Isaac, an abandoned infant found by regal women, and virgin births,[25] and a rejected female who falsely accuses of rape a Joseph-like Adonis, also the plot of Euripides' *Hippolytus*.[26] Melicertes' half-sister appears too, whose name like so many of Cadmus' kin remains today in the Hellespont. As Graves attests, this recurrence is not only with Euripides' plot in the *Hippolytus* but likewise shared in the *Bible* with the episode of Joseph and Potiphar's wife. The unjust accusation of a scorned woman may link a Hyksian network including Baal with Bellerophon as a plot of a most ancient narrative in Egypt's "Tale of Two Brothers," dating back to at least Seti II's reign.[27]

Another seal depicts winged messengers approaching an earthly king seated upon an ivory throne, likely resembling what the ivory legs supported; another shows a seated monarch grasping the paw of a sphinx; and yet another displays a bull rider cameo in agate.[28] According to the foremost authority of ancient cylinder seals, only seventy seals have been found in Greece, which includes this Theban horde.[29] The gold jewelry warrants further exposition but only makes redundant and amplifies our justified claims of a Hyksos presence and legacy in Greece traced from around the 14th Century BCE, trickling down via myth all the way to Socrates' time.[30] Plymouth Rock and the Mayflower replica obviously mark the Massachusetts Bay Colony site. Imagine if Pilgrim artifacts, such as a record of Squanto's having taught the Pilgrims to use fish as crop fertilizer, Governor Bradford's diary, were to be found in Greece and those findings authenticated, vetted: we would say that either the Massachusetts Bay Colony Pilgrims undoubtedly were in Greece too or else their artifacts were transported there.

As with the finds at Mycenae, the horse, chariot, and charioteer are Hyksos themes and also are found in the Thebes Museum on a ceramic *larnax*, a chest associated with Egyptian linen boxes but used for burial coffins in the case of the tombs only 19-kilometers from Thebes. Rocky Greece had little internal use for cavalry, let alone for chariot warfare.[31] Such iconography displays wishful thinking and, we say, recollection of a heritage.

In history, chariots appear first among the Hittites and Mitanni, with the Hyksos introducing the technology to Egypt.[32] They are only used infrequently in rocky Greece, beginning late in the 14th Century, though represented in Mycenae in art in the 16th Century and in Thebes in the 15th-13th Century.[33] The Theban *larnax* depicts funerary rites in addition to other scenes on the flat surfaces, on one a bull with a jumping acrobat. That theme links to Minoan Krete and with links with other Hyksos usage of the fashion including wall paintings in fresco at Avaris and at Alalakh, east of Ugarit.[34] Chariots in Krete came from the mainland, not the other way around.[35] Our thesis advances in contra-distinction to foundational suasion that the Hyksos, innovators of this equine-based technology in Egypt, brought it to Greece *before* homegrown Achaeans used it sparsely because of the aforementioned rough topography. As at Nilotic Avaris, Cretan Knossos, Syrian Alalakh, and Thebes of Greece, the practice commenced around the eastern Mediterranean, their artisans shared a painterly style in fresco, depicting bull jumping, and supplicating buxom priestesses; so since all three engage in war, weapons technology for attack, like chariots, appear in art though infrequently in Krete and Greece.

Seven gates of Thebes, cited in Aeschylus' title, offered entrance up onto the hilltop city, which extended five soccer fields by another eight, where centered was crowned the old and new Cadmeias.[36] Today's Thebes adapted to the modern "horse-drawn chariot," the automobile, with a grid of six by eight streets overlaying a small city with a population close to that of Eureka, California. The modern town encrusts a promising *tel* or *huyuk*, beneath which awaits dwellings to be excavated. Some apartments of the Houses of Kadmos, new and old, buried for millennia, exposed shyly ancient rooms and sanctuaries, nearly aligning with today's modern building and block.[37] Posthole digs have yielded troves of findings that evidence a Levantine heritage centuries earlier that so disturbed the racist Plato in his "Menexenus."[38] Off Pindarou Street, a lot deeded in a widow's will allowed archeologists in the 1960s to shaft-excavate adjacent to, but beneath, business properties to probe successfully the ancient Cadmeia. Here they found flamed-scorched ivory furnishings, a ceramic bathtub, and an ivory throne, as well as gaming die, crafted from agate and in other rare stone, cylinder seals with oriental representations, hollowed to wear as jewelry for sealing jars. Some include depictions of threatening demons beneath the star juxtaposed within a horn-like moon, the latter today likewise impressed in the design of twenty-two flags of Islamic member states of the United Nations.

Modern street and city names provide audio palimpsests of Hyksos ancestry. In Thebes, streets echo dramatis personae of theater, of *Antigonou*, and of more recent Turkish occupation, such as in Dologlou, the son of Dolou. From Anatolia to the mid-Mediterranean, cities recollect a son of Thebes, Heracles, whom Pausanias linked to Egypt:[39] Ereğli in Turkey, Heraklion on the island of Krete, and (in Italy) Ercolano in the shadow of Vesuvius and neighboring Naples—or Neo Polis. These place names today like habitual memories emerge to conscious awareness of ancient conceptual memories once in the lyrics of Pindar, Thebes' own poet, whose polis spawned not only the demigod but also a god, Dionysus. In Thebes, it's as if at night a strobe-light reveals scintilla of Canaanite/Phoenician heritage. Thebes is like Jerusalem, where at each intersection of the modern towns stories ring out, ejaculating episodes such as where Antigone defied her uncle by casting burial dirt upon her exposed brother, or where Cadmus' grandson Pentheus encountered cousin Dionysus at the agora, or where Oedipus tragically found his hanging wife/mother/father's widow.

Beneath municipal offices await ancient witnesses of catastrophe. For the last century they felt the probing of archeologists digging while each's social context revealed threatening challenges not unlike what Thebes of yore lived through: archeologists like Karemopoullos, alive during our 1929 global economic crash; Platon, contemporary of the Vietnam debacle; Spyropoulos, a witness to TV reporting of the leveling of Berlin's Wall, and now beneath the Commercial Bank of Greece, a Savings & Loan-like scrutiny endeavors to bring Greece from the verge of European Union ejection. Academic investigators have found and continue to find more evidence of Cadmeia and its Hyksos emigrants. Material finds note late-Helladic frescoes of parading women, who resemble those on the walls of Avaris in the Delta, recovered gold just like what the Uluburun wreck revealed from the Mediterranean, and finding bronze weapons wielded by soldiers who could either fight or run, and text in Linear B script, unique in Greece north of the Peloponnese. Some of Thebes' modern buildings align exactly with those below from Cadmus' time, as viewed by Pausanias at the end of the 2nd Century CE. What Pausanias described as sacred haunts had laid exposed for a millennium as a cultural memory that informed of the "history of history," until the onset of Christianity negated a heathen past, thus beginning and bringing to consciousness the modern chapter from the time of Christ.[40]

Exact dating of these spectacular ruins has been problematic as there appears to have been successive Cadmeia, from 16th to 12th centuries BCE when the 16th Century BCE Mycenaean Thebes was occupied.[41] The first

Hyksos generation would have left Egypt in about 1550 to retreat to the Levant where thrived Agenor, father of Cadmus, Thasos, Phoenix, Kilix, Europa, and their less obtrusive sibling Phineas.[42] Then later, around 1375 BCE, the western bound ship we call Uluburun from the Levant sank off the southern coast of Turkey only generations before the Trojan War. Concerning the dating of Cadmus, one pre-Bernal scholar in challenging the longevity of the eldest sibling summed up what other scholars from the previous century had estimated of his dates. One cited the Parian Chronicle, composed in Hellenistic times, which begins with Cadmus thriving in 1516 BCE, the equivalent year in our calendar; this date would fit with the Hyksos' exodus. Another scholar, a 4th Century CE Church Father, estimated by today's calendar Cadmus lived sometime between 1455—1285 BCE.[43] The Egyptian Canaanite harbingers, categorized by the Cadmus eponym, had edged northward to their ancestral land, then north to Ugarit, and west across the south coast of Anatolia, before reaching Thebes in mainland Greece, Thebes above the Peloponnese, where, earlier, the signifier Danaus had supplicated Argos from non-Semitic Egyptians seeking revenge. The maps of this area are peppered with Semitic names.[44]

The ancient city of Waset is what Greeks called Thebes, just as the California Town of Gualala was corrupted by later generations from Valhalla. Even a cursory Internet search reveals that Waset is what Egyptians called Thebes, the city up river and the capital that most resisted Hyksos incursions. Today, as noted, Egyptians call Egypt "Misr" as in Istanbul's Misr Bazaar, or the Egyptian Spice Market. Naming is problematic for conceptual memories: What is a Kansas or Arkansas? The Greeks called themselves Hellenes; it was the Romans that branded them Greeks, meaning the Old Ones. In our argument, the fleeing Hyksos adopted the name that they had earlier given to the city Thebes on the Nile. Tribal Cadmus, who founded Thebes north of Athens, called his new city in an old tradition, after its new status harkening back to its origins, as in the place names New York, Naples, and for that matter Carthage, a cognate in Hyksos' language—more examples to heighten the plausibility and likelihood of historical Hyksos foundations.

Now we arrive back to the language and place name deconstruction we promised as scribes a little while ago, or a few centuries ago, in and out of time. We do this analysis, as noted, with the aim of finding common culture and a way out of war, to advance peacefully the human race. The reason why we use Greek names for Egyptian cities today is simply because for a long time we couldn't read the Egyptian hieroglyphs and had no idea how to identify Egyptian cities: we therefore were forced to fall back on Greek and Roman references. By the time of deciphering Egyptian, the habit of using Greek names had already been firmly established, like already long-dried cement. We now know the proper, intrinsic and ancient place names of almost all Egyptian cities perfectly well, and either if those cities thrived during the 2nd century BCE, and not the 1st or if during the 1st and not the 2nd; but now we are linguistic creatures of habit and those habitual memories sustain our Eurocentrism.

Apparently the Greek Heracles/Hercules, who was from the Greek city of Thebes, had Egyptian parents and was named by the Greeks after the ancient Egyptian god Shu, whom the Greeks surprisingly referred to as Heracles.[45] The somewhat famous Pharaoh Senusret I was known by the Greeks as Heracles Kharops; he too was named after the god, and the Pharaoh Senusret I had the Egyptian Thebes as his capital city. It would make de facto sense that the Greeks started referring to Waset as Thebes because of this connection.[46]

That said of place names, we come back to the issue of Cadmus' imported alphabet and letters, its origin and dating. Did Cadmus, in aggregate, arrive in Thebes carrying the Phoenician Alphabet or Linear B, a syllabary, or some variant of the 18th Century BCE alphabet viewed on cave walls by Flinders Petrie, like Jeffers' "Hands," but identified a few years later by Petrie's colleague Sir Alan Gardiner, who happened to be Martin Bernal's grandfather? Some argue that, if the former, then the date must be contemporary with Solomon's reign (970-931 BCE), and the mythic Cadmus must be contemporary with those Phoenician hands that designed and built Solomon's grand temple,[47] and long after Linear B for a Greek tongue had been introduced or discovered. This dichotomy is not necessarily the case, says Bernal.[48] Such an either or argument is based on the tree metaphor of language growth. Tree design grows ascending but language ascends and descends. The root or rhizome metaphor is preferable here, as roots bifurcate and converge, which best patterns what Bernal calls transition waves. The point here is that the Phoenician script goes back to 1800 BCE with some letters. Bernal theorizes that letters Γ, Δ, H, N, O, derive from beyond the Hyksos entering Egypt during the 13th Dynasty.[49]

Linear B is a phonetic representation for a syllabary of Greek. Why can't a people have several scripts? Modern science still uses Greek letters, after all. "Alphabet" is phonic of α & β. Linear B was not ubiquitous in the area in question, found only at Thebes on mainland Greece but also elsewhere in several places in the Peloponnese, Pylos, and Mycenae. It was essentially used for tabulation and accounting. We believe that it was the language of currency of the *cosmopolitans*. As Athens, absent in Homer, was late in flourishing,

Thebes was the major polis of the mainland intersection and inhabited by worldly and well-traveled citizens who relied upon Linear B for commerce with Krete and Greek speaking poleis.[50]

The point is that the Hyksos script was being used during the second millennium. Letters converged, some lost, and others appearing over a thousand years of amalgamation. Consider our letters "c" "k" and "q" as Latin additions. These originally derive from Etruscan, and, at one time, each letter represented three different phonemes; however, by Julius' time, they denoted only one sound, but they hung on persistently in usage because of the morphemes being linked to specific meanings. This is why we don't currently spell light "lite." Orthography shuttles between phonic and lexical regularity. Phonetic usage would make spelling easier, but such Shavian reform would lose etymological history.[51] This quest to find the truth of when and in what form the Phoenician Alphabet arrived in Thebes is a heuristic: we believe that the Canaanite-derived Hyksos people's influence is foundational and that the tribal Cadmus brought it to Thebes. Consider how some of these words reach downward root-like, rhizome like, intersecting, crossing, down and sideways into the fertile soil of *prehistory*. Consider how the names of eighteen US states call out pre-Anglo heritage, many of these derive from Native American morphemes. Consider how modern California received its name from the Umayyads, Arabic that translates as the hearth of the Caliph. The first name of San Francisco was Yerba Buena, Spanish for a plant ubiquitous during Spanish/Mexican ownership. Chicago is a Native American name for the "stinking onion" plant found there until the 20th Century CE. This naming all comes from somewhere, so, when a town on the island Santorini (S. Irene) is called Phoinikia, it likely designates a Phoenician occupation.

At best, the *Bible* is a vast library of history, myth, exhortation, religious instruction, propaganda, beautiful lyricism, and song, a cumulative work of art that tells the story of both human history and human imagination. *The Old Testament Bible*, from its first to last pages, had an estimated 100-150 authors, many likely nearly-literate scriveners or scribe-priests, whose script spans nearly a thousand years of recording and amalgamating of older human stories.[52] Imagine the potential for heteroglossia, whisper-down-the-lane distortion, even if its communal intent were literal/historical truth telling?

And that was likely the *Bible's* literate scribes' intent. The genres of the *Bible* are what Bakhtin called monologic, authoritative voice sustaining an utterance deemed sacred to those listening, a stance of delivery lacking the dialogic, the open ended inquiry of a searcher, like Herodotus, who questions, who provide how others see the issue or source of information, an early

Hegel who insisted on thesis, anti-thesis and synthesis in dialectic. Typical books of the *Bible,* discounting its peoples and languages of composition, are often monological discourses of exhortation (Prophets), Myth or Sacred Narrative (Five books of the *Torah*), and they are often lyric (Psalms and the Song of Solomon). None of these modes lends itself to analysis of an objective sort, save for a check against what we know of its supposedly reported pre-*Bible* history. With monologic exhortation and with myth-retelling, historical mistakes can and do abound with Yam and Baal narratives morphing *cum* Exodus,[53] with "The Song of the Sea" when no Hebrews were present in Egypt at the time;[54] with the late citing of Nilotic cities that previous to the year 1000 BCE had yet to exist in Egypt or if they did, they retained another name that since 1000 BCE changed to the name attributed in the *Bible*; and also with the *Bible* only first correctly identifying an Egyptian pharaoh, Hequkheperre Shoshenq I (also known as Shishak), at a time when Rehaboam ruled in Judea.[55]

As noted, Phoinikia on Thera (modern Santorini) was likely occupied and named by Phoenicians. Sarah Morris, in her *Daidalos and the Origins of Greek Art* finds that Herodotus names Memblarious, a follower of Cadmus, as founder of Thera eight generations before those islanders sailed west to supposedly found Santorini.[56] We may make mistakes here, even with two scribes fact-checking and vetting each other, but a monologic is by its nature a mistake-prone lens for history.[57] One might even say that factual truth for checking of historical accuracy is not the methodology of sacred or revealed texts or any exhortation or allegorical literature's central mission. It is when interpreters and revisionists look back at works of literature that purport to be facts based on facts that the post-Herodotian rational mind chafes. Heinrich Schliemann famously said, "Today, I have looked upon the face of Agamemnon" when viewing the death masque covering the body he had just excavated.[58] Are we to take his excited utterance as literal truth, when we now know that Schliemann had found and unearthed a possible a Hyksos king, the body and death masque in gold, like poor kin of Tutankhamun's, possibly of a fleeing Semitic warrior who died four hundred years earlier than Agamemnon? This dialectic, or second take, makes Schliemann's discovery even more significant and advances our objective knowledge, advances us with it. Likewise, Wim van Binsbergen, of the Free University of Amsterdam, finds this kind of truth advancement in Bernal's *Black Athena* debate about the history and origin of languages and therefore the *Homo sapiens* who spoke them and named their places of *patria*. Van Binsbergen states:

> The history of writing systems in the Eastern Mediterranean and the Ancient Near East in general is pertinent to the *Black Athena* debate in various ways… First, literacy is a dominant feature of the Graeco-Roman classical civilization, and therefore any exploration of the latter's historical antecedents is bound to touch on writing systems, their genesis and spread. As a fourth-millennium invention, writing (though not of course the alphabet) at the height of Greek classical civilization had been in existence for a much longer period than separates us today from the Ancient Greeks. This sobering realization testifies to the plausibility of the *Black Athena* thesis claiming extensive 'Afroasiatic' (i.e. Ancient Egyptian and Semitic) 'roots' for classical civilization.[59]

Writing is ancient, alphabets too, and their migrations mirror Bernal's "wave" theory of the movements of both languages and peoples.[60] Just so, the Hyksos occupied Egypt and then were forced widely beyond and likely in following centuries to disperse yet more widely, spreading their cultural wave outward from the map's red center counter-clock wise around to Illyria on the Adriatic, if we take literally the legend of Cadmus and Harmonia's retirement. Bernal subtitled his first volume of *Black Athena* "The fabrication of Ancient Greece." His *Cadmean letters:* is subtitled "The transmission of the alphabet to the Aegean." In both works, Bernal holds that "'the alphabet of primary transmission' can only be a West Semitic context."[61] According to Wim van Binsbergen, Bernal partially credits the multicultural identity as well as the alphabet of the Greeks to the Syrians, Canaanites, Anatolians and Mesopotamians. He also strongly credits "... alleged *Egyptian* contributions, which mark Bernal's originality and constitute so many bones of contention."[62] As we scribes have labored to record here, Hyksos culture under the sail of the House of Cadmus and its descendants informed the very Egyptian culture that Bernal argues informed the Greek. Those Cadmians inhabited both places and left their abundant traces especially in Thebes north of Athens. Time and chance, further excavations, will reveal even more of the Hyksos as the fathers and mothers of much of what we call Egyptian and Greek, even the earlier foundation of the Hebrew peoples' *Torah* and their identity. Again, the Hyksos legacies fund the *Torah* too. What is to be learned from the linkage? We wish to beg no questions, aiming at a "third-eye" of truth, one that takes us beyond our limbic drives to what can be learned in order to do a better job of *making a rational new way to live, of making a new, cooperative and common- culture history.* History is obviously made up of human action, and only we humans can correct its past transgressions to propel it more deliberatively into the future, building positively on the achievements of the past, but not tolerating the past's war-like "solutions" to conflicts.

Herodotus' utterances, an expanding array of a dialogic prism, open his *History* by blaming the Phoenicians. The seminal event reported by Herodotus, which so upset the author and would resonate with his linguistic community, was the abduction of women from Argos, specifically Io. This proper noun is ubiquitous, as it appears in the name of the sea to the west of Greece and also in several narrative myths. Io, whose appeal ignited Zeus' arousal, is the unfortunate victim of jealous Hera's wrath. Turned literally into a heifer by Hera, Io, pestered by the Socratic biting icon, a gadfly, was driven east and then south into Egypt. There she transmogrified back to human form to bear a pharaoh.[63] This abduction, Herodotus' purported as historical fact, synchronize with the mythological guise that Pseudo Apollodorus subsequently established as Io, the heifer, in Egypt, who spawned the Pharaoh Apophis, or does it bear witness to Epaphus, as identified by Egyptian texts? Please consider this line of reasoning:

> . . . the inscribed cover on the cartouche of the Hyksos King Khian, retrieved at Knossos in a dump of M.M III A, is a witness of the exchanges that existed at the time of the pastoral kings in the Valley of the Nile and the Aegean world. Thus, again in an inverse sense, the excavations of Phoenicia and notably those of Ras Shamra have confirmed the importations and the Aegean influences in the Levant, in the Middle Bronze period before and during the epoch of the Hyksos.[64]

The Attic Greek word of Herodotus' title, "Ιστορία," denotes "inquiry" rather than that which we later comprehend as "chronology," part of the post-*Bible* dialogic. Post-*Bible* chronologizing begins with an accounting from a list of events from the time of Christ and the tradition that the religion slowly gained. These advances particularly included, subsequently, the founding in 850 CE of Paris' Notre Dame Cathedral, which by 2013, celebrated its 850th anniversary. Inquiry and chronology are not the same thing, as the former is deliberative and seeks a new understanding; the latter is a fixed record. This distinction is helpful in monitoring the waxing and waning of this building status, which sustained its Christian mission with the exception of when Napoleon I for fourteen years substituted all crosses and Christian icons of Jesus with those of "Lady Liberty."

Given that the Father of History birthed a new genre, history, or conceptual inquiry—not chronologic enumeration—it is a genre void of the optative mood and of the middle voice of poetry. Its stance, though essentially monologic, entails greater dialogic than the authoritative utterances of sacred texts. Herodotus' investigation cited on the first page of his Book One a cause, an abduction. By placing the Io episode as incipient, a conflict including Greek, Semitic and Egyptian cultures, he signified primacy, a recollection that we ask readers to consider as an echo that linked the Hyksos exodus a thousand years earlier than when either Greeks and the Hebrews composed written discourse. Hecataeus, too, is reported to cite Semites in Sparta, south of Argos, where Danaus landed.

The tales of Daedalus, a mortal avatar of Hephaestus and the Ugarit's Kothar wa Hasis evidences cultural memory of origins relating further back to the god Ptah, embedded as final consonants in name "Egypt."[65] Such matches and other allusions of Hellenosemitica pepper texts in many genres of the Greek canon;[66] especially, those narratives about Cadmus, and others about Danaus, and their progeny of mixed blood down many generation to multiracial Athens that disturbed Plato (see prelude of Chapter 7). The exclusive tone of Plato's "Menexenus" resonates with Ezra, recently returned to Jerusalem from Persia to find foreign blood mixed in God's people; this state of affairs was rectify by Nehemiah's and Ezra's community by institutionalizing ritual and festival, like the Sabbath, exclusive gatherings to separate out the impure from the pure. This confluence is a foundation of our case for the common linkage of Hyksos/Canaanite/Phoenician with the Greeks.

While Greek tragedians orchestrated dramas, Herodotus' fashioned the new genre of inquiry rather than kings' lists, or reportage of natural and human disasters. These genres led to a fading of two features of Greek grammar, mentioned above, a loss that signified a shift from mythopoeia toward a more rational epistemology. Among standard evolution of the language from Attic to *koine* and to demotic, the shift in Greek of the first two stages entails a change from one's voice as conduit channeling some divine inspiration for an attuned audience. When writer performs to an audience, a monologic secularizes; and when actors perform to one another, with chorus integrating what happened, all for an interloping audience, a new rational discourse leads to higher levels of civilization.

When fixed in texts, a more distanced stance for writer composing for audiences beyond the present and, perhaps, at another place in time, critical comprehension of meaning from available facts allows for theorizing, hypothesizing, and budding science. The vocative "O, Zeus" is an exhortation, inviting in second person engagement or signaling in another genre, drama, a citing in dramatic monologue performed before witnessing audiences. This feature fades by the time of *koine* Greek and subsequently in demotic Greek. In the opening passage of his *History*, Herodotus reports a cause of effects, and shares comparatively with readers how others report on the same cause, for the Persians recall the event differently. Well-travelled Herodotus and Mesopotamian Berossus, unlike homegrown Homer, spent time in Persian-occupied Egypt and were considered relatively worldly.[67] After Io's abduction by those from the Nile, Herodotus furthers his exposition with episodes and parallel acts of abuse and abduction of women down to that of Helen by Paris. Such a display of alternatives from which the reader can choose is far different a dialogic than the restrictive exhortations that "Knowledge is fear of the Lord." Herodotus may well have fantasized some particulars, but here is a fine and reasoning mind monologuing analytically beginning dialogic. That Herodotus chose the Argolid encounter to begin his enquiry for readers of his time who shared tacit familiarity of the subject signifies priority, as established on the opening page of "Book One;" his "Book Two" dealing similarly with Egypt.

History, the emerging genre of investigation as opposed to epic or recollection, reveals a shifting epistemology. This change of ratiocination can be described metaphorically, and perhaps glibly, in a depiction that favors left brain scrutiny and concentration rather than right brain chiming and comprehending.[68] In Book 1, Herodotus identified other cultural sources reporting on the same event, such as how the Persians accounted for what happened, a version in contrast with how Greeks attuned to Herodotus' writing during the Golden Age. The ears recognized onomastics, of Phoenicians and Egyptians that referred to Canaanites and the people of Misr of the Second Millennium. This kind of new triangulation of cultural perspectives and memory puts a fine lens on objective history and likewise on shared myths and, thus, advances truth.

Epic monologic stories elicit commonality by the recognizing of a singular event; exposition, on the other hand, elicits generalization derived from a series of events. In addition to prioritizing, logic subordinates chronology in enquiry, so different with Herodotus than in Homer's epic that chained together chronologically that "this happened and then that happened." As mentioned, the Argolid rape of fifty women preceded those several reported abuses that include Helen's abduction to Troy and analyzed cause with effect to synthesize novel meanings, all events having occurred in an earlier millennium, not in Herodotus' time, bridged by Herodotus' analytic mind, by the "Father

86   BIBLICAL TIME OUT OF MIND

of History." From the moment Helen faced Priam, the future promised an infinity of paths but only one led to Herodotus' home in Halicarnassus.

Less than a decade after World War II, Jean Berard, a latter-day Herodotus schooled in modern European critical thinking, returned to this same cause of effects. After the immoral anti-Semitic horrors committed in his Christian Europe, Berard grounds the Hyksos people as of Semitic origin, a contrast to the previous 20th Century academics then identifying Indo-Europeans as the Hyksos stock, for older scholarship scoffed that Semites were capable of conquering powerful pharaonic Egypt. Berard initiated debunking the sociology of knowledge of pre-World War II and earlier, a wedge further driven by Astour, Bernal, Morris, and those included in the Notes. Yet even Berard, too, reveals a racist epistemology:

> Without doubt, Io is the issue of the kings of Argos and for that reason her descendants such as Cadmos [Cadmus] cannot be regarded as pure Phoenicians. But it was the Phoenician sailors who removed them in order to take them across their country and across Egypt, comingling in both fact and generalized myth, as the myth figures are generalizations of historical tribal cultures. Then Io goes on a quest for her sons, and it is in Phoenicia that she searched; it is from the house of the queen of Bylos that Io retrieves them. Then, in a later epoch, the legend of Io is attached to the Syro-Palestinian region, to Iopolis and to Gaza.[69]

Berard's narrative accounts for the Greek source of the progeny of Io. His methodology or mechanism, his techne is "echo" and "match;" his words, too, grapple with fixing fluidity so difficult to capture from the past. His point of entrance likewise is as a European, a post-World War II speaker of Indo-European language. Berard, like Herodotus, patterns with his narrative a Greek beginning, middle, and end. Our present thesis "puts" Egypt as the source of ejaculated narratives of expulsions of Hyksian "impures," who polluted for more than a century the virginal Nilotic lands. "Thesis" itself is a Greek word used today on Krete busses for a ticket that "puts" one in a specific seat.

Our narratology patterns a beginning with a Hyksos expulsion from Egypt, a middle as chase, and an end in a post-Spartan Attica, traumatized the bewailing Plato about the pollution of Greek stock from a millennium's descent. Yes, Semitic Egyptians abducted a Greek maiden, who bore a Semitic Pharaoh of the Hyksos dynasties, whose descendants fled north and resided in Greece among other lands, similarly sensitive to reverberating echoes from the Hyksos expulsion. Unlike Berard's modern account, however, Cadmus, Danaus, Io, and Daedalus aren't all episodes of one story but episodes in separate narratives that cumulatively pattern an exodus of an epochal source of memory that was shared, transmogrified, and expropriated by others right down to the present day Mormons. Our thesis is more adequate, frankly, than Berard's "rapprochements," which approximates the connotative meaning "to match." Furthermore, to use Berard's diction, our thesis captures how Hebrew, Ugarit, and Hittite all "echo" the grand and true original Exodus that is objective fact. Please also consider the following analysis, though it truncates time, which our discussion has fleshed out:

> A fragment of the history of the "Impures" chased from Egypt, according to Hecataeus of Abdera [4th Century BCE], tells of a pestilence in Egypt resulting in the expulsion of foreigners with alien religious rituals. The most noble emigrants went to Greece and other places, under the guidance of Cadmos and Danaus except for a great segment that fled to Judea, under the guidance of Moses. Parts of this exodus narrative may contaminate the story of the expulsion of the Hyksos.[70]

Our analysis advances generally though challenges some aspects of Berard's argument in his 1951 essay. The Frenchman posited Semite Hyksos' raiding Greece too early, in the 18th and 17th centuries. We follow his lead by correcting the dating to when the pharaohs of the 18th Dynasty chased out of Egypt Hyksos refugees. Many of these occasionally settled and commenced commerce, only to be again routed until in time some settled in Greece between the 16th through the 13th centuries. Further, we find no evidence of Hebrews being in Egypt, nor the presence of Moses ever in Egypt, though surely the lawgiver presided east of the Jordan. The stories of a Nilotic Moses—the name, an infant abandoned like Oedipus or Dionysus and a number of legendary others, and his exodus—are appropriated from another peoples' history synthesized with earlier myths from neighboring cultures, an intuition pursued by Sigmund Freud in his *Moses and Monotheism*.

It is only during the reign of Solomon's successor Rehoboam in the 9th Century BCE that any Egyptian pharaoh is identified accurately. From this point on in the chronological reporting of the Bible, one can discern the emergence of worldly awareness and the fading of solipsistic isolationism. It is when Rehoboam's successor, Jeroboam, returned to Israel from Egypt that Biblical records and external facts agree in providing congruence with historical facts. It is plausible that Jeroboam was among the first Hebrews to have reached Egypt and perhaps it was during this sojourn that a precedent of Jewish mercenaries in time advanced up the Nile to the Nubian border at Elephantine. But, there is no evidence that Hebrews were in Egypt in the third and second millennia BCE. The first credible biblical and extra-biblical evidence puts Jews in Egypt over a hundred years into the first millennium BCE.

During the years following approximately the date Jeroboam returned to Israel, papyrus texts accumulated adjacent to a Jewish Temple near today's Sudan border. Perusing the extant papyrus texts from the Elephantine geniza, it is clear that this Jewish community deviated from Levantine Jews and clearly did not follow the ways of Moses nor reveal any awareness of the Great Lawgiver until a few texts of a quite late date. It appears that they worshiped gods, perhaps those gods related to the two golden cows that Jeroboam brought into Israel when he succeeded Rehoboam. From the year 1000 to 600, Egypt was as weak as it had been during the Second Intermediate period of the Hyksos, between 1800 to 1560 BCE, when an early migration of Semites, Canaanites, not Jews, settled in the Eastern delta and eventually took over northern Egypt. Later, in Rehobam's time during the Twenty-Second Dynasty, Libyans ruled Egypt, and subsequently Nubians, then Cassites, and eventually, Persians, and others dominated the vitiated land mocked by the Prophets. These are the centuries when Hebrew scribes, prophets, looked back and cast what Shlomo Sand titled his studies as "Inventions" of nationhood and cultural identity.[71] Only contemporary with Euripides' *Trojan Women*, is there a text—the Passover Letter, which evidences Moses. This letter was composed a half century after Herodotus visited Egypt while the region had become relatively yeasty linguistically, with alloglossia of Aramaic, Greek, Persian, Egyptian and written correspondences radiating out to various homelands. Note in the Passover Letter that in the second line there is the apostrophe to gods in the plural: "Yedaniah and his colleagues of the Judahite garrison, (from) your brother Hananiah. May the gods seek the welfare of my brothers."[72] Further, in investigation of earlier texts, one frequently finds both gods Yahweh and Anat and the evidence of sacrificing sheep in the traditional Egyptian customs.[73]

Three major events were recorded by nearly all peripheral states, not events experienced only by one Hebrew state itself: each documented or appropriated the Hyksos exodus, also the Thera volcanic eruption of 1500, and the invasion of the Sea Peoples since 1200. Between the mythic time of Abraham, Joseph, and Moses sojourning in Egypt and between kingdoms from Saul to

Jeraboam, a lacunae of nearly two hundred years spans 1200 to 1000 BCE, a gap that nearly every relevant nation acknowledged, the time of the Sea Peoples, implied by Amos 9:7.

First Millennial Jewish prophets from the time of Solomon wrote about Second Millennium patriarchs, but no unquestionable evidence has been found to establish their certitude. Greeks, on the other hand, wrote in drama, odes, epics, and histories about Second Millennium Greeks, and abundant evidence has been found for many of the cities that sent ships to Troy, from tiny Karian Mindos that financed two, to Mycenae of Agamemnon which sent many ships. Had second Millennium Hebrews been in Egypt, the acts and artifacts of both cultures should reflect that earlier inhabitation: neither does. Second and first half of the first Millennium Jews in Egypt would have noted the Sphinx or the Giza Pyramids, akin to a modern arriving to Paris noting the Eiffel tower. This Biblical record cites nothing of the kind.

Said differently, had Jews been in second to early first Millennium Egypt and not noted the Pyramids, Herodotus' historic mind, and modern Berard's with him, would have been violated. A Japanese student in Paris post 1899, when the Eiffel tower passed the Great Pyramids in height to become the tallest structure on earth, would surely note the tower's existence, just as the French might remark on a Left Bank visitor from Imperial Nippon saying "Wari, o'tenki, des nay?" or "Icura deska?"

We find credible Jeroboam approaching the Nile around approximately 890 BCE. We have some trouble with preceding dates, of Joash or Jetohoem, the father of Jeroboam; Solomon, and David as no external evidence corroborates these datings; likewise, the earliest that we can ascribe the dating and life of Moses, the lawgiver's, is about 1150. So we have a possible history of the first Jews in Egypt about 900 BCE. It is not until approximately 250 BCE that the uber-*Torah* or *The Old Testament* appears to have been amalgamated from earlier events and much earlier myths and with a political and religious intent, not historical, as in Herodotus' analytic intent. Consider the *Torah*'s many authors, drawing heavily on a Hyksos and heathen past, and the history of biblical history becomes clearer.

Here we scribes, guilty of anthologizing now ourselves, should address the theories of "Biblical Minimalism" and "Biblical Maximalism," being proponents of the truth first, seeking the Greek's middle ground or Aristotle's Golden Mean, but tending toward the "minimalism" that does not take *The Bible* as a literal record of historical fact or even as factual reporting of earlier myth. Then there follows the fascinating double-glinting axe blade mirror images of what may have happened, via the language stew, which Bakhtin called "heteroglossia," or modern "whisper-down-the-lane." Resulting utterances and texts via transmutations over time may have concatenated into exhortations like the Ten Commandments, which included nested palimpsests that came first and from whence they may all have come. Eventually, Hebrews, the scribes of the *Bible,* were finally ensconced to anthologize in Alexandria or Jamnia, post the birth of Jesus. None of this arguing for Hyksos fundings of biblical literature diminishes the grand human exhortation and art that the *Bible* is, a high-water and uniquely human accomplishment that just needs to be understood by both reason and by faith that we might live an even better history for the sake of our collective futures.

If we are now to find peace in the Middle East and thus in the entire Internet-connected and inseparably inter-twined world, we must be honest with each other about our aggressive, warty pasts, the Shah of Iran leading to the Ayatollah Khomeini and perhaps to hostage-taking, the abomination and perversion of historic Islam that is now ISIL having some twisted roots in others' imperialism and in past oppression. Social troubles that seem regional are not restricted to a state like contents of a glass. The unwarranted invasion of Iraq in 2003 displaced two million Sunna refugees west toward Syria to become the bitter foundation of ISIL. Who is accountable for the Assad government's not falling, as predicted, in six months' time: why now do we blame Assad's regime for ISIL'S creation? If there are absolute truths in the *Bible,* and we believe that there are as biblical moderates, one of them is that "the meek shall inherit the earth." We argue here and now that the meek are in fact precisely the meek by design because they do not wish to re-create cultural mistakes from the bloody and contentious past.

5
Narratological History
Historical Narratology

Thus I have traced the descent according to the account given by the Hellenes; but as the story is reported which the Persians tell, Perseus himself was an Assyrian and became a Hellene, whereas the ancestors of Perseus were not Hellenes; and as for the ancestors of Acrisios, . . . belonged not to Perseus in any way by kinship, they say that these were, as the Hellenes report, Egyptians. Let it suffice to have said so much about these matters [palimpsests of Greece] and as to the question how and by what exploits being Egyptians they received the scepters of royalty over the Dorians, we will omit these things, since others [Persian, Assyrians, and Egyptians] have told about them.[1]

To understand where we post-modern scribes plant our flag on biblical minimalism vs. maximalism interpretations, one should first understand what powerful historical, political and religious forces were mitigating to create the foundational literature that is the record of the Jewish people, specifically "The Book of Law," or "Deuteronomy," the basis of *The Torah* or *The Old Testament*.

Jewish culture and history are *remarkable* in the number of first *innovations* and the advancement of human civilization, interrupted sadly by a Mesopotamian-wide Assyrian takeover of both the lands of Israel and Judah noted earlier. This foundational text created a sustained tradition of monotheism in a polytheistic world; a first sustained worship of a single god and a first centralized and politically-sanctioned temple for worship; a written and read-aloud-as-record law coda for ethical behavior, although not the first; the radical sociological shift from extended families to nuclear ones; and a unique tradition of not eating pork that has lasted nearly 3,000 years to date to differentiate Hebrew ancestors, which accounts for the lack of pig bones in archaeological sites in ancient Israel and Judah. All of these innovations are the result of a primary cause, and that cause is human, not necessarily divine, unless one argues the plausibility, that these humans were divinely created in ignorance and then discovered, not invented, their supreme God/unknown creator. We scribes, not priests as were the first hundred to one hundred and fifty recorders of the *Bible* over many pre-Christian centuries, will leave that deduction or induction to you, dear readers. We offer, though, that all effects have causes, causes worth ruminating about if we are to understand those effects all around us. If we are to have present day peace in the Middle East and world-wide, we need to find common cultural ground and to celebrate those with differences. Studying war, the past causes and methodologies of it, can yield this hoped-for light, and, we scribes sincerely hope, can yield a ramping down of the human blood-lust that stems from hegemony and the nightmare of misguided xenophobia.

As far back as 6,000 years ago, the technology of weaponry, like the sword mythologized in the Arthur legend, resulted from smelting metals, forged tin and copper among stones and clay creating bronze, then cooled in water. Weapons forged in casting inform history entailed a sociology. Military service was mandatory for Semites, Greeks and in wartimes for Celtic farmers, who galvanized craft guilds that specialized in production, distribution, and archiving for tombs. Sword-smiths manipulated the elements of earth, wind and fire, conspired with magic derived from many like Imhotep, Kothar wa Hasis Haphaestus, or Vulcan.[2] Such secrets were guarded from all but immediate family; those fallen soldiers were often buried with their revered swords. The success of Roman conquest depended for centuries on iron, steel, sword-smithing—on double-edged short swords and shields and armor, on gladiators, a term for sword length, and on a new military strategy for fighting as a team. The sword is a cause for historical effects, just as Hyksos' chariots and horsemanship caused Egyptian and Greek incursion and exodus.

We should trace the true causes of the creation of the Jewish people next, how they came to be, when and where they emerged. Traces in the memories of Hebrews, Canaanite/Phoenicians, and Greeks, expressed in oral, written, or painterly texts, evidence happenings from the 16th Century BCE, though in some cases transmogrified, like how the Elizabethans recalled their historical memories. Institutional memory of another Semitic incursion into Europe in Shakespeare's day was manifested in dramas by William Rowley's 1618 *All's Lost by Lust* and by Thomas Heywood's 1592 *Four Prentices of London*. The plot of the former is set during the Moors' early presence in Spain, and of the latter in Jerusalem of 12th Century crusaders. Elizabethan playwrights expressed their conceptual memories, time-out-of-mind that extended an epoch, a similar extent as Herodotus and his contemporary tragedians from Golden Age of Greece remembered their conceptual memories back to when the Hyksos exited Egypt. Further than is assumed, institutional memories can extend millennia by orality, writing, art, and habit. New Grange tomb in Ireland took at least three generations to build, yet no plans or specs existed that modern-day workmen could use to complete the intricately crafted structure. Noting the Irish knack for story telling, some argue that the design for this tomb—and dozens of others—was set forth in yarns and tales.

The polytheistic Canaanite people and their god Baal surfaced in time in the Judaea Heights to compete with Yahweh among the earliest tribal Hebrews. Baal, the bull icon, was likely deemed an avatar of those bulls with tumbling acrobats at Avaris, ubiquitously depicted by roving Cretan artists. It was these who came to be called Jews via their location as a tribal place name. The Canaanites, not Hebrews who hadn't yet reached the Nile, occasioned the exodus subsequently appropriated and adapted in literature. Over a half millennium later, the Jews first with polytheistic gods and icons of Baal-like golden calves, co-opted from the Canaan god Baal, commenced economic forces that led to their civilization and religion on the banks of the Jordan River in about 800 BCE. The Jews *emerged* from the tribal pastoral nomads already inhabiting the general area south of the Assyrian empire; "there was no great migration" as also noted thoroughly earlier in our debunking of the *Exodus* story and in the publication and televised findings of Silberman and Finkelstein's *The Bible Unearthed*.[3] We argue the *Biblical* "Exodus" has its roots in a pharaonic pursuit to overthrow Hyksos overlords around mid-16th Century BCE, despite the later Moses' history-cum-myth of a Yahweh encounter on Mt Sinai. And despite the supposed resultant Jewish monotheism 500 years earlier, the first traceable Jewish culture began to coalesce in 900-800s BCE. The *original* Jewish herder people from east of the Jordan remained Canaan-influenced polytheists who worshiped both the stars, the mountains, earthquakes, and those famous golden calves persistently, long after the mythical shift to monotheism. Still alive in the conceptual memories of the Egyptians, Greeks, and Hebrews, the history of the Hyksos provided the template, upon which was enhanced the separation to the Red Sea rather than crossing a land bridge just north to escape the pursuing Egyptians. Here's why.

The first Jews were pastoral nomads who tended sheep, goats, and even likely pigs. They *emerged already in place* on the Jordan River basin and ranged short distances searching for fertile lands to feed their animals, first used for micro-tribal and extended family sustenance. In times of relative abundance, the herd's size could support more than the community in meat, cheese and milk, for trade of those very same pastoral products for the grain needed as feed in turn led to larger herds and more trade of herd products with other area tribes. This pastoral and somewhat picaresque economy of the first Jewish nomads *emerged and grew out of the fertile soil of the chaos and economic disruption of the areas later known as Israel and Judah, chaos caused by both the invasion of the Sea Peoples that effected not only all those tribes living on both banks of the Jordan River but the entire macro area and an Assyrian takeover at the end of the Bronze Age.*[4] These stunning disruptions were gradual for the soon-to-become Jewish nomads already living in the Canaan area. As herd sizes grew beyond subsistence, and with economic power fluid and tribal peoples relocating short to mid-distances, new opportunities to trade exchange came: the first Jews were resourceful and ambitious in pastoral terms, ahead of their time in so many ways.

By 900-800 BCE, in the very early Jewish settlement of Meta, olive oil pressing stones attest to the first commercial independence and identity of the first Israelites, as the relic stone presses with olive oil draining through channeled grooves, unearthed by archeologists, were clearly larger than those needed for individual family or even micro-tribal use. A connection exists even here between the Hyksos people, like the individual tribal mythic symbols Cadmus and Europa who stood for very real and foundational tribes long before Meta was built. For the tools to impress the soft plaster sealing olive oil jars tell a good part of the journey stories of the earlier Hyksos and Mesopotamian economies. It is a co-terminus story with those pressing the olives into oil who later emerged when Jewish pastoral herders of nomadic travel *fixed with place-named sites of commerce,* as the Jewish homeland with tangential agrarian lands to feed and sustain a homeland interrupted too often by conquers; just as the Hyksos had much earlier maintained in the Delta before expulsion from Egypt to points east, then north, then west to Greece.

Some contemporary thinkers argue that Jews years later derived genetically from these Canaanite Hyksos. This is plausible, even likely in isolated cases. However, the enmity of racial difference suggests otherwise, as the case of Hebrew Dinah and her lover Shechem reveals. Dinah is the feminine echo of the northern tribe of Dan, and Shechem is a Canaanite ethnonym remembered in the city of that name. Genesis 34 narrates how Dinah's Hebrew brethren negotiated fruition of the love by insisting the infidel and his race comply with mandatory circumcision, which they did. Then, when the conforming infidels were recovering the painful operation, the Hebrews massacred them; the narrative metonymically suggests an early genocide, obviously antithetical to a common culture deriving peacefully as promised in the "Book of Ruth", discussed in the last chapter. Rather than placing historic and literary blame, we scribes choose to seize the opportunity to ask humanity to do better, to attend to classical Hebrew innovations that mirror those in the Muslim world, seeking that necessary cultural bridge, if we are to have peace. This refutes the notion of ethnic blending of Canaanite with Hebrews.

Two early Jewish city-states, Israel and Judea, followed that first small settlement of Meta in approximately 900-800 BCE, in what was southern Palestine. Israel, to the north (but south and west of the dominant Assyrian empire), offered more fertile land, rolling hills, verdant grasses, abundant water access, a Jordan River valley emptying into the Dead Sea. It was (and is) more suited to agriculture. Yet, it was the more barren land area of Judah further to the south that first housed the then small settlement that later became, after the Assyrian takeover, a ten-times larger and more prosperous city/state due to a documented exodus in the 8th to 7th Century BCE from Assyrians overlords. Pastoral nomadic tribes subsisting upon micro-economies governed by barter occupied these areas. At an earlier "moment in time" the first monotheist Hebrews had gained economic traction in an area they already inhabited from historical Canaanites. And their rapid although small scale economic rise led to a centralization of politics, to a religious monotheism and a politically sanctioned temple adjacent to the King's palace, to a nuclear family life sociology, and to a prohibition on eating pork, innovations which all make ultimate sense if one considers the historical forces at work.

Young Hebrew prophet Josiah emerged as the political leader of Judah by the 7th Century BCE. The Yahweh of Israel had been postulated as the one god by the 8th Century, although polytheistic worship of Canaanite inspired icons of stars, mountains, bulls and golden calves persisted until at least the 6th Century BCE.[5] Also in the 7th Century, "The Book of Law" or "Deuteronomy" emerged likewise as *one* of man's earliest code of written law of behavior and consequences or spiritual and legal crimes and prohibitions and of exhortations to behave ethically, a major innovation of the Jewish community among the indigenous others. Here the prophet/king Josiah practiced *innovative politics of religion and identity* that make sense for much of what came after, including eventually the foundations of the modern state of Israel.

Josiah apparently saw the need for identity creation and had the moment to do so for his people and his rule. The earlier incursions of the Sea Peoples and then the Assyrian invasion had rung the final death knell of the Bronze Age for Canaanite and Hebrew. With iron surfacing with abundant ore and easy smelting, the emerging Jewish nomads gained economic power and occupied the two homelands with a first larger population in Israel to the north and then a large shift to the south to Jerusalem in Judah. In time the Assyrians returned south into Israel, allowing untouched Judea to gain from political opportunities for power and for identity for the people to centralize government and construct a temple, in short, an *ascension to authority*. By the 7th

Century BCE, Jerusalem grew as a center of a small region on the southern edge of Palestine as the capital city/state, but the setting lacked sufficient water for drinking and irrigation to support the Assyrian-fleeing former Israel residents previously displaced and now heading south. One of Josiah's many geniuses, besides recognizing a moment in time/history for immortality and a new thinking/rule, was the engineering marvel of a 500-meter canal system to trough an underground well-spring creek out of a Jerusalem cave into the heart of his rapidly expanding city as its virtual lifeblood in an arid climate. This engineering innovation alone led to others that more than border on the religious, the political, as well as those of ethnic identity. One could argue that Yahweh provided the water that led to his dominance as the one god. Following Herodotus' lead, we scribes will simply keep recording, not make that judgmental leap from fact to value.

The channeling of water for humans and animals, with crop irrigation, was *key* for economic growth in Jerusalem and *in establishing the distinct identity of the Jewish people.* Seizing the opportunity for centralization of power, religious authority, law-pronouncing, command and ongoing rule, Josiah ordered that a temple to Yahweh be built right behind his emerging palace in Jerusalem, again declaring Yahweh as the one god and citing Asherah as Yahweh's wife, a polytheistic vestige that pays unintentional homage to the Canaanite ancestors.[6] Over time, the new religious authorities eliminated worship of Asherah, but the goddess/wife served as a link to poly-theism and to Canaanite influence. According to an archeological review, "the preponderance of archaeological artifacts provides evidence of various religious practices that coexisted in Judah alongside the official worship of Yahweh."[7]

Josiah declared "Deuteronomy" as "The Book of Laws" to be enforced by rule and sponsored single family housing in Jerusalem, rather than the communal and tribal living of the nomadic life. He declared *his rule* as the one rule, himself the arbiter of objective religious truth, all strokes of genius if one's goal is to maintain power and forge identity for a people whose epistemology must *differ* in some important ways from the polytheistic, nomadic, extended tribal families from which the "new" people descended.[8] Unfortunately, human nature and blood-lust were and are what they are, and Josiah's new empire of centralized political power, centralized and state-sanctioned religion, centralized irrigation and a commerce center that provided identity for a people emerged and relocated slightly from their historical and genealogical origin. But this came to an abrupt 5th Century BCE end when the Assyrians again marched south from Mesopotamia, destroying and erasing all but the Jewish concepts formed and made part of cumulative traditions, collective memory, and habitual, perhaps conscious patterns of behavior. The Assyrians had done so just after the Egyptians killed Josiah. The collective memory led the Jewish Priest Ezra to reassert the *Torah* in 458 BCE, as the Assyrians had put the light of the states of Israel and Judah, with Jerusalem within it, on hold. In time, they became semi-autonomous under Greek hegemony that ended when Romans assumed the Hellenic mantle to destroy and disseminate survivors after Titus' invasion in 67 CE. But right after World War II, the light emerged from the dark until when the Israeli homeland was re-planned, and after 1967, the State of Israel was re-established in its current 20th-21st Century CE form.

It now seems productive to come back to the thorny question of biblical Minimalism and Maximalism and whether these two binary opposite theories can have a golden mean or middle ground between. This deciding on literal vs. figurative interpretation of *Bible* narratives is central, as so many claims of rule, hegemony and war stem from interpretations of biblical guarantees of homelands, sovereignty and past possession of lands and resources.

While we scribes plant our flag on the ignored Hyksos whose records were foundations for many biblical stories and myths, we do not wish to be either dogmatic or closed-minded. In other words, we do not wish to suffer from hardening of the opinions, an academic and a social disease. We hope not to be priests for any church, just reasonably accurate recorders/investigators, standing on the back of some Hebrew scholars like Smolo Sand and Bezalel Porton,[9] and other non-Jewish scholars who are already out ahead of us in this investigation of the *Bible* and its unavoidably similar subject of the historical study of the state of Israel. We hope to honor traditions by investigating with the best of modern scientific and archeological inquiries which of the Biblical stories might have a basis in other-cultured historical facts. Also, without favoring dogma over what we find to be truths, we refrain from turning away from that which was recorded earlier as history and attenuated as legends or myths by people remote from the Nile, who recall social and/or habitual memories.

Biblical minimalism, (also known as the Copenhagen School for several of its prominent figures taught at Copenhagen University) is a trend birthed in the 1990's in Biblical scholarship. *It* makes two primary claims: first, that the *Bible* cannot be considered reliable evidence for what actually happened in ancient Israel; and second, that the state of "Israel" itself is a difficult topic for historical or literary study.[10] Minimalism is hardly a unified movement, more so a label applied to several scholars at several different universities who hold similar views, primarily Niels Peter Lemche and Thomas L. Thompson at the University of Copenhagen, Philip R. Davies, and Keith Whitelam. Minimalism philosophy of *Bible* interpretation caused intense debate during the 1990s—the term "minimalists" in fact being a derogatory term tagged by its opponents, who were thusly dubbed in counter-point "maximalists," but in fact neither faction fully accepted the other's label. The Maximalists, or neo-Albrightians, were comprised of two distinct groups, the first represented by the archaeologist William Dever and the influential journal *Biblical Archaeology Review*, the second faction represented by conservative evangelical Christians such as *Bible* scholar Iain Provan and Egyptologist Kenneth Kitchen.[11]

Minimalism maintains that the *Bible* is not an anthology of literal or historic truths: rather, it is a relativistic work of metaphor, allegory, instruction, a moral and figurative or connotative tome. Maximalism maintains that *The Bible* is the absolute literary record of historical and denotative truths: a coda of historical fact faithfully recorded. Minimalist/maximalist debates were/are occasionally heated, sometimes featuring unfortunate name-calling, almost making one echo Rodney King's famous line, "Can't we all just get along?" Many scholars stay in the middle ground between minimalists and maximalists, critically examining the arguments of both schools objectively. Since the recent origin of the terms of biblical interpretation, while a few of the minimalist arguments have been challenged or rejected, most others have been refined and adopted into the mainstream of biblical scholarship.[12]

Chief among the minimalist contentions is one we share vociferously: that most of the events and myths recorded by the *Torah's* many authors in the 5th through 2nd centuries BCE are recollected and re-constructed literary and figurative works that provide intentionally-distorted records of facts and myths from at least several centuries (and several other cultures) earlier. Only when the differing communal intents of the scribe/priests, those in charge of emerging pre-literacy, is subtracted from the amalgamated record can we find a few gems of historical truth in the literary record. That said, however, we scribes would likely characterize ourselves as open-minded minimalists who would love to embrace the certainty of the maximalists if the preponderance of the evidence just pointed that way.

Unfortunately for the current maximalists, by the beginning of the 20th Century, the stories of the Creation, Noah's ark, and the Tower of Babel (in brief, chapters 1 to 11 of the "Book of Genesis") had ceased to be taken literally by most scholars. The "new" starting point for biblical history was thereafter regarded as the stories of Abraham, Isaac, and the other Hebrew patriarchs. Chiefly due to the publication of two books, Thomas Thompson's *The Historicity of the Patriarchal Narratives* and John Van Seters' *Abraham in History and Tradition*, it became widely accepted that the remaining chapters of Genesis were equally non-historical.[13] At about the same time, archaeology and comparative sociology combined to convince most *Bible* scholars that there was equally no factual basis to the biblical stories of the Exodus and the fictional Israelite conquest of Canaan.[14]

By the 1980s, the *Bible's* stories of the Patriarchs and the Exodus and Conquest were no longer accepted as historical, but biblical historians continued to use the *Bible* as a primary source and to take the form of narrative records of political events arranged in chronological order as presented in the *Bible,* with the major role played by Judean kings and other important Hebrew individuals. Newer tools and archeological approaches have been brought to bear on scholars' knowledge of ancient Palestine's history, notably new archaeological methods and approaches (e.g. the age of surface surveys, used to map population changes which were invisible in the biblical narrative), and the social sciences (such as Robert Coote and Keith Whitlam's *The Emergence of Early Israel in Historical Perspective*, which used sociological data to successfully argue that it was *kingship* that formed Israel, not the other way round).[15]

By the 1990s, a school of thought emerged holding that the entire enterprise of studying ancient Israel was seriously flawed by an over-reliance on the biblical text, which was too problematic (untrustworthy) to be used even selectively as a source for Israel's past, and that Israel itself was in any case itself a problematic subject. This is from the very movement that came to be known as biblical minimalism and its motivations are primarily truth-telling, not devaluing innovative and valuable literary, ethnic and cultural traditions.[16]

Scholars who have been called "minimalists" are not a single group, and in fact they deny that they form a group. Philip Davies points out that while he argues that the bulk of the *Bible* can be dated to the Persian period (5th Century BCE), Niels Peter Lemche prefers the Hellenistic period (3rd to 2nd centuries BCE), while Whitelam gives no opinion on dating the *Bible's* anthological composition. Similarly, while Lemche holds that the Tel Dan stele (an inscription from the mid-9th Century BCE which seems to mention the name of David) is probably a *forgery*, Davies and Whitelam do not necessarily agree. In short, the minimalists do not agree on much more than the fact that the *Bible* is a doubtful and biased source of information about ancient Israel.[17]

The first of the minimalists' two claims is based on the recognition that history-writing is never objective (Bakhtin's term used here is heteroglossia), such discourse involving the selection of data and the construction of a narrative using preconceived notions about the *meaning* of the past. Thus, "history" is never neutral or objective: this realization raises questions about the accuracy of any historical account, a fact not lost on your scribes here. The minimalists caution that the literary form of the biblical books is so apparent and that the authors' intentions so obvious that modern scholars should be *extremely cautious* in taking the stories at literal value; even more importantly, even if the *Bible* does preserve some *accurate* historical information, we currently lack the means to sift that information from the inventions with which that literal information has been mixed as a work of *literature*.[18] The minimalists make a wholesale claim that the *Bible* is vacuous as an historical source; rather, they suggest that its proper use is in understanding the time and place in which it was written, a period which most of them place in either the Persian or the Hellenistic period.

The second claim is that "Israel" itself is a difficult concept to define in terms of historiography or science. There is, first, the idealized Israel, which the *Bible's* authors imagined "biblical Israel." Niels Peter Lemche states: "The Israelite nation as explained by the biblical writers has little in the way of a historical background. It is a highly ideological construct created by ancient scholars of Jewish tradition in order to legitimize their own religious community and its religio-political claims on land and religious exclusivity."[19]

Modern biblical scholars take aspects of "biblical Israel" and marry them with data from archaeological and non-biblical sources to create their own version of a past Israel: this composite is called generally "Ancient Israel" to differentiate it from the *present* 1967 state. Neither version bears much congruence to the *real but fragile* Jewish kingdom discussed previously and destroyed by Assyria in about the 7th-5th Century BCE—the real and objective "historical Israel" which *is* documented and vetted. The most productive topics for Jewish history-writing in this post-modern period are likely either this documented historical Israel or else the biblical Israel, the first a historical reality and the second an intellectual *creation* of the biblical authors.[20] Linked with this dichotomy of approaches to the truth is the observation that modern biblical scholars have concentrated their attentions almost exclusively on Israel and Judah, and their religious histories, sometimes ignoring that these two locations may have been only part of a wider, albeit later emerging community than the *Bible* notes. The Jewish picture is subsumed by and emerges from Canaanite tradition due to the influence of the Assyrian invasion and the conquest of the Palestine region by the Sea Peoples.

Philip Davies' book *In Search of Ancient Israel* "popularized the scholarly conversation and crystallized the import of the emerging scholarly positions" regarding the history of Israel between the 10th and 6th centuries BCE.[21] Put differently, it crystalized current research and thinking rather than proposing an original take. Regardless, the book was a watershed work in that it stitched together the interpretations that emerged from archaeology, the study of historical texts, sociology and anthropology.

Davies argued that scholars need to distinguish between the three meanings of the word Israel: the documented, historical ancient kingdom (historical Israel that emerges later than claimed); the idealized Israel of the biblical authors writing in the Persian era and seeking to unify the post-exilic Jerusalem community by *creating* a common past (biblical Israel); and the Israel that had been re-created by modern scholars over the past century or so by blending together the first two (which he termed ancient Israel, in recognition of the use of this term in scholarly histories). "Ancient Israel," Davies argued, was especially troublesome for biblical scholars who ran the risk of placing too much confidence in their reconstructions, resulting from their relying too heavily on "biblical Israel," he felt.[22] Davies holds that the *Bible's* highly ideological version of a Jewish society had already ceased to exist when the bulk of the biblical books concerning it reached their final form in the centuries right before the time of Christ.

In his book *The Invention of Ancient Israel* and subtitled "The Silencing of Palestinian History,"[23] chastises his peers for their concentration on Israel and Judah to the exclusion of the many other peoples and kingdoms that had existed earlier in Bronze and Iron Age Palestine, including the Hyksos people. Palestinian history for the period from 13th Century to the 2nd century BCE has been largely ignored, he claims, and scholars have concentrated instead on the political, social, and above all the *religious* developments in the small city/state of Israel.[24] This line of reasoning, Whitelam argues, supports the contemporary claim to the land of Palestine by the descendants of Israel, while keeping biblical studies in the realm of religion rather than in *history*, where he feels they belong.

Thomas L. Thompson's book *The Mythic Past,* subtitled in the US *Biblical Archaeology and the Myth of Israel*, contained the "Myth of Israel" phrase almost guaranteed to cause controversy in America.[25] The European subtitle, "How Writers Create a Past," was likely more descriptive of its actual theme, which is the need to treat the *Bible* as *literature* rather than as *history*: "The *Bible's* language is not an historical language. It is a language of high literature, of story, of sermon and of song. It is a tool of philosophy and moral instruction." This was Thompson's attempt to set the minimalist position before a wider public;

however, the effect of Thompson's book became the cause of a criticism by William Dever.[26] His work *What Did The Biblical Writers Know and When Did They Know It?* led to an instructive public dispute between the two authors, which crystalized the debate to make what seemed like opposing views somehow oddly synthesizable. We hope our monograph will, perhaps, achieve just what these two scholars/scribes/non-priests are approaching.

The tenets of the minimalists generated considerable controversy during the 1990s through early part of the 21st Century. To be fair, some conservative scholars, motivated according to the minimalists, by their evangelical Christian orientations, have reacted defensively. In arguing against the minimalist claims that essential books of the *Bible* were composed during the Persian or Hellenistic periods, they seek to show that the details of the *Bible* were in fact *consistent* with having been written earlier. A notable work in this camp was Kenneth Kitchen's *On the Reliability of the Old Testament*.[27] Avi Hurvitz compared biblical Hebrew with the Hebrew language from ancient inscriptions and found the diction consistent with the period right before the Persian period, some time prior to 587 BCE, thus questioning the key minimalist contention that the biblical books were written several centuries after the events they describe.[28] Taking a disparate approach, *A Biblical History of Israel*, the authors Iain Provan, V. Philips Long, and Tremper Longman III argued that the criterion for distrust set by the minimalists—that the *Bible* should be regarded as unreliable unless passages are directly confirmed by external sources—is *unreasonable*, for that the *Bible* should be deemed reliable unless directly falsified by empirical evidence, such as carbon dating of archeological dig finds.[29] We scribes ponder here persistent questions and a genuine desire for contemporary Muslim and Hebrew cultures to find their shared and common grounds, their histories built next door to each other, before flash-points ignite again. To do this we must be honest about the marvelous, real but mythologized and heteroglossic history of the *Bible*.

In the academic mainstream, a growing number of scholars see significant, even radical, contradictions between the *Bible's* version of history and the documented *reality of history*, while even some scholars who continue to take the *Bible* for their objective point-of-view see it as having a reliability as the level of detailed investigation increases. As a consequence, the study of Israel's past has thankfully moved *beyond* the minimalist/maximalist debate. Historians of ancient Israel have now adapted their methodologies by relying less on the *Bible* and more on sociological models and empirical archaeological evidence.[30] Scholars such as Lester Grabbe, author of *Ancient Israel: What Do We Know and How Do We Know It?*;[31] Victor Matthews, *Studying the*

Ancient Israelites: A Guide to Sources and Methods;[32] and Hans Barstad, *History and the Hebrew Bible*,[33] simply seek to put the evidence before the reader and explain the issues, rather than attempting to write histories. Others such as K.L. Knoll, *Canaan and Israel in Antiquity*,[34] attempt to include smaller and younger Israel in a broader treatment of ancient Palestine. This is not to say that the ideas of the minimalists are completely adopted in modern study of ancient Israel. For example, Mario Liverani's 2005 *Israel's History and the History of Israel*,[35] accepts that the biblical sources are from the Persian period—Herodotus' period of approximately mid-5th Century BCE. But he believes that the minimalists have not truly understood that context nor adequately recognized the importance of the ancient sources used by the *Bible* authors. Liverani, a would-be maximalist, holds positions that do not fit either a minimalist or a maximalist position and that are typical of those now being expressed by 21st Century biblical scholars who seek middle ground.[36] Liverani's philosophy may be the golden mean or middle ground between our favored-for-empirical-and rational-reasons *minimalism* and our sought-after-quested-for-*maximalism*. It holds that the *Bible's* many authors, while reporting late-to-the-party events and myths far after their common coin currency had been spent by other cultures like the Hyksos people, they owed a real debt to the Hyksos' past. Cadmus, Europa, the whole Hyksos familial mythic tribe stood for the historical reality of a picaresque people who so informed the Egyptian and Greek cultures that serve, along with the later Israelites, as the well-spring of the *Bible,* history's most famous work of literature and the touchstone, however metaphoric and figurative, of the history of history.

Consider all that has been argued above; consider what follows as we seek peace through common culture. The *Bible* is a depository of many cultures that by 400 BCE became crystalized as Jewish. Its gemlike identity derives from significant traces of older cultures of half a millennium: the Hyksos, Assyrian, and Egyptian, in that order. In retreat the Hyksos spread its Canaanite culture east. Then through Land of Canaan north counterclockwise up the Levant and west across the southern coast of the inland Hittite empire to the Aegean and Greece, dissipating over time, of a millennium—and remembered in Plato's hostility in the "Menexenus." The *Bible* contains lingering presence as does the present day map of the eastern Mediterranean and the Aegean of the Hyksos people or at the very least traces of the Canaanites.

On the earthquake-raked Thera, we earlier cited today's village of Phoinikia, still with lingering associations of Phoenix on the island otherwise known as the modern Santorini. Herodotus alluded to Memblarious, *a follower of Cadmus,* had founded Thera eight generations before the islanders sailed west sometime before Troy to found the polis of Sparta.[37] Second millennium Greece was not a Greece of the Greeks but a stew of many including Greek, Hittite, Phrygian, Thracian, and for our argument Semitic, all fusing their cultures, like Israel, into a gemlike identity of Golden Age Greece of the 5th Century BCE. The Theban Pindar[38] claims interestingly that it was Cadmus himself who built altars to the sea-god Poseidon. Sarah Morris, in her work "*Daidalos and the Origins of Greek Art"* includes helpful chapters on "Danaus" (Danaus) and "Kadmos" (Cadmus, Quadmus, etc). Her fascinating thesis argues that Daidalos, who fashioned his son's unfortunately lethal wings, is a *proto-artist* whose medium was metals, specifically bronze.

The Hyksos, or Canaanites, were among the very first historical metal *urgos,* those "doers of deed" of metal-making.[39] The richest veins of iron used in forging were at Krete, its cousin island of Thera, the richest veins of iron of all, and at inland Greek Thebes, a metallurgical source, from which another atomic element derives, Cadmium. The locative and eponym deriving from the name Cadmus likely contributed to naming the element Cadmium. This essential element accounts for yellow pigment in the background painting of the Cretan-style goddess on display in the Thebes Museum. Plausibly, these names and artifacts connect back to the Hyksos of the second millennium BCE. The related figure associated with metals, the legendary mortal Daidalos, treated in Sarah Morris' study, is a theophanic avatar of Kothar wa Hasis, the smith *god* of the Ugarit, much like the Olympian Hephaestus, or the Roman Vulcan.

We likewise advance that it was the Hyksos who introduced the military technology of the chariot to Egypt, which in due time required stronger components made from metal, from metal-smithing, in the form of axels and other weapons. The subjects of metals, their names and locations, *further* our thesis of Hyksos' influence on both the *Bible* and its authors' older sources. Sometime after they were forced to flee Egypt after long dominance, it was perhaps the Hyksos people who were among the earliest to discover iron and its sources in mines. To make bronze, one needs tin and copper, the very name of copper-rich Cyprus; the source of tin in Anatolia was scarce with far away England, with Afghanistan providing surplus. Semites *were* frequently in England, a point that John Steinbeck notes to his editor in a letter as an appendix to *The Acts of King Arthur*[40] and later Theodore of Syria, who reintroduced arithmetic into England in order to synchronize Easter dates in the 7th Century.[41]

The mastery of composing graphemes by these populations is analogous to developing metallurgy, military technology, and onomastics of person and place names. Numeracy and literacy are usually associated with rationality and civilization, as these skills also elicit magic and tyranny. The final Hyksos pharaoh's name appearing on the Rhind mathematical papyrus, mentioned above, heralded the Egyptians' overthrow with a vengeance remembered down to Queen Hatshepsut's reign (1479—1458 BCE).

Leonard Shlain[42] (1998) and Deborah Tarn Steiner[43] (1994), two very different authors, one a pioneer of laparoscopic surgery and the other a classicist, enumerate the downside of advances from the effects on writing and reading on human neuroplasticity: for the former literacy relates to miscegenation and for the latter to tyranny. Steiner in *The Tyrant's Writ: Myths and Images of Writing in Ancient Greece* finds that imprinting oaths onto tokens to full-blown texts of kings most often tyrannized populations of Egypt, the Levant, and Greece. Steiner asserts that "semata that allow individuals separated by time and space to communicate with one another and the gods" can take on ritual transactions among mortals and between mortals and immortals so that the resultant text-fetish glows with metaphoric radiance that crouches the masses shielding their eyes in terror.

Numeracy and literacy surely advanced economies and, fortunately, here is where evidence lingers among the dust of millennia past. For those tools used for sealing olive oil jars are evidence of the path of the Hyksos' picaresque trajectory north and then west. Scribes of oriental tyrants regularly wrote directives, propaganda, and symbols that ended up embossed on seals for impressing ceramics, scattered as shards around the Mediterranean via sea-faring and land-based traders. Talismans, kings' cursed tablets, and legal decrees trade upon the imaginations of the time among cultural communities, who received tiding from those trading across time and space as if the king were present in majesty during the arrival and final purchase and consumption. According to Berard:

> Egyptian or eastern objects found in the Aegean Basin start from an epoch much more remote from the Theban New Empire; and that much of these articles are datable in an exact manner. Thus the inscribed cover on the cartouche of Hyksos king Khian, retrieved at Knossos in a dump of MM III A, is a witness of the exchanges that existed at the time of the pastoral kings in the Valley of the Nile and the Aegean world. Thus, again in an inverse sense, the excavations of Phoenicia and notably those of Ras Shamra have confirmed the importations and the Aegean influences in the Levant, in the Middle Bronze period, before and during the epoch of the Hyksos.[44]

Berard would agree with what we've argued here is valid about the Hyksos' influence in the region and its lingering, foundational effects. He, above, provided substantial textual evidence for grounding for the Hyskos presence, the argument affirmed additionally by the fact of a Hyksos pharaoh's presence appears on the Rhind Math papyrus, which we will soon likewise discuss again.[45]

In addition to the evidence of cylinder seals and inscribed cartouches that recollected the Hyksos, there are cultural references of the Land of Canaan that abound in the *Bible*. Here follow some biblical references as a relevant but selective list in summary. Cadmonites (also Kadmonites or Qadmonites) are often identified as the ancient "Canaanites";[46] "Benekadem" are identified in multiple books as "sons of Cadmus" or else as "of the East."[47] In addition to the Cadmus references in the *Bible,* which we ironically contend that the biblical authors got *right,* there are frequent onomasticons relating to the Greek myth about Cadmus' family: three of Cadmus' five sons' names echo in the Moses story. The name of Cadmus' brother Phineas, who searches for his lost sister ends up in Bulgaria, appears in at least three separate times, the first of which is involved directly with Moses and *Exodus*. Cadmus' brother Phoenix appears in the *Bible* and extra-biblically as both a tribe and a location.

The book of *Joshua* 13:3-6 says: "From Sihor, which is before Egypt, even unto the borders of Ekron northward, which is counted to the Canaanite: five lords of the Philistines; the Gazathites, and the Ashdothites, the Eshkalonites, the Gittites, and the Ekronites; also the Avites:

> 4 From the south, all of the land of the Canannites, and Mearah that is beside the Sindonians, unto Aphek, to the borders of the Amorites:
> 5 And the land of the Giblites, and all Lebanon, toward the sunrising, from Baalgod under mount Hermon unto the entering into Hamath.
> 6 All the inhabitants of the hill country from Lebanon unto Misrephoth-maim, and all the Sidonians, them will I drive out from before the children of Israel: only divide thou it by lot unto the Israelites for an inheritance, as I have commanded thee."

Phineas in Greek myth is Cadmus' brother, and the *Bible* says of one of his name in *Exodus*:

> 6:25, "And Eleazar, Aaron's son, took him one of the daughters of

Putiel to wife; and she bore him Phinehas: these are the heads of the fathers of the Levites according to their families...
6: 26 These are that Aaron and Moses, to whom the LORD said, Bring out the children of Israel from the land of Egypt according to their armies."

In *Exodus* 25:6-16, Phineas has to kill so the Hebrews can avoid the plague. In *Joshua* 22: 32-3, 32nd paragraph we find: "And Phinehas the son of Eleazar the priest, and the princes, returned from the children of Reuben, and from the children of God, out of the land of Gilead, unto the land of Canaan, to the children of Israel, and brought them the word again. Verse 33 continues, "And the thing pleased the children of Israel; and the children of Israel blessed God; and did not intend to go up against them in battle, to destroy the land wherein the children of Ruben and God dwelt."

In 1 Samuel 4:6-19, Phineas has the Ark of the Covenant, and, eventually, facing Philistines is killed. 1 Samuel 14:3 likewise contains an extensive genealogy of Phineas. There are references to 2nd millennium correspondences among the Kings of Egypt, Hittite, Amurru, and Greece, all of which reveal accessibility and travel and trade between the lands and kingdoms. Until the tsunami-like catastrophe of invading Sea Peoples, occurring around 1250 BCE, the peoples of these nations would have remembered the fleeing Hyksos and Thera volcanic eruption as the most significant natural and geopolitical event of its region.

Sequential Hittite correspondences, dating between 1500 to 1250 BCE, register troublesome rogues disrupting Hittite hegemony in buffer regions to what is known today as Lykia, Miletus and Lesbos, which might offer evidence of geopolitical cooperation both with and against the Hyksos.[48] There is no mention in any cache of documents, Syrian Ugarit, Hittite Hattusa, Egypt Amarna, or anywhere in Israel regardless of the cost of research and the expense of excavation that identifies any Hebrew presence, but there *is* a clear awareness of Semitic speaking Canaanites (e.g. Hyksos).

Likewise, Cadmus' name itself is a Semitic word denoting both locational and temporal meanings, and which appears, as noted, in the *Bible* several times. In a way, the meaning of Cadmus both in place and tribal name relates to "Caliph", as in the state's name California. "Khaliph" means the "one who follows"; Cadmus means "the one before." Strikingly, "Adam Cadmon" is in Jewish esoteric thought envisioning a demiurge that preceded the Adam of *Genisus*. Also coincidental, "Cadmoen" of Bede's time is the first English poet.

The biblical "benequadminites" are much like "benejamin," or Benjamin, which means "the son of the south." Qudminites are the "Sons of the East" where the sun arises. Outside the *Bible,* other evidence places Cadmus in Syria near where the Orontes enters the Mediterranean Sea. Great works of literature often echo biblical allusions, and fact can become fiction when time goes out of mind, out of chronology.

Clearly, Semites traveled extensively. Variations of the Northwest Semitic are found around the Mediterranean, shared by sibling languages such as Canaanite, Hebrew, Punic, and speakers of Aramaic. Linguistic codes that lack vowels and rely upon only consonants appear widely and reveal early presence (triconsonantalism, today with e-mail and URLs occurs regularly as an efficient means of texting, e.g. "R U thr"). An old Tuscan title for Mercury was Cadmus, which appears in different authors' works under the various but related forms of Cadmilus, Casinillus, and Camillus. Otfried Müller cites these references.[49] Many early superstitions of both the Greeks and the Romans were derived from the Egypto-Tuscans. In a previous passage, Müller describes Cadmus in terms exactly suitable to the Egypto-Tuscan Neph the author of production.[50] We have elsewhere met the assertion that a son of Ishmael was called Cadmeh.[51] that a town in Cadmeth is mentioned in *Joshua* xiii. 18; and that an ancient people of Canaan were called Cadmonim.[52] Why such an in-depth linguistic analysis and conjecture? We humans, ancient, classical, modern and to the 21st Century CE are more the same than we are divided, that we have, if not a common ancestry, a common culture through common values, that might bind us together and bring an end to nationalistic violence.

All of this biblical and extra biblical evidence creates more than adequate plausibility that the Hyksos people influenced much of what we know of the history of history, but what of their direct effect on Hebrews? Well, the Canaanite influence on Hebrews is definite and established; similarly, there are no pig bones found in Avaris sites, but there *are* camel bones unearthed, and there is the telling legend surviving of cooking a kid (calf) in mother's milk. Here evidence of absence is not absence of evidence. This Hyksos link is syllogistic. A *major premise* is that the Hyksos people were Canaanite and in the land of Canaan. A *minor premise* is that the Canaanites influenced Hebrew lore and biblical record. Thus, we must *conclude with entailment and validity*, that the Hyksos definitely influenced the Hebrew.

The importance of *all* this analysis and interpretation is amplified in its contemporary import, given current conflicts. Consider this "fact" again to see another example of why this is the case: that aforementioned famous nineteenth century German Heinrich Schliemann may have mistaken a *Hyksos* for a Greek king when uttering famously, "Today, I have looked upon the face of Agamemnon." The death masque covering the face he excavated could have been a fleeing Semitic, a Hyksos warrior, who died some four hundred years earlier than the famous conqueror of Troy, who in Homer's famous tale was murdered at Mycenae by his wife and lover Aegisthus. The dating of the Mycenaean shaft tombs has long been established as occurring during the correct century of the Hyksos exodus: the 16th Century BCE. And consider this: just 25-meters beyond Lion Gate and to the right was found a stone carving from another grave in Circle A, this one representing a *charioteer with a horse*, grave memorabilia or κτερ-ίσματα. The dating and the innovative war technology introduced by Hyksos to Egypt and rarely cited in rocky Greece heightens the plausibility of our thesis.

But more dramatic is the several death masks that Schliemann found that so excited the 19th Century German—gold sheets crudely wrought, which anticipated Egyptian masques of the 18th dynasty. Also outside the polygonal walls of Mycenae, down the ramparts, is Circle B, with Rho graves' architecture exactly that of the Ugarit, other further proof of the Hyksos' earlier-than-Hebrew legacy.[53] Hence, art, architecture, and fashion are congruent with 16th to 14th Century Nilotic culture.

From 1600 BCE until the Sea Peoples devastating incursions, the Argolid in central Peloponnese reigned supreme, much as Thebes did until two generations before the Trojan War.[54] Or, for that matter, Athens, five hundred years later, which like Jerusalem, ruled during the first half of the First Millennium. Here is the source of legends, of the Io myth, that of Danaas, from several traditions, including Hebrew, Greek and Ugarit (Canaanite or proto-Phoenician). The father of the protagonist in the Ugarit "Poem of Aquat" is named Daniel, literature that might date from prior to 14th Century BCE, a plot that perhaps Herodotus remembered a thousand years later when he documented the commencement of Semites locating in Greece in his *Histories*. Only a score or two kilometers north lay Mycenae, founded by Perseus, whose mother was Danae, echoing directly the daughters of Danaas. With the southern mainland of Greece founded by Phoenicians, Greek findings evidence the Hyksos arriving during the early part of the Late Helladic period in Thebes.[55]

The odious thesis of *race* was nearly demolished with the fall of the Third Reich, although it persisted for a time in South Africa, the US, and Israel to name a few nations. Its unpleasant whiffs linger certainly, and our thesis' ambiguity may be seen to sustain its premises, but this is far from our intention. Let us explain. As a very important aside, it might be wise to disentangle and separate the issue of race from culture. Hebrews certainly appropriated much of the Canaanite culture. Were some Hyksos progenitors of some future Jews? Undoubtedly, they were. But culture and race are two different but overlapping categories, and emphasis on the latter has resulted in a high percentage of human history's human carnage. We Americans may enjoy Italian food, for example, but would likely not have joined Mussolini's fascists in the 1920s.

During World War II, however, we hesitated ordering pasta at restaurants or sushi for fear of a lack of patriotism. Race assumes a packaging of genes to deliver our gene bundle from 1630. With each birth, our deck of genes is cut in two. With a 20-year span a conservative range for reproducing, approximately five generations can result per century. For instance, each of us entails the genes of 32 different people over the last century who would include great-great-grandparents. The next century accounts for genes from 1,024 sources; the next century, 32,768; the next, 1,048,586; the 5th Century, 33,554,432, a diluting of the genetic ancestry seismically. Each one of us resulted from coupling of some female and male, lover or rapist, and going back a half-millennium year result in huge numbers of forbearers who flooded our gene pool with non-cultural DNA. Now this is a hypothetical number of course, but in times of chaos and war with resulting rape and Romeo and Julieting, the gene flood number is still quite large, unless a person's gene source derives sololy from some sequestered Pyrenees mountainous community like that filmed in Buneul in his 1933 horror documentary, *Land Without Bread*.[56] Unfortunately, until of lately, humans the world over only remember the fraternal males who carry monikers through genealogical time like "Gage" or "Freeman."

Over five generations, progenitors must factor in huge figures that recently accounted for the future king of England, William or Harry, who count an Asian Indian grandmother among his more tightly knit and well documented heritage. Precious few of us who come from kings or queens without dilution via the common man or woman.[57] Let's discard race, however, in this objective thought experiment and our meta-view of man's ancestry, and let's turn our attention to *culture* before Marie Le Pen's party dangerously resurges in France.

The gap in time between the Hyksos expulsion from Egypt in 1550 BCE and the crystalizing of Jewish culture during Solomon's successor's time in the 800's BCE spans 700 years, events of emerging aggregates that result in autonomous Jewish culture, not from autochthony or theochthony, of springing from the ground or from the Deity. Some of the 1550 BCE Hyksos from the Delta were possibly ancestors of Rehaboam's cohort, but to claim the identity of that cohort being encapsulated only in the Delta is a logical non-sequitar. Race is essentially always a bogus thesis, typically a political tool to forge nationalism and fraught with nationalism's often unfortunate consequences such as Other-ing. Culture, on the other hand, implies choice to a certain extent. Will I play up my English or Italian identity? Either can be worn by any, draped here or sewn upon the human pastiche. Professor Gage's intellectual identity and culture is more Jewish American than any of those with whom he grew up as a result of his education and quest for an intellectual life. By analogy, first millennium Jews were more culturally Hyksos/Canaanite and Assyrian than they were Egyptian, Hittite, or Greek in terms of diet, dress, and flavor of governance, as well established by Thompson.[58]

We excited scribes will now try to push the selected gems of history out of delightful literary dross toward a summary, a placing of all this whispering loudly down the lane of history into the context of the world we live in *now*. Tonight we will hold our smart phones up to the night sky and let Google Sky Map (™), a free download we recommend, show us the same sky and constellations that the Hyksos would have seen so long ago, seeing even further into the stellar past and into a larger creation… If we can program in the right Egyptian and Greek locations and keep up with the big story of the Hyksos' picturesque journey, that is…We believe that we can and will see the past truly, even if it means that some of the Hebrew grand tradition is pure, post-hoc heteroglossic invention for the understandable reasons of modern nation building and of race preservation. There are other cultures, which share the same geography and similar histories, namely Muslim ones.

An example might serve here. There was apparently not much writing on papyrus after the Hebrew exile, but clearly the century following the life of Jesus accounts for a large amount of Hebrew writing on papyrus. Use of Hebrew for community usage likewise has a revisionist history. The Hebrew of contemporary Israel is a reconstruction, as we've noted elsewhere about both the Hebrew and Irish languages. Hebrew was the sacred language of ritual in history but served only rarely as the *koine* of speech or writing in Jewish communities, as evidenced in the case of Jesus' language, who spoke Aramaic.

Likewise, Paul spoke Greek. The grammar of Hebrew itself was not formulated until the 9th Century CE in Arab Europe when other scholars followed the lead of the Arab grammarians in Al Andalusia, who first formulated the syntax of Hebrew's brother tongue Arabic.[59] This one example of a time out of mind language morphing out of both myth and history illustrates literally that a spoken and written language assumed to be ancient but really is not; it also illustrates figuratively that perception can become reality, even if that reality is not essentially real. If the Abrahamic tradition of one of the three great religions of the world contains much that is only figuratively true, then perhaps the job of one seeking an absolute value of common culture and peace-making among competing religious claims, border disputes and outright warring, is to find and celebrate those intersecting histories and traditions that foster peace, like those found in the *Sermon on the Mount*.

The humane and forgiving values expressed there might serve as a coda for peace, a high-water mark for civilization, which, if practiced, would yield peace and understanding. "Blessed are the meek, /for they shall inherit the earth. . . / You have heard that it was said, 'Love your neighbor and hate your enemy' / But I tell you, love your enemies and pray for those who persecute you. . ."[60]

Consider, too, the Native American Creator's "Instructions" on how to live in harmony and how that oral tradition offers benefits or reimagined truths as well as the dangers of heteroglossia, from the primal Creation story to 21st Century Facebook: Martin Bohl recent Facebook post: "Elder's Meditation of the Day"—"IN THE BEGINNING were the Instructions. . . The Instruction was to live in a good way and be respectful to everybody and everything."—Vickie Downey, TEWA/Tesuque Pueblo. Don Coyhis likewise says: "A long time ago, in the beginning, the Creator gave to all people and to all things the Wisdom and the knowledge of how to live in harmony. Some tribes call these teachings the original Instructions, the original teachings, or the Great Laws. All of Nature still lives and survives according to these teachings. In modern times, human beings are searching for the Instructions. Many churches claim they have these Instructions. Where are these teachings? The Instructions are written in our hearts."[61]

Human kind must follow inner moral compasses. We co-scribes will try valiantly anyway in the pages to come, as a solemn promise to you and to our shared humanity, that we might come together to where we should go and to ensure that this planet survives with us humans on it, stewards of the shared environment and of peace.

The stakes couldn't be higher: the very survival of our species, the survival of our shared planet. If we are to play our best ethical game, Hebrews, Muslims, and Christians alike, we must agree on the rules, which really all come down to one uber-rule: to do the genuine very best we can to find and enhance common ground, to really listen to others, to deliberate action together in unity, to wage peace together."

6
Sociality of Knowledge
A Social Life of Information, Conclusions, and Implications for Peace

Now I have an idea that Melampus the son of Amytheon knew all about this ceremony [Dionysian]; for it was he who introduced the name of Dionysus into Greece, together with the sacrifice in his honor and the phallic procession. He did not, however, fully comprehend the doctrine, or communicate it in its entirety; its more perfect development was the work of later teachers. Nevertheless it was Melampus who introduced the phallic procession, and from Melampus the Greeks learned the rites which they now performed. Melampus, in my view, was an able man who acquired the art of divination and brought into Greece, with little change, a number of things which he had learned in Egypt, and among them the worship of Dionysus. I will never admit that the similar ceremonies performed in Greece and Egypt are the result of mere coincidence—had that been so, our rites would have been more Greek in character and less recent in origin. Nor will I allow that the Egyptians ever took over from Greece either this custom or any other. Probably Melampus got his knowledge of the worship of Dionysus through Cadmus of Tyre and the people who came with him from Phoenicia to the country now called Boeotia.[1]

EVIDENCE OF THE HYKSOS FOUNDATIONAL THESIS ABOUNDS. Scholar Beltz says succinctly: "Canaanites were descendants of Hyksos."[2] Most authorities acknowledge that Hyksos were Canaanites but do not know their origin. The base in Egypt was centered at Avaris, west of present day Suez. Hyksos had commerce with Byblos, Ugarit, Ebla and Krete when Israel clearly wasn't around, either as an agricultural center or as a nation. The Hittites weren't a maritime power but were clearly a land-based empire. Some Avaris archeological finds support the *Bible* argument. Among the excavation, no pig bones were found among twenty animal mummies, though absence of evidence isn't necessarily evidence of absence.[3] There is consensus that the Hyksos clearly introduced horse chariots and the loom to the region. A millennium later, Herodotus reports that wearing wool was taboo according to the Egyptians, an example of habitual memory of Hyksos oppressors.

Previous to the Hyksos domination, Egypt had no interest in animals as transport or as a means for conquest. Cosmology held that, should an Egyptian die beyond ancestral boundaries, his being would not enter the afterlife. Hence, other than mercenaries, there was little Egyptian aggression abroad until after the Hyksos expulsion from Egypt, with any dead likely resulting from Egyptians in pursuit of the legendary Cadmus' tribal people in flight. Hyksos had a profound effect upon Nilotic culture. The Apis Bull, a traditional festival and icon of Egypt, might well have been spread by the Hyksos. Not to overextend speculation, but clearly the Avaris frescos with motif of the bull acrobats against a labyrinthine wall pattern share much with the Minotaur myth and other paintings in Krete's Knossos and in the Cadmeia I in Thebes, excavated in the 1960s. Could this be evidence for the descendants the myth of Cadmus? Cadmus' sister was kidnaped by a bull, and Cadmus was guided by a cow with crescent markings on both flanks from Delphi to where he founded Thebes. At Thebes, Cadmus built an altar to the goddess Onga, the Hyksos equivalent of Athena.[4]

A tonsured head upon a mushroom colossus, found by Bietak, recalls fashions of earlier headdress styles, only connected to the culture of pre-Canaanite Ebla just south of Aleppo in Syria, dating from before 1900 BCE.[5] A cylinder seal from Avaris possibly associates with the Canaanite sea god Yam, aggressively posed upon a pedestal, underscored by a snake; it also depicts a boat with Baal in bull form looming over a lion. In Ebla was found a regal scepter bearing the name of a Hyksos king at Avaris.[6] Ceramic molds for casting bronze tools and weapons were infrequently found in Egypt previous to Hyksos occupation.[7] In Avaris, there is the practice of donkey burials within the tomb; we find evidence of a previous caravan economy converted to a sedentary one: here there are cemeteries built within walls, clearly no longer evidencing a nomadic people.

If the Hebrews existed in Egypt before 1000 BCE, why was it necessary for them to cross the Red Sea when the land bridge provides an easy escape to Gaza? The famous Moses crossing of the sea more closely suggests a non-anthropological subjugation of the same sea that becomes animated in the Yam/Baal struggle. In our search for peace, we look at literary and archeological evidence of exodus', real and imagined, as well as traces of military and cultural war footprints from land and sea. In this insistence of ours on the real Hyksos exodus from Egypt serving as the appropriate model for the Hebrew one created through heteroglossia and out of real time, we are not casting blame for a very human and also a culture-building exercise in fiction. As suggested before and in Chapter 7, other European nation states as well as non-European ones practice similar feats of fantasy and appropriation. What we are doing, we hope, is finding common cultural bridges that might unite cultures, religions, and peoples with presently competing and contentious claims. We are aiming for a bridge to peace, in our shared time.

In the 1970s Gage gained access into the reserved stacks of the Louvre, where he photographed the Cadmus amphorae and kylix of the First Millennium, a remembered habitual memory of fleeing Canaanites? Perhaps. We are focusing down sharply on cultures crossed and dominated in the paths of fleeing Hyksos, some of whom intermarried and advanced commerce, while fore ranks migrated counterclockwise all the way to Greece and Sicily and Illyria: first where Hebrews would occupy, north to Ugarit and the Hittites, and west to Greece, with Krete in between.[8] It is Cadmus and his family's itinerary that interests us, he being not an historical figure but an ethnonym, a representative of the Canaanite Exodus, as mentioned. Before this myth is that of Danaus of Aeschylus' tragedy *The Suppliants*. Danaaus' story clearly tells of fifty maiden daughters of Danaus fleeing farther from their fifty sons, Aegyptian cousins set on rape, to the Peloponnese; further, Danaans are one of the three names Homer uses to describe the Greeks assaulting Troy and, subsequently, one of the twelve tribal names of Hebrews. The girls' flight, dramatized by a 5th Century Greek tragedian patterns Hyksos' escape of the previous millennium.

Our thesis, where we began and where we find our "end" of peace, is that a lawgiver Moses, historical or legendary, historicized a divine plan by drafting a book that included Hebrew palimpsests of episodes of a flight from Egypt upon the wave of Hyksos exoduses. Hebrews progressively and beautifully historicized earlier Canaanite myths in the later-anthologized *Torah*. The ancient mythic battle between the sea and the supreme god become an historical event out of time in the derivative narrative of Yahweh opening the sea to allow a warrior king to escape Egypt. Four biblical traditions associate Hebrews with Egypt: "The Echo" in Genesis 1 and 2; "The Family of Nations" in Genesis 10; "Joseph"; and the Moses story.[9]

However, the Hebrews imagined the lawgiver Moses, a Jew with an Egyptian name, thereby appropriating the Canaanite Hyksos, as the Hebrews appropriated Canaanite poetic parallelism, metaphor, and *agon*, as well as the earlier tale of Noah from a millennium earlier via the Akkadian Gilgamesh.

Language memes accretes to carry along vestiges of prior hegemonies from one age to another. There is more Arabic in our present English language, for that matter more Arabic present in French, Italian, Spanish, or Portuguese, than there is Egyptian influence from 1400 BCE through to the birth of Christ on the Hebrew language and thought. What influence of Egyptian on Hebrew one does find comes increasingly as they approach the time of Christ. Proximity influences languages, especially occupation of one culture by another, such as the Arab presence in Spain for nearly eight hundred years.

The Spanish "Olé" uttered as the bull passes by is just an echo of "Allah." This is habitual, non-conscious memory living in language. Many revealed language texts of the *Old Testament, New Testament, Quran, Torah, Hadith*, and Christian are all distinctly Middle Eastern, not Egyptian. Hebrew scribes believed they were writing about "What Happened" in composing, over centuries, *The Torah* (recording accounts, identities, and commemorations), those human bids for identity, but they were often mistaken commemorations, sometimes ones deliberately distorting myth as history. This does not diminish the beauty of the uber-book as a didactic work of art, of myth and of history, one whose psalms, songs, parables and books present the best of mankind in empathy and altruism (morphed in *The New Testament* to such high-water moral instructions as "The Sermon on the Mount," "The Parable of the Good Samaritan" and "The Parable of the Prodigal Son"). This is a distinctly human achievement: the use of third-eye imagination for recording the made-up or transcribed pinnacles of moral civilization, as well as the use of negative literary examples of conquest and punishment used to instill fear or revolution for immoral practices.

In the *Old Testament*, we meet the best and worst of man, recorded and invented, flinching and unflinching, all revealing important moral truths through a beautiful blend of poetry, song, allegory, parable, myth and history.

At least two important ideas are in play here: models of history and categories of memory, as there are at least two sides to every story, if not seven. As noted in our "beginning" of the search for peace, Martin Bernal wrote several seminal titles on this topic since 1987.[10] His undergirding thesis is that two models of interpretation of ancient history exist, the ancient and the Aryan models. The former includes Herodotus, Pausanias, Pherekydes, the *Bible*, the *Book of the Dead*, etc. These reported on what happened from a vantage point closer to what had been happening. In contrast is the Aryan model, which extends from 1780 to the 20th Century. These more modern voices reported upon what happened in the ancient and medieval past. Influenced by Newton and the Enlightenment, they hypothesized in historical interpretations how racial fictions best explain what happens, as in laws of nature. Non-French European intellectuals, living particularly in the many principalities after 1871 to be called Germany and the clustering of states to be called Italy wrote jealously, lacking a Charlemagne, to ground the notion of nation/state. England had invented an Arthur, as equivalent of the Emperor. Seemingly to spawn myths to found political identity, dozens from now forgotten territories from Saxony to Savoy resemble today's troublesome areas between the Black and Caspian Sea, where and when all hated all Others.

With Bernal, Israeli historian Shmolo Sand, likewise, identifies in his two titles how 19th Century German Jewish scholars reacted to major German Enlightenment authors' anti-Semitic folk theories.[11] In *The Invention of the Jewish People* and *The Invention of the Land of Israel: from Holy Land to Homeland*, Sand cites how Jewish scholars from post Enlightenment milieu propagated the Israeli nationalistic myth, a thesis that Jewish scholar Sand tries to defuse as being the enemy of potential peace with the Arab world. The Aryan classists' model, criticized by both Bernal and Sand, produced acknowledgedly a lot of good work in archeology, but their racist starting premises prepared the way for Hitler. Bernal says that scholars should revisit the ancients and prefer what he has modeled as an alternative theory for historical interpretation, as your present scribes seek to do here.

In his early trips to Syria, Professor Gage had a revelation about the Hyksos influence upon Greek myth and, subsequently, was gratified to find in Bernal's ancient model some confirmation. Though bothered by Bernal's title and his lack of emphasis on the Canaanite role, which Sarah Morris also felt that Bernal had missed, Gage's work on the "ancient model" at Humboldt State University in 1987 caught the attention of Prof. Medsker of the Graduate School at Claremont University. In that same year the first volume of *Black Athena* was published, Gage delivered a paper at Claremont's Institute of Antiquities. Having recently returned from Syria with insights anticipating what Bernal would publish that year and what Morris did in 1996, Gage argued that Bernal played down the role of Semitic influences upon Greece.[12]

Bernal emphasized that direct Egyptian conquest across to Greece seemed more seismic through conquest than what resulted over a greater period of time from both commerce and war. We hold that rather than in one swoop after the parting of any sea in the best Hollywood tradition, the intruder Hyksos' exoduses was more a series of evacuations and departures following the initial disgorging around 1560 BCE, then with departures frog-jumping beyond the latest reach of Egyptians, with periods of settling after conquering and fostering commerce. Many of these former relatives of pharaohs ventured increasingly as entrepreneurs who developed more hospitable potential markets in Anatolia and the Aegean. Eventually, these too became prey again to escape further north and west across the southern coast of the non-maritime Hittites, when new Pharaohs like Rameses II took up pursuit and whose son it was who first recorded Hebrews in history (and these not in Egypt but in the highlands east of the River Jordan which his armies had overrun). Sometimes the Nilotic vendetta was furthered with opportunistic local mercenaries, who may have lost what the Egyptians had lost when first the Canaanites invaded in the 18th Century BCE.

In addition to models of historical reportage is memory, the gradual drift north of Semites lived in traces in the conceptual memories of those settling in Greece from as early as the 16th Century and later, remembered in oral and written texts, as institutional memory, dramas, histories, odes, and panegyrics. Should conventional thought hold that institutional memory fails beyond four centuries, consider the past in England in the dramas of Shakespeare's day, as referred to in the last chapter. William Rowley's 1618 play *All's Lost by Lust* and by Thomas Heywood's 1592 play *Four Prentices of London* feature as settings and subjects of another Semitic incursion into Europe that began in 711—the Moors early presence in Spain—and the Western Crusades incursion into Palestine in the early 12th Century respectively. The point here is this: memory of English playwrights extended back to 711 from 1600, a time gap greater than that of Herodotus and the historical event of the Hyksos exodus.

Memory has been differentiated by Deborah Holland, art historian at Cambridge, as occurring in three categories of the personal, the conceptual, and the habitual.[13] Using Bakhtin's theories, Gage modified Holland's troika in two more recent papers, one on Shakespeare delivered at the 2010 Authorship Conference at Ashland, Oregon, and the other on historical medieval queens of the south who married north, delivered at the Sixth International Congress of von Humboldt Travel Writing in Morocco in 2011. Personal memory for we scribes includes accidental discoveries. For example, in the case of Gage, his accidental memories of a 1958-59 trip "hitchhiking" from Berkeley to Damascus; for Freeman, reflections of a lifelong-friend lost recently to a motorcycle accident and of their many good past-times together. These personal and accidental memories are the Proustian *Remembrance of Things Past*, associations tied to one's private place and family, to sounds, to smells, to sensory triggers of eidetic imagery with intuitive notions of identity. Conceptual memory, on the other hand, is social and derives from *patria*, from socially embraced community foundations. Societal conceptualization are ideologies embodied as stated missions of and learned by testing in school, such as the functionality of tripartite governance. Parenthetically, Geary points out the public school in France was instituted early in the 20th Century in order to standardize French as the national language, when nearly half of today's France spoke other languages and dialects, for language education is the spine of conceptual memories.[14]

Habitual memory is what grabs us scribes here as it reveals earlier palimpsests, morphological layers of behavioral manners, not societally acknowledged matters. Habitual memories explain why Christians in Spain frequently yell "Allah" that is now "Olé" as already mentioned. This is the tacit and unconscious knowledge that governs why we ate ice cream last and not first at last night's dinner. It is what elicits from the youngest why on Easter in celebrating the crucifixion of Jesus gardens are planted with what result from what bunnies do. Though often unconscious, habitual memories reveal cultural and institutional histories quiescent of Time out of Mind; the Hyksos deracination from Egypt is an early palimpsest that accounts for behaviors associated with the alphabet; myths; recurring themes and memes of abduction, the founding of cities, building temples or citadels; likewise it imprints on maps and memories the onomastics of *topos*, of place.

After Bernal in relevance comes Michael Astour's *Hellenosemitica*.[15] His study is the most thorough elaboration of Cadmus, Danaus, and other evidence of mid-second millennium Canaanite exoduses. Of note, both these eminent biblical scholars are Jewish as are their kindred spirit scholars Niels Lemche, Israel Finkelstein, George Mendelman and Norman Gottwald. Their etymological probing provides us with some crucial references in our argument. Coincidentally, they are congruent with the contemporary Israeli historian Shmolo Sand, whose investigations lead to how the 19th Century European intellectuals bought Bernal's Aryan model that eventually led to Hitler's atrocities and subsequently further its misappropriation in his homeland today. Like the VW automobile and Bayer aspirin, classical scholarship often ignores its family ties to obscene nationalism. Incidentally, Geary's *Myth of Nations: the Medieval Origins of Europe* provides a strong parallel argument to our own that often some take myth to project back into dim history to falsify historical precedents.[16] But we scribes have promised readers a beginning, a middle and an eventual end. . .

That Cadmean Thebes in Boeotia north of Athens is the same name as the Capital of Egypt suggests a link of habitual memories, with all those sphinxes extant. As alluded to earlier, the capital in Egypt is a Greek name and not what the Nilotic population called itself, just as Egyptian peasants today refer to themselves as the Mirs, though the cosmopolitan used the diction most familiar. The remnant of the Hyksos, arriving under Egyptian duress in Greece with "Cadmus," and, according to myth, founding the city Thebes, reveals a name that is surely linked to the pre-Hebraic, Semitic east. Platon in 1963 excavated the Cadmeia I and II at Thebes to find those very same cylinder seals that Gage filmed at the Greek museum. Only three seals were Mycenae Greek; 34 others were Syrian-Babylonian.[17]

One seal dated around the 14th BCE depicts a human strangling snakes in each hand, a motif that, too, appears on coins and emblems of alliances a thousand years later in Theban affairs. This could depict Heracles' well-known feat. Heracles is from Thebes, according to several versions of the myth. Some link Heracles to Melqart, a proto-Heracles of Syrian origin. The Melqart or Melicertes kills a lion bare-handed. The practice continues today by Sheiks, according to one of Gage's students at Aleppo University. Another example of personal memory, Professor Gage prizes a photograph with the elder at dinner in the grandfather's home in Aleppo's medina, a living link to the time of Heracles.

Cadmus, like Phoenix, is a mythic representation of colonizing Canaanite Hyksos. Kadmonites [see also Kadmos, Cadmos, Cadmus, Kadmeia, Cadmeia] in the *Bible* are the ancient Canaanites.[18] Pausanias reports of Cadmus who led a Phoenician army in Boeotia.[19] Spelling can cause modern readers confusion, as "q," "k," and "c" are interchangeable.[20] To reiterate in order to underscore the habitual memory, "Bene-kadem" translates as sons of Cadmus, or of the sons of the East or that which is before—a locative or orientation relating to the sun.[21] Hence, mythic Cadmus, source of the alphabet that carries his brother's name, Phoenix, may refer to the syllabary in Linear B, which dates approximately at the time as Canaanite/Cadmean colonization of Thebes. This would accord with the early dating provided by the Hellenistic Parian calendar.[22] Bernal designates in Chart 2 of *Cadmean Letters* the Semitic source of each letter's graphemic appearance.[23] Not only are the letters identical, but these letters sequence similarly, further indicating a Canaanite/Phoenician morphology of much of human kind's habitual memory. This memory remains paramount in every alphabet today.[24]

The Cadmean Alphabet is triconsonantal that lacks vowels, so we beg patience with our alphabet soup. Cadmus is a cognate of the atomic element Cadmium, mined to this day near Thebes and used in yellow coloration. Cadmus' wife, child of love and war, is Harmonia, or Concord in Latin, as in Paris' Place de Concorde. In lore, their wedding gift, a necklace was a recycled present that Zeus first gave to to Cadmus' sister Europa.[25] In Ugarit, there was a man named "qdm."[25] These elements are not accidental nor random but once carried the conceptual memories of an ancient people, and they coalesce to form a clear picture. Cadmus' brother, Phoenix, in various forms imprints the map of the entire Eastern Mediterranean. On the island of Kythera near Thera, there is Phoinikus.[26] Likewise, there is a port of Phoenix on the south-coast of Krete.[27] There is the harbor Phoenikus of Erythrae. On Thera/Santorini, still stands a Phoinikia, which Gage visited in 1987. Near Bodrum, there is a Finike. Relatedly, Canaanites' Byblos, Beirut, Tyre, Sidon, and Arvad are all identified as Phoenician cities.[28] Consider state and county names of the United States: what habitual memories haunt beneath today's onomasticon?

In addition to etymological alphabet soup, there is genre, there are literary memes persisting through habitual memories and appropriated subsequently. As mentioned, the Canaanite influence on Hebrews also shows in that all three sets of the commandments, in Exodus 23:19b; Exodus 34:26b; and Deuteronomy 14:21b, there appears a curious caveat among each: "Do not cook a kid in its mother's milk." This taboo reveals a former cuisine of ritual, approved of in the Ugarit text "The Poem of Dawn and Sunset."[29]

Further, as cited above, the name Cadmus is a Semitic word denoting both temporal and locational references, a grapheme that appears frequently in Genesis. 15:18-21:

> 18 In the same day the LORD made a covenant with Abram, saying, Unto thy seed have I given this land, from the river of Egypt unto the great river, the river Euphrates:
> 19 The Kenites, and the Kenizzites, and the Kadmonites,
> 20 And the Hittites, and the Perizzites, and the Rephaims,
> 21 And the Amorites, and the Canaanites, and the Girgashites, and the Jebusites.'

In orientation, "Cadmus" is tangibly related to "Caliph," as in the Khalif or Caliphate. The latter translates as "the one who follows"; while "Cadmus" is "the one who came before." In esoteric Jewish thought, Adam Kadmon is envisioned the demiurge, who preceded Adam. A son of Ishmael was called Cadmeh in Genesis xxv. 15, and he may share the cognate with a town named Cadmeth, mentioned in Joshua. xiii. 18. Further, an ancient people of Canaan were called the Cadmonim in Genesis. xv. 19. Curiously, Caedmon is also the earliest known English poet.

It all begins with the sun: to reveal habitual memory of orientation, the biblical bene-quadminites are akin to bene-yemin, or Benjamin: the "sons of the south." Here again evidence of the Hyksos presence is ubiquitous in language, place names, myth, the *Old Testament* itself. Thus, Quadminites are the "sons of the east," where the sun arises, as sons of Benjamin are those to the right of the rising sun while in another Northwestern Semitic language, though not Hebrew, a similar construction translates as "sons of the north," to the left when orienting to the rising sun.

Another but quite modern example of habitual memory occurred in Israel in 2004 when Ariel Sharon created the "Kadima Party," implicitly conveying the notion of primacy, a perfect example of a linguistic meme. Only 10 miles south of Aleppo is a town of Qadene. Triconsonantalism of Semitic languages provide heuristics not valued by Indo-European languages that fetishize spelling, though truncations in today's e-mail and for some time in advertising, as in "Toys R Us," appear to be favoring the former and the rebus.

These names document that the *Bible* displays undeniable intertextuality, a debt shared with Ugarit literature, and with cousin Greek myths. Along with other onomastics; the names of three of the five sons, the brothers of Europa in the Greek story, appear curiously in the *Bible* but more tellingly is the fact that all three relate to Moses. Phoenix is cited in the *Bible* as both a name and a location. Phineas or Phinehas, the Hyksos brother who ends in Bulgaria in search of his sister, appears as three persons. The first is involved with Moses and the Exodus story.

Phineas, Cadmus' brother, appears often in the *Bible*. Exodus 6:25 records:

> '25 And Eleazar Aaron's son took him one of the daughters of Putiel to wife; and she bare him Phineas: these are the heads of the fathers of the Levites according to their families.
> 26 These are that Aaron and Moses, to whom the LORD said, Bring out the children of Israel from the land of Egypt according to their armies.'

In Numbers 25:6-16, Phineas kills a married couple, so that the Hebrews can avoid a plague.

Joshua 22:32-3:

> 32 And Phinehas the son of Eleazar the priest, and the princes,

returned from the children of Reuben, and from the children of Gad, out of the land of Gilead, unto the land of Canaan, to the children of Israel, and brought them word again.

33 And the thing pleased the children of Israel; and the children of Israel blessed God, and did not intend to go up against them in battle, to destroy the land wherein the children of Reuben and Gad dwelt.

In 1 Samuel 4:6-19, Phineas has the Ark of the Covenant, and, facing the Philistines, dies. In 1 Samuel 14:3, we find Phineas' whole genealogy also supports the drift of Bernal's, Astour's, Gordon's and Billigmeyer's arguments about rich Hyksos fundings of an earlier time in the very same region. We scribes do not cite this literary evidence for the Hyksos presence in an academic vacuum.

We hope to show that what can be learned from lost and forgotten hegemonic traditions has important application to the here and now, to the ongoing Arab/Israeli conflict, to recent and ongoing events in Syria, to what is likely to appear next in our online newspaper, television, and Internet headlines about geopolitical affairs, Other-ing, and ethnic or nationalistic aggression and infighting. We are seeking peace and world human harmony out of an ancient map that ought to be studied for not only its historic interest but more importantly for its potential to resist erasing the past and unite us in a common past and cultural ancestry.

If we consider the Abrahamic episode of Hagar impregnated by her husband and then being driven into the desert, we hear similarities in two others sources: Ugarit/Greek, with Baal, horned Canaanite God, impregnating Anat, a cow-like figure, who flies likewise to the desert (but not necessarily Egypt), and we see the connection too with Io in Aeschylus' drama. The heifer Io goes to Egypt and gives birth to Apophis, an identified Pharaoh of the Hyksos dynasties. He is the ancestor of Danaus, sought by Aegyptus, whose sons rape the daughters of Danaus. "Danaans," by-the-way and not to be redundant, is one of the three names Homer uses in the *Iliad* and the *Odyssey*, and Dan is the northern most of the Hebrew tribes. And Dinah of Genesis 34 is a feminine equivalent.

The altar of Athens' Parthenon was public, still situated and in front of the east tympanum. Killing to eat wasn't shameful to Socrates and his friends. But when Christianity overtook ancient religions, all pagan places of worship, all altars were brought within for the exclusive community to celebrate a mystery. Every emerging culture realized the ugly truth that, unlike their gods, we mortals eat and defecate - while our gods don't. Sacrifice was necessary for bountiful crops and game to nourish those of emerging cultures to endure and reproduce, just as Joseph Campbell found again and again in his myth investigations and just as Margaret Mead observed among primitive tribes. But in Canaanite lore, this fact was ritualized in a deity, later resembling if not identical to the god Baal as a cow and kid killer. And what makes the biggest splash for suppliants obeisant to their gods: killing one's literal kid. At the heart of all this ugly reality, human sacrifice emerges recognizably, like images of a photo from a chemical bath.

The *Biblical* echo of the Abraham and Isaac episode touches upon a loathsome practice of Semitic infanticide among these descendants. As cited above, the Commandments include the edict of not boiling a calf in its mother's milk, a commandment passed directly from the Hyksos to the Hebrews and the latter's moral objection to human sacrifice. We have come a long way, thanks to the Jews. Supermarkets like "Safeway" anesthetize shoppers from the means by which much food is obtained. Even the name denotes a "safe" way to feed oneself without risk of injury or death (or a failed crop). Meat wrapped in plastic boats distances us from our mortal reliance and human need as carnivores requiring meat to eat.

The Ugarit culture provides abundant resemblances of the Hyksos history as well. Among the extant libraries, four mythic narratives, with fragments, were found and subsequently translated in the 1930s by Gastor: the "Poem of Baal," the "Poem of Aquat," the "Poem of King Krete," and the "Poem of Dawn and Dusk."[30] As noted, these texts predate the Hebrew pastoral tribes. The Sea People razed Ugarit around 1225 BCE,[31] so the texts may go back further, perhaps to "1500-1350" ("a century of the most widely accepted date for the 'Exodus').[32] Ugarit was written in cuneiform, but the sequence of letters is very nearly what became the Greek sequence and letter graphemes some several hundreds of years later.[33] As previously noted, Cadmus brought the alphabet to Greece, and Herodotus in the 450's BCE and Pausanias in 115 CE both reported seeing Cadmean letters on pots in Thebes.[34]

The "Poem of King Krete" implies the value and fact of eastern Mediterranean intercourse. It provides no evidence of the presence of Hebrews but much evidence that Hebrews subsequently "borrowed and adapted Canaanites ideas."[35] And the Ugarit language is so closely related to Hebrew that the texts have unlocked many biblical ambiguities. Psalm 29 echoes directly the Hymn to Baal.[36] Psalms 68.4 language "He who rides the clouds" is used earlier by the Ugarit poets.[37] Synonymous and antithetical parallelism of these poems is seen likewise in a modern parallel with the

Psalms and with Walt Whitman's gorgeous poetry.

In the "Poem of Baal," Baal and his sister Anat struggle with Yam, the sea god, and with Mot, the god of the underworld, and, in the poem, Anat is depicted as wrestling with the waters like Leviathan, or the Red Sea, Psalms 77. In Judges, Anat appears as "house of" and "son of" in four passages. Likewise, the *Bible* references God as Yahweh and as Elohim. Elohim is the plural of "El," and El is a principal protagonist of the Ugarit Poem of Baal. Many scholars feel that there were several sources conflated into the Torah, that there is not one *Bible* but several. The Bull god of El is similar to the Bull god of Jacob. Psalms 82.1.[38] Eloist texts of around 932 BCE are usually identified as the second oldest source of the *Bible* and are of Canaanite origin, according to Beltz. If you read the whole, the two, Yahweh and El, are nearly interchangeable, with no tension suggested. But in Ugarit texts there is a generational conflict, as El is the father of Baal as in Greek myth Cronos is father of Zeus and the one who tried to eat him along with his siblings.[39]

"The Poem of Dawn and Dusk" tells of El by the seashore aroused by his two daughters. Astour explains how the daughter, Dusk, links etymologically with Europa.[40] She is the very evening star escaping to the West, just as Europa did. Is this related to the symbol of the moon rendered as a habitual memory in subsequent Muslim iconography? Envision the crescent moon with the planet Venus above the horned bull riding west away from Cadmus and brothers on the Lebanese seashore… Is the morning star a signifier of Cadmus in pursuit of Europa? We think so, and not just as a historical or literary curiosity but as common ground between the ethnic groups and religions, potentially uniting, not dividing, the politics of humankind through shared common history and common myth. It is in these Time Out of Mind human commonalities that jump generations and bend centuries to teach us moral lessons in which we find promising human lessons of peace.

We scribes of post-modern peace-making must continue the search for common cultural ground that emphasizes shared foundations rather than focus on differences; we advance forward in the conviction that building bridges from habitual memories of the ancient and present personal pasts augur social harmony.

Extra-biblical evidence cites Cadmus as being in Syria near where the Orontes enters the Mediterranean. The country near Ugarit includes Mons Cassius or Jabal Acra, associated with Cadmus, who retrieved Zeus' sinews in Greek myth. In addition to geography, in religion, there are many parallels with Greek and Ugarit myths, Baal/Zeus, such as "the rider of the clouds," the thunder god source of rain, of fertility. Moreover, Yam/Poseidon correlate

126 BIBLICAL TIME OUT OF MIND

with the sea. Mot/Hades correlate with death/underworld. Preceding the Olympians and Baal with his sister Anat are the older generations like El and in Greece the Titan Gaia and her husband Ouranos, a word still in Modern Greek for "heaven" (the arching back and up castrated father, leaving open from mother earth a gap between him and her, the gap being "chaos" the realm of humans). Is Yahweh a son of El or of Elohim? Is Adam Kadmon of Jewish mysticism an Ouranos of the Titans? The Titan offspring Baal and Cadmus both built temples, like Solomon actualized.[41]

Consider Isaiah 27:1 for *Biblical* as motifemes derived from Ugarit but still resonating also in the Hebrew authors' contemporaries, the Greeks:

> In that day the LORD with his sore and great and strong sword shall punish leviathan the piercing serpent, even leviathan that crooked serpent; and he shall slay the dragon that is in the sea.

Further consider Psalm 104, dated 200 BCE:

> 1 Bless the LORD, O my soul. O LORD my God, thou art very great; thou art clothed with honour and majesty.
> 2 Who coverest thyself with light as with a garment: who stretchest out the heavens like a curtain:
> 3 Who layeth the beams of his chambers in the waters: who maketh the clouds his chariot: who walketh upon the wings of the wind:
> 4 Who maketh his angels spirits; his ministers a flaming fire:
> 5 Who laid the foundations of the earth, that it should not be removed forever.
> 6 Thou coveredst it with the deep as with a garment: the waters stood above the mountains.
> 7 At thy rebuke they fled; at thy voice of thy thunder they hasten away.
> 8 They go up by the mountains; they go down by the valleys unto the place which thou hast founded for them.
> 9 Thou hast set a bound that they may not pass over; that they turn not again to cover the earth.
> 10 He sendeth the springs into the valleys, which run among the hills.
> 11 They give drink to every beast of the field: the wild asses quench their thirst.
> 12 By them shall the fowls of the heaven have their habitation, which sing among the branches.

13 He watereth the hills from his chambers: the earth is satisfied with the fruit of thy works.
14 He causeth the grass to grow for the cattle, and herb for the service of man: that he may bring forth food out of the earth;
15 And wine that maketh glad the heart of man, and oil to make his face to shine, and bread which strengtheneth man's heart.
16 The trees of the LORD are full of sap; the cedars of Lebanon, which he hath planted;
17 Where the birds make their nests: as for the stork, the fir trees are her house.
18 The high hills are a refuge for the wild goats; and the rocks for the conies.
19 He appointed the moon for seasons: the sun knoweth his going down.
20 Thou makest darkness, and it is night: wherein all the beasts of the forest do creep forth.
21 The young lions roar after their prey, and seek their meat from God.
22 The sun ariseth, they gather themselves together, and lay them down in their dens.
23 Man goeth forth unto his work and to his labour until the evening.
24 O LORD, how manifold are thy works! in wisdom hast thou made them all: the earth is full of thy riches.
25 So is this great and wide sea, wherein are things creeping innumerable, both small and great beasts.
26 There go the ships: there is that leviathan, whom thou hast made to play therein.
27 These wait all upon thee; that thou mayest give them their meat in due season.
28 That thou givest them they gather: thou openest thine hand, they are filled with good.
29 Thou hidest thy face, they are troubled: thou takest away their breath, they die, and return to their dust.
30 Thou sendest forth thy spirit, they are created: and thou renewest the face of the earth.
31 The glory of the LORD shall endure forever: the LORD shall rejoice in his works.
32 He looketh on the earth, and it trembleth: he toucheth the hills, and they smoke.

> 33 I will sing unto the LORD as long as I live: I will sing praise to my God while I have my being.
> 34 My meditation of him shall be sweet: I will be glad in the LORD.
> 35 Let the sinners be consumed out of the earth, and let the wicked be no more. Bless thou the LORD, O my soul. Praise ye the LORD'.

The Ugarit "Poem of King Krete" has a principal *Job*-like plot of replacing deceased progeny, of facing death, of regeneration and of new progeny, overcoming but facing a son's challenge. It opens with despair as the King has lost his family, likely to violence. And in dream, god El asks if Krete wants a new kingdom. He, instead, wants progeny, to hell with what he had, gold, chariots, etc, all of it, useless without family to share: he wants a new station, a new place and a new homestead. If King Krete were a Hyksos, what had he before the revolution? Krete is to purge, sacrifice, and advance to a new kingdom, not to hold fast, or regain Avaris? Krete does pursue the dream and gains all, but then he must acquiesce as promised. Shlain writes of how woman finds fulfillment in bearing children; man simulating birth in creating art.[42] This theme appears again and again. God, as creator of Eve, and the Greek god, Hephaestus, creator of Pandora for Prometheus' brother Epimetheus; El Shataqat as a male creating/crafting and a female conceiving are likewise motifs that repeat in parallel across religions and ethnicity. Additionally, Morris delineated a case paralleling the metallurgic deities, Chousor and Kothar wa Hasis and the Greek Hephaestus and the Egyptian Ptah, whose name imprints in Greek orthography as "pt" the name for Egypt, absent in Misr.[43]

Please consider these references as sustained echoes in Exodus 31:

> 1 And the LORD spake unto Moses, saying,
> 2 See, I have called by name Bezaleel the son of Uri, the son of Hur, of the tribe of Judah:
> 3 And I have filled him with the spirit of God, in wisdom, and in understanding, and in knowledge, and in all manner of workmanship,
> 4 To devise cunning works, to work in gold, and in silver, and in brass,
> 5 And in cutting of stones, to set them, and in carving of timber, to work in all manner of workmanship.

Next to last, consider the Hittite legacy discussed previously, this time in the meta-perspective light of common ground. The 2nd millennium BCE correspondences among Kings of Egypt and the Hittites, among the Hittites and likely the Greeks and Amurru, reveal accessibility, cosmopolitanism, and fluid communication that evidence other kinds of socio-political connections. Predating the 1250 BCE invasions of the Sea People, these kingdoms of nations would have possibly retained conceptual memories of fleeing Hyksos, of the previous—of more than a century—or habitually remembered disruptions caused by them as they migrated north into previously untroubled regions.

Sequential correspondence dated between 1500 to 1250, regarding the collaboration of Greeks to arrest troublesome rogues disrupting the inland Hittite hegemony in buffer regions of what is known today as Karia, and Lykia, of Miletus, and Lesbos, just west of modern Turkey all evidence a geopolitical cooperation according to Michael Wood, author of *In Search of the Trojan War* 1998).[44] No mention among the cache of documents identifies Hebrews, but references in the *Bible* cite Hittites. The correspondence record indicate a clear and feared awareness of Greek speaking troublemakers in the region of Kylikia or Cilicia, who could be of multiethnic Hellenic communities like Thebes and Sparta.

Hyksos, Canaanite, and Phoenicia are palimpsests of Semitic warlords, once ruling the arguably most populated, civilized land in the world of the time. These unhoused aristocrats, rich in memories, continued to multiply inclusively with overrun tribes in Hyksos' escape to institutionalize conceptual memories imprinted down to the time of Herodotus. Their case is quite different from Hebrews whose racial exclusivity, excepting the "Book of Ruth", forbid race mixing. Both born in eastern Aegean, Thales (624—546 BCE), the First Philosopher, and Pythagoras (570—495), of theorem fame, had a Phoenician parent, though granted these lived in the region long after the demise of the second millennium giants, which included the Hittites Empire. Hittite kings' letters were found and verified, vetted; one scholar, Fourier, argues evidence that a few of these letters cite prominent heroes of the Trojan.[45] With the Internet, scholarship predictably will further discoveries of this kind of ancient web of communication that may lead to not only understanding but to ethical growth.

Last: consider the evidence from Cretan culture. Cadmus' family and Krete relate directly as well. The union of Zeus and his sister resulted in the offspring on Krete of Minos, Rhadamanthus, and Sarpedon.[46] Researcher Joe Shaw, at Kommos, Krete, identified a Canaanite temple. This dates as

Canaanite / Phoenician Temple. Komos, Krete. Circa 1150 BCE. Located in present day Greece. Excavated by Dr J. Shaw.

early as the Sea Peoples, a continuity down to 1000 BCE. Gage's wide travels have plotted Cadmeon/Hyksos' influence. He has been to the island where Memblarias, a cousin of Cadmus founded a colony, a descendent who left his name there: Thera.[47] The Thera wall frescoes noted earlier are of that same Cretan style also found in Greek Thebes. The frescoes resemble that of Egyptian Avaris. These artifacts indicate a cosmopolitan and regional sharing of tastes, fashions, and erudition that suggest a period of multicultural harmony. And as cited often above, mythic connections proclaim ties with Thera, Sparta, the Argolid, and Boeotia. . . And now it is time to quote some wise and elegant poetry.

As T.S. Elliot wrote in his Four Quartets, "in my end / is my beginning."[48] So it is here, beginning our end with perhaps the most impressive example of heteroglossia of literatures and the soundness of the Torah's Hebrew authors appropriating much old myth and recollection, as if it were recent literal history that for certainty are often much older and often mythical, not archaeologically verified fact.

As fans of ancient literature or poetry know, Gilgamesh was a Sumerian king who lived and reigned in Mesopotamia about 2500 BCE.[49] Gilgamesh sought a kind of immortality by his protagonist's role in this seminal epic, which records the hero's struggle and defeat of the monster Humbaba (sometimes translated as Huwawa). In 1853 the poem finally was translated by George Smith.[50] The poem is on one level a kind of didactic and multi-layered passion play, telling as it does the story of our venerable goddess Ishtar and her attempted seduction of Gilgamesh. Gilgamesh resists her advances, not out of a value of fidelity but instead because the great king is disturbed by Ishtar's poor treatment of her most recent former lover. Discussed earlier, the myth of the Goddess Ishtar, qua-Anat, qua-Inanna, is longitudinal across centuries, as goddess status rightly allows: Ishtar both provides and uses her sex promiscuously to acquire and destroy power, yet all while remaining a virgin in some accounts! The Epic of Gilgamesh, then, is in part an ancient story of human good struggling against the temptation of Ishtar's wiles, but it contains a second layer of moral conflict. The protagonist Gilgamesh conquers the ogre who guards the dark forest, the evil Humbaba, who threatens to "disembowel" Gilgamesh and "feed his entrails to the birds." In what was yet to become classic fashion, Gilgamesh destroys the ogre/monster Humbaba, he of the muscled face and grotesque teeth, just as Gilgamesh triumphs over Ishtar's lust, thus assuring, with the epic, his legend and memorialized.[51] But it is neither one of these two primal layers that fascinates us most about the world's oldest extant written literature of length and of its region's subsequent Greco-Roman culture. Joseph Campbell's "one story" and "mono-myth" resonate loudly here.

On Easter Day in 1984 just outside Ain Devar in the duckbill of Syria, Professor Gage stood on the banks of the Tigris River, looking east toward Nineveh and beyond to Iraq, the Mesopotamia of ancient conquest and influence of Greek and Hebrew culture beyond what is acknowledged. Gage's host pointed out Jabal Judi, a summit in the far distance, saying, "That is the mountain where Noah began sailing—he landed north at Ararat." Nineveh, where the oldest Flood Tablet was found, featured a prototype Noah in an episode in the Gilgamesh epic predating anything in the *Bible*. Prof. Gage's Fulbright predecessor in Aleppo was John Maier, who co-authored "The Gilgamesh" with Gage's teacher, the novelist, John Gardner, having been killed the year before in a motorcycle accident. The seed of an essay was planted that day on the banks of the Tigris River. Two years later Gage was in the British Museum's Western Asiatic Department, holding this very clay and palm-sized Muscle Face, Humbaba. Gilgamesh's antagonist the monster was defeated, the Ur-Other, like so many Others since who have been vilified, the monster of the epic poem who challenged King's Gilgamesh's absolute rule. Depending on point-of-view, any person may substitute this ancient monster tale any contemporary example of their vilified group proves that we humans have not advanced nearly as far as millennia since civilization would suggest: consider cold-war Russians, Cubans, Americans, the British, Irish or

Scotts, the Sandinistas, Baathists, and Sunnis, Palestinians, Jews, Catholics, Muslims, Shintos, Buddhists, Native or First Americans, atheists . . . any group that can be objectified by category and not by its individual citizens' content of character.

A decade and more after Darwin published the *Origin of Species*, George Smith, perhaps at the same desk in the British Museum that Fulbright scholar Gage was assigned, attuned with the pre-Old Testament example of how there is little new under the heteroglossic sun. Reading the ancient cuneiform on clay, nearly the size of the clay Humbaba mask, Smith recognized that embedded in the Gilgamesh epic was much of the Noah and the Ark tale from the *Bible*. Known currently as the "Flood Tablet", the Museum had acquired it following excavation at Nineveh. A millennium older than Smith's text of 6th Century BCE, Gardner and Maier in the early 1980s translated the Sin-Leqi-Unninni's version of Gilgamesh; this version bookends with Smith's later text.

Consider the multitudes of oral and written expressions of this tale layering the conscious memories of those of the Fertile Crescent all these years and how avatars of its protagonists and antagonists grafted upon new tribal memories, with other Flood Story avatars.[52] In nearly all of them, a deity, to purge evil earth, instructs a protagonist to assemble creatures two-by-two aboard a rectilinear barge, "an acre was its whole floor-space; ten dozen cubits the height of each wall; the dozen cubits its deck, square on each side."[53] After the Great Flood, these protagonists all similarly send out birds to signal safe harbor, which ushers in another kind of second coming for all species.

Darwin's thesis, other excavators' findings, and Smith's translations initiated what has been sustained to now with Gage's colleagues' tome not only raise questions about Hebrew authors appropriating much older myths and recollections but in fact confirm them. That epic tales, including this iconic Noah story, would be appropriated by the many anthologizers, semi-literate folks meaning to tell the human didactic story, is a completely understandable series of acts cumulatively fixed in the artifact called *The Bible* and fixed then in time as if these events were true history, not as the metaphors that these stories often are, and not as earlier myth and legend. To pretend away or to ignore the influence of other cultures, predominantly of the east, and the historic and mythic pasts of those influencing cultures on the Hebrew creation of the *Bible* and its instructive place in human history, really as the seminal marker, is to turn a blind eye to Joseph Campbell's "one story" and is to invent what already exists. If we humans are to learn from the mistakes of our historical and literary pasts, we must acknowledge those pasts objectively, admitting all cultural influences and pro-generators, finding that common cultural ground—and sometimes common ancestry—as mentioned repeatedly above.

In writing this book, we scribes have other, related observations, all smaller tributaries of water running toward a big, flooding river of peace that we hope again covers our planet in another sea change. Our arc/ark is one of collectivism on a human and animal-bearing wooden ship of common culture. Our personal experiences have seasoned in the writing and discovery of this project; even habitual memory has aged a little. As we humans get older, experiences both sweet and bitter and everything in between, become more momentous and deliberative. The personal joys become more profound and lasting, the sorrows still cutting deeply, but our ability to move on, to learn from the past grows.

We scribes have learned this savoring of the personal life, all of it, and practice it every day, like yoga, learning how to learn all the more, seizing the chance to become better individual people, inhabiting and savoring a better world for all, breathing in and out. In prolonged meditating on the counter-clockwise flowing Hyksos' river of influence, we've found positive lessons of invention and influence, as well as negative ones of war, hegemony and expulsion, ripple effects frozen and fixed in time in *The Bible* and in Time Out of Mind before it, stilled in it and accelerating beyond it.

We've grown together, we collaborating scribes, and we've learned a personal lesson that the family unit is and has been, throughout the history of history, the most primary force of all. Like our friends the canines, whom we and our spouses and children all love, we are animals in packs, dependent on each other, imprinted on not only leaders but on each other as a collective of individuals with common interests. Mortal life and real time are too short not to emphasize this very human finding, the third eye discovery of our research.

We abridgers of millennia have discovered a new syllogism, a new logic we want to now share.

Our syllogism of hope for peace is this one:

1. Major Premise is that the family unit is most important!
   1a) The accompanying minor premise is that…
   Whether through birth or adoption, everyone comes from a family!
2. The inevitable conclusion is that 2a) Everyone's family tribes are most important!
   2b) Another entailed conclusion is that we humans are all the same in

this valid truth and that we ought never to act otherwise; the belief that we humans are fundamentally different is folly and is dangerous to our survival as a species.

2c) Another conclusion is that all cultures are comprised of large webs of family units, those of farm, village, town, city, empire; hence,

The Major Premise II): All cultures are made of a web of families…
Minor premise IIa) all families are important…
Therefore, III) All cultures are important!

When we realize this finding of truth with validity, we will know as a species that wars borne of Othering and of difference are an archaic waste of thorns that bar entrance to the verdant garden of universal respect and dignity. Wars are born of Othering and of emphasizing difference, the puffing up of xenophobic nationalism against the enemy-other, the monster; hence, the cure for war is collectivism in a common world culture that emphasizes what we share as our human core values: family, farm, village, town, city, with no more need of empire, ever again, for empires kill and always have killed. Empires are borne of dirt, and dirt they shall become.

May this new paradigm of common culture grow out of empires' rotting decay into a fertile potting soil which morphs into a tall and perennial green and yellow sunflower that reaches photo-synthetically, year after year, toward our shared sky so blue that we can reach up and touch it together as if it were an azure, three-dimensional human painting. This is the message of Jeffers' cloud of hands, the message of Joseph Campbell's study of myths, and our best take-away truth. This is the epochal bottom line that matters.

And now we find our end. . . . It will be a better one if our readers come along and talk with us, share ideas for a better way, as in Frost's "A Tuft of Flowers," where "Men work together, I told him from the heart,/whether they work together or apart." James Moffett called this "a plurality of consciousness," and it is a plurality that just might save us, make us better.

(James Moffett, *The Universal Schoolhouse: Spiritual Awakening Through Education.*)

7
Maps & Territory
The Laughter of Our Grandchildren and Why We Must Forge Peace Now

> Such was the natural nobility of this city; so sound and healthy was the spirit of freedom among us, and the instinctual dislike of the barbarian, because we are pure Hellenes, having no admixture of barbarism in us. For we are not like many others, descendants of Pelops or Cadmus or Egyptus or Danaus, who are by nature barbarians, and yet pass as Hellenes, and dwell in the midst of us; but we are pure Hellenes, uncontaminated by any for an element, and therefore the hatred of the foreigner has passed unadulterated in the life-blood of the city.[1]

HANDS SILHOUETTED ON CAVE WALLS SIGNAL signs from time out of mind. They are futile, heroic, human, all at once. From Athabaskan anonymity to the post-modern, we scribes attune to these signs, they, not us, unhinged from time's mortal constraints. Our planet is at the meridian. In time and in space, our relation to the planet has returned to where it was in the 13th Century: before Copernicus de-centered earth, before Darwin branched out evolving species from the great Chain of Being, and before Freud imposed powerful but non-conscious forces that rationalize deep limbic urges. So, now we can return to a kind of positive optimism based on efficacious agency. Yet, humanity is running out of time, unable to outrun it, despite and because of technological progress; natural resources are dwindling, and our toxic garbage is polluting earth, air, and water. Humankind is inescapably, save for petroglyphs and time capsules, centered in space and time, we are midway—10 to the 28th power from the smallest speck of Dark Energy to 10 to the 28th power of the size of the Universe itself. As graphed by time, we are Earth-centered between 14.4 billion years since the Big Bang and 14.4 billion more until the cosmic whimper, although we humans ourselves are a flickering flash of a species whose gnat-like lifespan might be abruptly shortened by a rapacious appetite for over-consumption.[2]

It is high time for us to expunge the temporal notion that humans inherited the earth wholesale, and, for the security of the planet, we need to understand that we have planet earth on loan from our grandchildren. Only a few generations remain for humans to prolong, salvage, what we've all enjoyed historically. We are by nature and should be optimists, rational optimists, who have faith in the catalytic potential of mind and in the potential for love to prevail over all.[3] And love or at minimum respect for differences must prevail.

A Hyksos-like Exodus isn't a valid option for we humans anymore in a shrunken world in time and place, as Venus is too hot and Mars too dry. America's space shuttle program has ended and NASA near moribund. Earth's the right place for love, says sage Robert Frost in his poem "Birches", who hadn't a hint where love might be better. Our birch branches that the two of us have been climbing for these scores of pages began in a shadowy Mediterranean time four millennium ago with an all-but forgotten primal story. The Hyksos/Biblical Canaanite story of rich versions of historical diasporas morphed into myth and chelated racial codes that later become human narratives of ethnic energy, which assured survival potential for some, destruction for others. We suspect it has always been thus, as long as there have been "civilized" *Homo sapiens*: a 6,000-year blink of time's eye in the long run of evolution and cosmic play out since the Big Bang.

Let's focus down upon central stage, its foreground illuminating the setting of Jerusalem, a potential flash point of global significance against the backdrop of aging horrors of the last century's holocaust. Our Klieg lights have investigated history/myths/maps, how myth and fantasy appropriate historical recollection to gird identity and legitimize communal missions, such as the nation state, and how we the audience of Earth ponder outcomes, of how chariots, swords, plowshares and knives may turn into peace building arts. Act One featured episodes entailing King Solomon's Temple, and now purported buried at Temple Mount beneath the storied Muslim Dome of the Rock.

Why is this so important? Archeology may trigger the end of us before our beloved grandchildren are born; the very archeology that we have relied upon as methodology to re-reveal the Hyksos as the historical source of the original Biblical Exodus can be likewise mis-used by nationalists to precipitate global violence. The German National Socialists' use of cultural mythology launched a World War that led to the State of Israel, a cosmic irony. Many acreages all over the world of land are palimpsests awaiting those with myth, archaeologists, and an army to substantiate their identities for treasured texts. For two centuries now, peoples, especially those living for epochs in the home of the three Abrahamic religions, have become suspicious of archeologists purporting to advance science, perhaps functioning as Trojan Horses for imperial interests.

Americans, stemming from a land with little more remembered history than painted aboriginal hands in caves, have trouble understanding why these paranoids could get so upset about treasure-claims until recent shale-oil frackers blew methane into our drinking water that sometimes lights on fire when we turn on our taps.

Please let us explain by heteroglossic overview, by playing "whisper down the lane" in a new way with new rules; with a paradigm that requires that truth's distortion be kept to a minimum. This objective is now never more important, the importance of an undistorted human look back, for, should any now desecrate the Muslim shrine at Temple Mount under pretext of archeology or any other reason, there might not be enough war-heads to impede the fanatical and the simply pious Muslims from responding, lemming-like, to such a shocking potential Armageddon. Tearing down Holy Centers layered upon earlier Holy Centers leads inevitably to human carnage, whether Sikh, Jewish, Muslim, Christian, or any other religion.

For the present Israeli government to finalize its transformation of an inclusive Holy Land into a mutually-exclusive Hebrew Homeland by rationalizing the archeological excavation of the early 8th century CE shrine where, according to the *Qur'an*, Mohamed himself ascended to Heaven is potentially the hot button to prematurely end those six millennia of civilization, if not of human life itself. Thus, that argued for rational optimism and the new rules of "whisper down the lane" must need application. The stakes couldn't be higher. The time for distortion and its intolerance has ended as methane drinking water is not the only thing that might catch fire catastrophically. The human race might, nay, our whole planet might, spin inflamed into deep space that doesn't care much for one temporary sparkler fizzling in the black.

We two have been addressing pre-Christian sources of mythologies that are like nuclear atoms from root to bole to branch to seasonal green leaf, tracking the transmogrifying Hyksos original Exodus and its historic and mythical reach. Gage co-writes with one foot in a time before the H-bomb and the other foot planted where nearly all living beings have both feet in a time of awaiting a possible apocalypse apprehensively. Freeman, a nanosecond younger, is a team-mate with both feet on apprehensive, shaky ground. A significant percentage of Gage's cohort in Europe never lived to see their tenth birthday, tragically, because they were Jewish, and because of the folly of race distinction. The slightly younger of us, Freeman, whose name, like Gage's, means something stemming back from the Middle-Ages, both denotatively and connotatively, is a former resident of the far-East in the 1960's and currently the West; he has visited the sites of Hiroshima and Nagasaki where the bomb ended an era. Freeman now occasionally drives his Irish daughter's well-made Mazda 3, manufactured in that very Phoenix-like Hiroshima of the 21st century. Both Freeman and Gage seek to have their grandchildren prosper and endure, just as all humans should wish; hence, we of the audience are compelled to be more strident at mid-Act III, having witnessed the converging episodes that have revealed dramatis personae of the egomaniacal facing the simply mad fundamentalists, acting despite whimpering pleas of an arrogant and uninformed superpower, with a fawning and impotent United Nations.

The title of a recent talk at Freeman's community college says it all, "May This Never Happen Again."[4] Settled among the furnishings of the Fireside Lounge, Bucks County Community College, organizers of the "Bux/Mont Coalition for Peace Action" with "Hibakusha Stories" Groups, featured Clifton Truman Daniel, Harry Truman's grandson; Setsuko Thurlow, a Hiroshima factory worker; and Yasuaki Yamashita, a Nagasaki survivor. The evening exhorted a compelling argument in-itself for the necessary new paradigm, the truthful look back and forward, so that our grandchildren might have grandchildren too. During this chilling look back at where we have been, or have been forced to be by misunderstood events and from lessons unlearned, we are spurred from a hard look at the legacy of Othering, at the hard facts on both west and east "sides of the ball" that escalated to the sad expediency of saving military lives by taking civilian ones, spurred by the democratically-dangerous greatest-good-for-the-greatest-number utilitarian philosophy. Setsuko spoke of her school-age co-workers wandering blindly in the fallout and white mushrooming heat at Hiroshima, holding their melted eyeballs in their charred hands, crying out like ghost chimera early-warning sirens, in unutterable pain and anguish, instantly on the way to dying, all in a molecularly disastrous moment.

Yasuaki Yamashita, he then of Nagasaki, told witness of his family and neighbors instantly vaporizing while he was both lucky and unlucky enough to be at work, a few kilometers from the hellish epi-center, where formerly human shadow paintings were left by the Enola Gay's sister, not much unlike the blast-frozen chimera shadows of the residents of Pompeii, telling of radiation hospitals still half-full of patients now, over sixty years later. It was more than Vesuvius erupting that led Yasuaki to live an ex-patriot in Mexico since the late 1940's, only returning once to relive the unthinkable.

Euphemisms like the very names of the two A-bombs', Little Boy and Fat

Man, underscore the importance of playing the game in the new way. Within two months after that August 6 fateful Hiroshima message from "Little Boy," one hundred thousand souls had died, most of them civilians, likely far more, as hospital record keeping was skimpy to non-existent, notes forbidden. At Nagasaki, three days later, "Fat Boy" taught seventy-five thousand that the end can come in a moment.[5] Say the boys' names now in Hiroshima or Nagasaki, and one might get an inkling of the Muslim rage that further Israeli excavation at Temple Mount might engender. We humans simply *have to learn, to be acutely aware of and to honor other cultures, if we are to persist*. For example, had we learned from the brutalities of the Christian Crusaders, would the Japanese, primarily Shinto's and Buddhists, have attacked Pearl Harbor by surprise in the way that the Crusaders often came in darkness and by dawn? Would the Allies have killed 225,000 via two unkind "boys" in order to send a lethal message that might have been much more humanely sent by dropping Little Boy right in Fuji-San's iconic crater, destroying far fewer lives but making the same forceful, world-altering point?[6]

Myth, narrative and ritual can sometimes augur suicidal results, by giving rise, if distorted, to xenophobia or to worse. Should we never forget, lest we repeat the aggressive mistakes of the historical past? Should we acknowledge crimes, learning from both our failures and our successes, and then get on with our Candidian gardening? After all, there are parents and children to be fed. This is the question Joseph O'Neill addresses in *The Blood-Dark Tract*, a study of his two grandfathers imprisoned in mid-20th Century as terrorists, asking: "At what point [are] we released from participation in the injustices of the past?"[7]

We had better study solutions. We are interested in displays of manual-mode override ethical thinking. We scribes feel that this kind of innovation is ever more necessary now, in the post-nuclear age.

In order to return to the Temple Mount context, we need to air another story that the Western world has mostly silenced, taken off its palate, cleansed, numbed tongued and bleached out of its paintings…This story can begin around World War II when the zeitgeist celebrated a heritage then designated as Greco Roman, in a genre Bernal referred to as the "Arian Model of History." The unparalleled horrors of Auschwitz transmogrified this heritage with a zeitgeist model subsequently referred to as the Christian Classical past, a heritage subsequently becoming the dominant curriculum of both schooling and state. The reality of the Sixth Day War in 1967 further versioned a Judeo-Christian appellation. To attune to another narrative in order to better understand, it would be wise to consider to Richard Bulliet's title, *A Case for an Islamic-Christian Civilization*, for, if we don't pay apt attention to this narrative, we will likely fail to understand why the Temple Mount as example and metaphor are so crucial to our species' survival: "The past and future of the *West cannot be fully comprehended without appreciation of the twinned relationship it has had with Islam* over some fourteen centuries. The same is true of the Islamic world."[8]

As historians, we acquire methodology in order to analyze texts, archeological finds, and philology, and then analyze with startling advances in genome research with new and frankly explosive data now emerging from DNA studies. Reviewing the rigor, the scientizing about language and race investigations since the 19th Century and since J. G. Fickte's notion that land, language, and territory are commensurate concepts, we must acknowledge after two World Wars and the unnatural demise of millions that what we are addressing here, our failure to learn from past heteroglossic justifications for Empire has been a ruinous and lethal zeitgeist heritage for we humans. Humankind has learned from science that pure racial identity is nonsense, or we should have learned so by now.

Use of language and names for demarcating borders is a ruinous and recent European construct.[9] Stories of unique human origins are most often fraudulent whimsy.[10] Some stories can and do get innocent people killed. Stories of homeland, of nationhood, of language, do galvanize us to action, but can our grandchildren endure our demand for identity distinctions beyond the folkloric? Smolo Sand's recent book puts the very Israeli homeland, and phrases like "the land of the Jews," squarely under the microscope.

"Every marginal *mythos* or trivial legend from which it is possible to exploit an ounce of legitimacy for territorial rights and demarcation becomes an *ideological weapon* and then an important building block in the construction of national memory."[11] Since the Six Day War, when President Johnson requested the victors to *identify borders*, all Israeli leaders have echoed Prime Minister Levi Eshcol's response "not at the moment," to do so or not do so only for the time being to preserve the option of future hegemony. The *Eretz* Israeli or the Greater Land of Israel could extend from the Nile to the Euphrates. When Americans wake up to how the Israeli Lobby and Christian Lobbyists with Neoconservative mendacity continue to lead the US into war, Israel may be perceived as threatening the Jewish people and the Jewish State itself.[12] The story of the ashes of Moses' red heifer exemplify both the absurdity and the threat. The heifer's purity is supposedly proven via its limited confines of having lived under Moses' care.[13] Accordingly, these ashes still exist beneath as sanctification, allowing observant Jews to plan to search for these many hundreds of year old ashes. In 1952, after the Qumran scrolls were discovered in a Jordanian cave, some searchers found hints that the ashes still exist in the ruins of Solomon's Temple in Jerusalem upon which stands the Al-Aqsa Mosque. This treasure hunt seems to legitimize excavating the Moslem sacred shrine much like Schliemann's voiding trough.[14] Should this logic prevail and lunatic or state sanctioned archeologists decide to dig up the mosque, Muslims from Detroit to Jakarta to Mogadishu, to Rabat to Parisian *banlieues* will magnetize in anger to the Holy Land of Canaan and perhaps light that last human sparkler flame. We humans need to find a better way.

Likewise seeking both truth and peace, Sand documents how the phrase the Land of Canaan became the Land of Israel after the destruction of the Temple and then later when modernized in the 19th Century by German Jewish intellectuals to match anti-Semitic Germanophils' questionable scientizing that wed together race, language, and territory.[15] He further analyzes today's political alliance of Zionist and Christian fundamentalists to validate colonialism in the Middle East, which augurs the very destruction of the Jewish state, for ". . . homelands did not produce nationalism but rather homelands emerged from nationalism."[16] Neoconservatives' very definition of advocating the aggressive promotion of "democracy" and promotion of "American national interest" in international affairs via means of military force vastly heightens the likelihood that military aggression will in fact be used to advance territorial and nationalistic agendas. Our languages, the stories we tell in them, do more than reveal us; they make us who we are and will be as well. We thus must choose our languages and our stories.

Hebrew and Irish are recently recreated languages, though the latter didn't take hold because Aran Islanders found absurd academic surveyors. Can our densely populated earth anymore afford the traditional concepts of sovereignty and nationhood, as they have often proven deadly over the millennia? We are more than implying that there may come a time, and soon, when the human race may need a common culture of *civilization*, of equal parts appreciation and empathy, as the binder gluing us *together in common* rather than distinct and prideful cultures, more than humanity prizes both our oft-dangerous race or religious distinctions and our independent nation-building. The term "commons" is no longer the park in Harrogate, England, of Lockean reference, but it *is* a commons, as in common civilization.[17] This commons of drinkable water, fresh air, and graze-able turf for cows and sheep is neither Western nor Eastern, but rather is global and is a commons that includes quinoa, kiwi, and sumac too. It is a modernity of signifiers: heads bowed down from Aleppo to Eureka to New and Freetown, no longer over worry beads or prayer books but huddled over iPhones. On the other hand, there is culture, passion driven in quest of identity formation, which disrupts civilization. Youths igniting themselves in terrorist proclamation against injustice destroys any potential of common ground. Rather youths finding a shared vision not of Otherness but of sameness promises conversing across the shared world with cohorts. Cultural identity of exclusion provides an excuse circumscribed in a banana leaf called reason to plow under familial homes and the venerable olive groves of descendants on ancient lands for eons of ongoing destruction. Civilization and Culture, according to Terry Eagleton, are in opposition, like Nietzsche's concepts of Apollonian and Dionysian, potentials that can open to negotiating, that warrant distinguishing for analytical understanding.[18]

One impassioned youth of culture was Bobby Sands who found common ground beyond his martyrdom. The IRA hunger striker protesting against the British overlong occupation of Northern Ireland, famously and lastly said, before he died: "The best revenge is the laughter of your grandchildren." Bobby Sands' grandchildren have since laughed. Too many of us of civilization have caved into the good life of consumerism and entertainment, desiccated of any passion, and ought instead to draw from Sands' paradoxical wisdom to acknowledge that all of us have earth on loan from our grandchildren.[19]

But in this post-nuclear age, a time of dangerous heritages colliding in potentially higher-stakes hegemony, will Sands' grandchildren inherit an earth where they too can have grandchildren, those who look for common ground and no longer look to persecute the other as different? For this optimistic human scenario to come to pass, lessons of the past and present *must* be attended to in order to find the uniting and common grounds so often alluded to previously. In a surprising way, we, one of us a Unitarian, one an agnostic who now more than ever believes in peace, are together exposing not a vengeful God likely derived from 2nd Millennium Hyksos but, rather, the New Testament teachings of Jesus, who was foremost a peacemaker among men, especially in His common-ground sermons of peace like "The Sermon on the Mount." Where we have trouble philosophically is with fundamentalist misapplications of sound religious texts and principles distorted to divide by identity and to divide from other religions, equally valid, ethical and civilization traditions. The Neoconservative trend, starting in the 1960's and waxing and waning in the fifty years since, is accepting of the heteroglossic distortion of identity tales if those narratives match zealous notions of spreading unique nationalism and democracy, expanding borders, a nationalistic mitosis.

That there have been three seminal cultural paradigms of modern western life—the Greeks, Romans, and Arabs—is in no way ignoring the contributions of China, or India, or Africa, or the indigenous First Nation peoples of America, Australian, or Polynesia. But given the Temple Mount potential for Earth Death, or Armageddon, the loci of needed attention is on how Hellenized Rome, Al Andalusian Europe, and the Modern state of Israel have shaped humankind's gravest political challenge. Under the Islamic principle of dhimmi, the rule of Ottomans (1453—1914) , the Safavid (1501—1736), and the Moguls (1526—1707) dynasties administered successfully and in relative peace their empires and what was then thriving international commerce before the British ruled the Empire where the sun never set on its dominion.[20]

The United Kingdom of Queen Victoria to Winston Churchill led the state with the largest Muslim populations for a century; but the US lacks such experience and wisdom when it comes to how best to govern globally, inclusively of Muslim cultures. Readers might know about China and Africa and India, yet may know so little about the Islamic world, one of the three afore-mentioned genuinely great heritages. For the most part, this heritage celebrated dhimma, allowing other religions to thrive and perpetuate culture through education in their languages, though virulent Islamists are stunningly ignorant of both history and their own religion. That notorious void, theirs as well as ours, sometimes deliberate but more often benign ignorance, may prove as dangerous as Al-Qaida has and the minuscule fraction of Islamists who are now already sufficiently motivated to become terrorists. Knowing the Other, its potential for malice and its achievements worthy of respect and veneration is a requisite of ethical Empire. Is the US ready to fill this role? Or will we succumb to an ostrich-like isolationism until a China attempts to fulfill it in their own way?

Let's review the fact that within a decade of Mohammed's death in 632 CE, his successors struck in silver and gold the first universal currency, for Byzantium and Persia had mutually exclusive currencies. Then Islam reached within nine-tenth of the miles to the English Channel, and Shakespeare still used the gold Moroccan coin.[21] The Muslim inclusive currency extended from 711 CE on the Atlantic and soon spread to the Pacific. Terms from the Muslim heritage have since peppered the diction of English, and every European language, only slightly less dusted than Latin, and for that matter than Greek. But a good amount of that Greek entered the West from Semites after Rome by way of Gibraltar—that is long, long before there was a Rome when Cadmus' sister Europa arrived in Krete on her white bull.

These facts and stories are not in the common curriculum of the schools nor even common knowledge, yet we live in a Modernity considerably shaped by Muslims. How many schooled in Europe and America know that some of our glorious First Crusaders indulged in the specter of cannibalism?[22] That perhaps the greatest blood-letting was against fellow Christians of Southern France, the Cathars of the Albigensian Crusade?[23] The Christian Crusaders themselves reported their canbnibalism to the Pope but it was downplayed: the East has always known of it. Not knowing what nearly every Arab knows conceptually isn't helpful in peace-building through common ground and culture. Do we recognize the Arabic commonality in the state name of California? Have we tallied the spices of these Muslim word names that categorized into patterns of those very linguistic codes that denote, embody, and connote the good and satisfying life of material comforts of civilization, which can be shared by any here on earth? Historians of the Food TV circuit have distinguished the history of European cuisine as pre-and post-Arab Europe: during the latter, class differences were evidenced in the variety of what wealthy dined upon and how it was prepared, while in pre-Arab Europe all classes ate the same way; the rich only ate more quantity than the poor.

Our place and food names say much about where we have been, where our cultures come from, and how much we have in common… To know of these facts, to understand commonality, is to be civilized and not sequestered relatively alone in some distinct culture. Understanding human common ground is a value for realizing an ideal, a quest for peace-building. To know this is to realize that there is Muslim Radicalism, Islamism, and that there is Islamic Civilization, the Muslim religion of many cultures, just as there is Christian radicalism and Christian religion but also many Christian cultures. To be ignorant of this huge distinction is to dangerously misunderstand our world. Such stupidity matches the fallacious and divisive tradition of Osama bin Laden. This cancer heightens rage to make indistinguishable the illogic of "Most terrorists are Muslims" and "Most Muslims are terrorists." English diction differentiates saffron, sesame, asparagus and artichoke, but our language, though of late more global, still lacks a distinguishing term that denotes mouth-burning hot from spicy. Our world languages need to interfuse, which has been occurring through amalgamating, the process of which is already speeding up due to a technologically-shrinking planet; this is but one common culture index that gives us wordmongers rational optimistic hope for the future.

So, for the politicians of the world, we direct attention to a central stage, Temple Mount. Why is it so crucial to Islam? It is located in Jerusalem, the Holy city of the Jews as well as to Christians, the site of Jesus' crucifixion, so why do Muslims likewise claim it as their Holy Shrine? According to the author of *The Ornament of the World: How Muslims, Jews, and Christians Created a Culture of Tolerance in Medieval Spain*, Europe in 1187 first learned of the importance of Temple Mount to Muslims when an Englishman translated and made available *Mohamed's Ladder*, a narrative as sacred to Islam as *Golgotha* is to Christians.[24] In Sura 17, a line in the *Qur'an* speaks of Mohammed's "Night Journey of the Prophet and Archangel Gabriel." Only a phrase refers to a dream or a-temporal journey from Mecca to Jerusalem, rather than an historical and real sojourn. Subsequently, in the *Hadith,* further narratives pattern three cycles: 1. the journey, or *esra*; 2. the ladder, or *miraj*; and 3. a combination of the *esra* and *miraj*. Europeans learned of Mohamed's journey, including Dante, Goethe, and America's earliest writer of note, Washington Irving, who wrote a two volume *Life of Mohammed*. These three cycles gave rise to a genre of Muslim secular literature.[25]

The blind poet Abul ala al-Ma'arri (d. 1058 CE), then Ibn Arabi (d. 1240) fleshed out versions of this quest with analogous characters, the pilgrim and symbolic *doppelganger*, philosopher and theologian, anticipating Dante and Vergil, (or Sal Paradise and Dean Moriarty in Kerouac's *On the Road*). Early in Spain and in southern France, several translations were initiated by Peter the Venerable in the mid-1100s and later by Alphonse X in the 1260s. The Castilian King employed Florentines like Dante's teacher Brunetto Latini, who likely influenced the *Commedia*. Its source is of the Prophet traveling with Gabriel from Mecca to Jerusalem, where the two arrived on Temple Mount and ascend to explore hell, purgatory, and heaven, where Mohammed met God. Reciprocally, the Muslim episode returned to Europe as Roman Catholic dogma. Purgatory, embraced until lately by Roman Catholicism, would be thoroughly rejected by Protestants in the time of Luther.

The narrative of Mohammed's Journey and the Hebrew Exodus share similar sacred episodes for believers and warrant open-minded interpretation rather than literalism while respected by all for harmonious and inclusive multiculturalism, especially among those living in Jerusalem. Yet, review of demographics reveal a half century of expunging of Arab Christians and other orthodoxies while settlements are built over land owned for epochs. The total population of Christians may appear constant as the number expelled has been filled with Western fundamentalist Christians colonizing Holy sites. In the 1950's, Jerusalem had a sizable minority of Christian Arabs. Today, with a total population of more than a million and a half, less than 1% Arab Christians live in the city.[26] Christians from the US have been arriving, while its indigenous Arab co-religionists have been driven out of this city of three religions.[27] The US hears virtually nothing about expunging Christians from the Holy City, but one can view elsewhere on TV the irony of fundamentalist Christians lauding and contributing to Israelis building settlements over Arab land.

Identities change with changing landscapes, via exodus and its corollary immigration, and they can change with changing mental landscapes too. The Syrian who moved to Oakland is no longer the person he or she was in Aleppo; for you cannot go home again, as Thomas Wolfe knew. The river you step into changes with each step, but Greek sage Heraclitus implied that you yourself also change with each step too. Save for some in the brain, our cells change completely on a seven year cycle. So, what is a homeland that is ironically comprised of cellularly-changing individuals; what defines homelands and their seminal roles in human behavior and, in particular, what defines homelands' roles in chronic war-waging, the worst of us, that blood-red road map of human history we seek here to erase?

Let's recall the fact that eighty percent of the worlds' current refugees are Muslims, because of war, origins, and desertification. These Muslims so closely resemble those Jews fleeing ancient homes in Judea in 67 CE and again more recently those whom the Allied Armies liberated to found their very fragile state in 1948. Why do so many Muslims care so much about Temple Mount as a contested homeland? Why the intense and contested territorial claims of patria or homeland?

The Latin for education is *educur*, to bring forth from within. We need, collectively, to educate ourselves about the way forward. If religion and language bring us together, rather than dividing us, then the great religions and languages of the world may advance us through common ground and bonds. New research into why we believe what we believe with religiosity may well educate us as to what must be done to move forward, to deter potential annihilation, to, instead, prosper. This rational, Herodotus-like inquiry is already extending to the study of the evolutionary basis of religion. Archaeology, social science, natural science must all be vigorously employed in order to understand our hardwired instinct for religious behavior as an "evolved" and evolving "part of human nature."[28] There must be a deliberative peace-making. This rational discussion needs to be purposeful in discovering, as did Campbell, Herodotus and Saint Thomas Aquinas, the real connections between evolution, psychology, genetics and anthropology to reach an essential "turning point, and advancement, in the science-religion debate."[29] This synergistic investigation about what is true (our common goals of peace, harmony and an end to the horror of war, Hiroshima ending the ancient war paradigm with a mega-blast) and what is both true and false. Realizing Bahktin's hetroglossia of texts where truth becomes religious falsity sometimes morphing back to truth, or staying persistent, with a new cultural spin as new truth, is all the more necessary if we are to persist and advance as a race. Survival is also a necessary pre-requisite to advancement. Without peace and working together toward peace, we are lost, as in the human-less planet of the Bill Hotchkiss poem where, "these mountains do not cry for tragedy/ do not cry for peace/ will applaud with claps of thunder/ when the human race/ is gone."[30]

We do not seek to be dilettantes, nor even scientists or philosophers grappling with the deepest problems of both disciplines in order to determine right from wrong behavior. We have been arguing, hopefully with some success, using an amalgam of neuroscience and literary criticism to re-examine, that we humans need a synthesis of action in how to solve the classic high-stakes problem of how to get disparate individual nations, religions and ethnicities to start cooperating for the survival of both our common race and of our planet.

Groups and different heteroglossic ethnic and literary traditions with deep-seated but different morals and values need to coalesce around a common civilization emerging from nations and fading nationhood because of a common historical fact: the seeds of our three religions all stem from a several hundred mile square common region that encompasses as epicenter Jerusalem, Temple Mount in specific, and radially out to Egypt, Greece, Syria, Turkey, present day Iraq, and ancient Mesopotamia, or the fertile Crescent of religious birth. Rather than concentrating on the different, on competing branches of the common human roots, let us ascend the tree up to reach for the sky of sunlight, for generative photosynthesis, so that we humans and our earth may grow and prosper and not poison the common vine with war, pollution, with wanton disregard for our brothers, sisters, all living species and the planet which sustains us all. *Biblical* and *Quranic* literatures about where we have been and where we should be headed, our moral compass, might provide a common "moral currency" that ought to serve as a firm basis for cooperation between rivals, Arab, Israeli, Christian or any faction, if we attend deeply to all of that common Yahweh, Mohammed and Jesus' teaching ground. "If our planet is to have a peaceful and prosperous future such a common moral currency is urgently needed."[31]

The Greek word *ekphrasis* derives from *ek* and *phrasis* and translates roughly as *out* and *speak*, signifying, two very human traits: to get the story out or, alternatively, to draw their seminal and picaresque stories out from others, to speak the important genesis stories that must be spoken in order not to exclude but to find common ground that we might work together to live on. Originally, "the word (*ekphrasis*) simply meant a description of something, but in the twentieth century it has come to mean more narrowly a dramatic description of a work of art."[32] We speak out here one last time about the way out of intra-species discord and war toward peace-making. Acts of violence with artifacts of war are our human legacy, while stunning in their ancient proofs of how *little* we humans have advanced beyond competing claims of nations toward civilization. Much of philosophy is that very search for the common moral currency that will bring the race together, rational optimism saving us if we can attend. That common ethical currency, like the 7th Century Arabic universal currency, spices and place names, in whatever Western-Eastern fusion it may take, is vital. The very planet's present symbiosis is likewise at stake.

The neuroscientist-moral philosopher Joshua Greene has, in his *Moral Tribes* and other landmark books, demonstrated that our biological brains drive social instincts that turn "Me into Us" as beneficial to Darwin's natural selection and to preservation of deep gene-pools. Greene, however, has likewise acknowledged that we are hard-wired to also turn that beneficial "Us" against "Them." Perhaps his even more important finding is that we "can do something about it."[33] Joshua Greene uses the effective extended metaphor of a dual-mode camera for our brains and our moral behavior. The brain's limbic "point-and-shoot" automatic settings allow us the biologic functions necessary to life that extend all the way up to camera taxa to life-efficient emotions, instincts and drives.

These, set by evolution, are automatic programs, modified by inherited culture and personal experience sustained in memories, but programs undergirded from days of hunter gatherings, of fight and flight, of warring over resources and territory, and, at their highest reach, lead "Me" to "Us" for our collective survival.[34] Ultimately, there is what the neuroscientist/prophet deems a "manual override mode," which can be the best of us, and what we in our scribal book have been vigorously espousing: the rational pre-programmed and conceptual override of the mental and camera manual mode. Here it is both necessary and marvelous that we might surpass evolution/social animal reactions of "Me" to "Us" and then beyond our tribal "Us against Them" to an "all" of all living creatures at the banquet table sharing communal supper together. "Our tribal emotions make us fight—sometimes with bombs, sometimes with words, often with life-and-death stakes."[35] So, for Greene and for us, our brain's marvelous manual operation mode lets us

MAPS & TERRITORY 149

innovate with a growing capacity for deliberative *reasoning*, making us Uber-thinking nimble, more able to solve problems like our ancient warring nature dragged into present time beyond its (if it ever had such) functional value.

Greene, and utilitarians Jeremy Bentham and John Stuart Mill before him, found that the greatest-good-for-the-greatest-number to be special, despite the tyranny of the majority historical flaw previously discussed. While Greene is aware of this flaw and the sometimes over-simplistic way that this rational philosophy is applied, he also asserts utilitarianism as a shining example on the hill of manual-mode brain achievement and the two "universally accessible moral values that reason has discovered: happiness and impartiality."[36] Greene also finds that utilitarianism-collectivism to be the very kind of "meta-morality" that our manual camera brain is capable of *discovering*, a way out of the blood-thirsty mess of human history. It is our best human work, but only so far in 6,000 years of civilization, and we can likely do better still, that rational optimism leading us forward. Please consider how this supposedly "quaint relic of the nineteenth century," utilitarianism, might apply in the following too real refugee scenario, also explored previously in reference to the Arab refugees' plight.

> As you read this, there are millions of people who desperately need food, water, and medicine. Many more lack access to education, protection from persecution, political representation, and other important things that affluent people take for granted. For example, as I write, Oxfam America, a highly regarded international aid organization, is providing clean water, food, sanitation, and other forms of economic support to more than 300,000 civilians caught in the conflict in the Darfur region of Sudan. A small donation to Oxfam America-less than $100-can make a big difference to one of these people. You often hear that you can save Someone's life for 'just a few dollars....' (the actual) cost of saving a life is about $2,500, according to GiveWell, taking into account all true costs and all of the un-Certainties. That's not a few dollars, but it is well within reach of middle-class people And, over time, even some poor people.[37]

While Greene uses this save-a-life example, of course, in hopes of motivating altruism and actually saving lives through collectivist giving to good organizations like Oxfam, he also uses the example to demonstrate utilitarianism as an achievement of rational optimism and the manual mode override of our instincts and limbic past. Another instance of Greene's advancing of civilization via breakthrough "manual-mode" thinking is the blurring and eventual erasing of borderlines that divide.

Maps in the minds of habitual memories linger for the politicians to bring to consciousness. The abstraction named "Syria" may dwell to legitimize expansion; from the BCE period, minds could reach east to the Tigris, south to Sinai and north even to the Magnesia River in Western Anatolia, where Punic Hannibal finally retreated from the Romans: he, in Bursa; Syria the other side of that river. Hafes Al Asad's imagination, whose son now rules, included much of the ancient boundary. The post-World War I map is coming apart under his son, Bashar.

Ethnicities grounded in culture and language are violently asserting their identities and maps upon a bloody territory. Kurds, Druze, Armenian, Yazidis, and the remaining dozen groups are engendering homelands of imagined or historically legitimized boundaries. The superpowers accommodate as today's allies, some with support and some cynically to impose national boundaries as accidents awaiting. Within these new faux states, superpowers in time divide to recolonize to exploit with commercialism. Think how the former USSR cookie-cut out Kyrgyzstan, to include opposing factions of Kyrgyzs and Uzbeks, awaiting the clashes in 2010. Superpowers exploit by triggering local hostilities among neighbors, forcing supplication to compete for pittances in order to suppress the Other, who was yesterday their neighbor. Nationalisms imagined out of faux history and based on race and language with imagined borders are the sociological nuclear waste dumps ready to pollute earth's aquifers everywhere. But the greatest flash point is clearly the land long ago receiving the ancient Hyksos exodus.

Our discourse of *Biblical Time Out of Mind* draws much from genre theory and myth theory, especially after Alan Dundes and later Rachel Havrelock: the former's methodology differentiates story and myth as sacred narrative, and the latter, in debt to the late Berkeley anthropologist who linked myth to mapping and foundations. A premise of Myth Theory is that there is no Ur-myth, but instead variations of heteroglossia crafted and accreted by the context of each subsequent author's sociology of knowledge: Dictys, Sanchuiathon, Manetho, Josephus, and other authors of Biblical texts. Out of the darkness of past folklore ripens Medea, on the one hand recalled malignantly by Euripides, who plots the mother achieving revenge for her husband's adultery by causing the deaths of her own offspring. From another, Medea reappears in the telling as the nurturer of mad Heracles guiding the hero to health; and again, in another version, Medea causes, yes causes, her children's death in an ill-advised attempt to make them immortal.[38] So, context gives form to utterance in subject, substance, and genre, depending upon the age, from where it comes, and from the language bearing it. In the feminism-aware 21st Century US, novelist Anita Diamamt published *The Red Tent*, featuring Dinah of Gen. 34 whose story is congruent of what we describe below as the Ezra/Nehemian map of the Hebrew Promised Land. Or, consider the 1978 film directed by Jules Dassin, *A Dream of Passion*, in which the protagonist, an actress preparing for the Medea role, finds direction from an imprisoned woman, found guilty of infanticide.[39]

Havrelock in *River Jordan: the Mythology of a Dividing Line*, enumerates *Biblical* foundation stories that explicitly or implicitly bound territory identified as the Land of the Hebrews, four of which bear on our thesis pertaining to myths and maps.[40] In all is the River Jordan, which to this day functions as boundary separating peoples. As with myth, none of these is the Ur-map, but cumulatively they afford sufficient ambiguity from which politicians in differing social contexts can fashion the Land of Israel.

Since each maps derives cartologically from sacred narratives, the following designate the Land of the Jews over history: 1. the Priestly map, composed by hereditary priests; 2, the Deuteronomic, the map authored during Assyrian troubles; 3. the Ezra (7:12) and Nehemiah, the map of a restored Israel; and 4. the Book of Ruth, a map entailing the populations that compose the nation.[41] Though at first appearing Pollyannaish, Havrelock's conclusion after a fine scholarly foray warrants the apt attention of all parties as they too, with us, have the Earth on loan from our grandchildren. If the contestants can restrain from the literalness of myth-derived boundaries and consider first both ecology and demographics, there may be peace in the Holy Land after all, as is our fervent hope.

The first pair of texts, the Priestly and Deuteronomic, explicitly identify borders but differ concerning the eastern-most boundary. The former cites the Jordan River; the Deuteronomic, the Euphrates. Havrelock avoids the question of historical dating of texts, but this is essential to our argument. The Deuteronomist texts were written around 620 BCE after the fall of the northern state and on the verge of the death of Josiah and conquest of Jerusalem, long after Homer on the Aegean composed the *Iliad*.[42] The social context and literary purpose is evident. Under the pressure of an impending Assyrian conquest, the people of Judea developed text that set legal precedents for future Jewish governance. This example supports the Hegelian analysis at the heart of Thompson's Harvard dissertation: one force engages an antagonist. The result is a synthesis wherein both victor and defeated adopt the ways of the other.[43]

One hundred and fifty years later, the Priestly tradition derived mostly from the destruction of Jerusalem to the return under Nehemiah in the time of Herodotus in Greece. Scholars judge that these authors were like the Founding Fathers of the US. After more than a decade of chaos under the Articles of Confederation, all but three of the signers of the Declaration of Independence sequestered in Harrisburg to draft a plan for the future. Likewise, after decades from return, the Priestly scribes drafted the plan that accounts for much of the Pentateuch, an anthology of myth and veiled historical happenings to establish Jerusalem as the cult center of the Jewish peoples.[44]

The creation story is about boundaries, of light and darkness, of human and animal, morning and night and so on that girds readers for dividing up the land into an Us and Them. Genesis 5: 1-32 narrates the heritage of the Jews in a manner not unlike Mesopotamian creation myths, though denoting humans as separate from gods, like Marduk. Much of the Priestly texts include Egypt and its occupation of the Land of Canaan. Central to our thesis, texts posit Moses as east of the Jordan, denied access in the West Bank, to further complicate the ambiguities of the several maps. As the Lord's fulfilled promise for their victimization, Hebrews borrowed the view of Canaan from the Nile: Genesis 28:10-22, 32; Joshua. 1-4; Judges12/1-6; 2 Samuel 17:22, 19:16-41; Kings 2:2. ; Numbers 34:2. and much of Ezekiel, especially 28.[45]

In contrast, Deuteronomic texts emerged around the time when Nabopolassar of Babylon (658 - 605) extinguished the Assyrians by taking Nineveh in 615 BCE. Composed largely in the milieu of the Prophets Nahum and Jeremiah during the rule of Josiah, Deuteronomy includes citations in Joshua, and passages from both Samuels and from Kings, which are expansionist in citing the Euphrates as the eastern border (Deuteronomy 11:24; Joshua 1:4).[46] Both the Priestly and Deuteronomic traditions convey explicitly for Jews, Christians, and Muslims an analogical determinism hard to question in the closed minds of the irrational fundamentalists of any religion. Those mesmerized by advocates of the Red Heifer, or the lemming-like suasion of the Rev. Jim Jones, or followers of ISIL can and have led to horrors, horrors that might have been and may be prevented by a prescription of critical thinking.

The other pair of sources of *Biblical* texts that generate maps derives from Havrelock's gendered analysis. From "Ezra" and "Ruth," the makeup of intra-Israel implicitly map how to deal with the Other within—by exclusion or inclusion? These map Jewish nations resulting from how to address the populations within, exclusive in regards to emigration for fear of previous race mixing or as inclusive, as a bound land embracing all settlers and immigrants.

The latter is very like the dilemma President Obama faces with the Dreamers, who have thrived for some time in the US. A bounded state comprised of both Jew and non-Jew is similar to the situation in occupied Palestine today, a concern of both those uprooted by the newcomers and by those recently returning to Jerusalem to assume governance after World War II, who conceptually remember the narratives of Nehemiah and Ezra, when the exiled return to restore. On the other hand, the novella, "The Story of Ruth," like the Joseph story, for its setting is idealized in the remote past that lead to the birth of the iconic King David.

Shifting from maps to myth/historical contexts, these generative texts reveal a major premise of our thesis. Featuring the grandmother of King David, "The Story of Ruth" was composed pre-exile, near contemporary with Homer (8th Century BCE); while Ezra lived and benefited from the Persian King Artaxerxes I (465—424 BCE). The social context and literary purpose is evident. For "Ruth," a novella, it reveals the peaceful days before the Assyrian conquest when Hebrew and Moabites interacted in a growing economy of political autonomy. It is instructive to consider how differently those at Jamnia after the birth of Christ arranged the Hebrew *Bible*. They appeared to value Ruth less compared with the Christian *Bible* of Jerome. Of the three major categories of the Hebrew *Bible*, the compilers placed "The Book of Ruth" among the "Writings," those lesser texts compared with "The Law" and the "Prophets." Christians who anthologized the Old Testament positioned "The Book of Ruth" between Judges and 1 Samuel.

King Artaxerxes I had granted Hebrews freedom to return to Israel. Many like Nehemiah and Ezra had advanced in Persian bureaucracy for the King to assign them as compradors in their homeland. Nehemiah returned to govern Jerusalem, followed by Ezra, resulting in the rebuilding of the Temple. These events occur around the time of Herodotus' travel writing, who never cited the presence of the Hebrews. Nehemiah and Ezra, with Genesis 34, for that matter, advance an Israel exclusive of only Jews. Among their accomplishments was instituting for the first time the Sabbath as a day of rest. Such a policy, with attendant rituals, obviates settlers and foreigners from corrupting Jewish blood with pollution. Ezra's reforms sought to cleanse Jerusalem by establishing ritual to separate believers from those non-observers like Moabites, Ammonites, and others marrying with the seed of God.

Ruth is set before King David's reign and provides an ethnonym of that Book in the *Bible*. She, the Moabite wife of a deceased Jew, returns to Canaan to care for her Hebrew mother-in-law, where she marries another Jew, the father of the Hebrews' most glorious King. David, too, as well as Solomon, had foreign wives about whom many prophets, like Ezra, would blame for betraying the Lord's people.

The Jordan River emerged from Biblical texts as both a horizontal and vertical signifier for Jews and Christians respectively, but, as with any artificial marker, such lines split some of the twelve tribes with Gad and Reuben with half of Manassas east of the river.[47] The Jordan is where John the Baptist baptized Jesus, and the waters, as any pure waters do, promise ascension to Heaven through baptism. Today, though, capitalism and state exploitation have resulted in at least three claims for the location in the *New Testament* where John baptized Jesus, claims by either Israel or Jordan to cash in on US dollars.[48]

After World War I, by carving up the conquered Ottoman Empire, the British and the French at Versailles, along with subsequent diplomacy, imposed boundaries, maps derived from the *Bible*, of what the Zionists would realize as the state of Israel in 1948. In that context, please consider the following citation as a prescription for peace through common resources, such as waterways, and for the future of the diverse people who share them:

> "If the resources are seen as belonging to future as well as the current citizens, then current practices can be called into question from the future-oriented perspective of the environmental movement. If we perceive resources as part of inalienable human rights and respectable place and time, then we can perhaps be persuaded by bioregional theories of human organization that would disregard state boundaries and reimagine commonalities in terms of the waterways that support them."[49]

It is this common cultural long-view of both our race's and the planet's survival that may save us yet.

Clearly, human narratives and history are rhizoidal plantings in earth. Stories surface, as memes, from settings of the past, the now, or the prophetic, to entertain, to motivate, and to realize events as mulch fertilizer back to the history of the stories' causes. Here at the meridian in cosmic existence, how can humankind craft a peace-building narrative that acknowledges that there is little time left for "fussing and fighting my friends," as John Lennon attuned years ago.[50] We must attend deeply to the past in order to move forward; and move forward we must, out of the past, that we not stay stuck in the muck and mire of archaic empires.

The fleeing Hyksos cast counterclockwise up the Levant clusters of refugees whose historical memories blossom into utterances of an ancient beginning, middle, and end, but, as Faulkner acknowledged, not necessarily in that order. The Ur-exodus got repeated in versions with every generation of each groups' refugees and in some cases manifested into form and elegance, such as the extant *Pentateuch* and Aeschylus' *Suppliants*, and the works of the lost Sanchuiathon.

The operative question persists: how much can historical events, historical interpretation, and myth reformulate fact? Scholars have established how the rhizomes of narratology result from historical cannibalism at Antioch and Ma'arat al-Numan (called "Marre" or "Ma'arri" al-Numan in Crusader texts) of the First Crusade.[51] This is a fact at first expunged back home in the West, then sublimated out of these historical events into narratives and grafted as romances in episodes of the King Arthur story, other chansons de geste, and especially *Richard Coer de Lyon*.[52] The patterns of accommodating ugly truths, like eating human flesh, wove backward and forward in a variety of genres, as letters, memoir, reportage, chronicles, case study, biography, parable, fable, and epic eventuating into Modern Times into science fiction and motion pictures. Christian de Troyes and other Languedoc poets have left 217 ballads resulting in evidence of how poets departed from religious subjects to secular content. Some of these poets, weaned on the previous centuries' raging contrarian thesis, questioned that Christians at communion literally eat God, a premise of the Albigensians, which eventuated in the Cathars' genocide. The taboo violations of cousins, on their Christian crusade, eating Saracens at al Ma'arra (1099 CE) was a horrid irony needing censorship back in Europe or sublimations for the health of the cultures' socioses. How did the myth of Arthur resolve historical fact into epic? Poets voiced secularized yarns about King Arthur from literary scraps from which the green thumb of Geoffrey of Monmouth planted, and the like of Mallory, Tennyson, and current TV scriptwriters composing to root modern English nationalism, over all the shared European garden.

Geraldine Heng's study the *Empire of Magic: Medieval Romance and the Politics of Cultural Fantasy* demonstrates aptly our thesis. The inspiration behind the sudden appearance in the 12th Century of the King Arthur romances derives not from long lost historical events in England when the Welsh/Roman civilization lingered as an onslaught of Saxon, Jute, and Pick infiltration overwhelmed the island, but rather from then-contemporary events of Christian crusader violence in the East. Even the Lancelot Guinevere adultery may derived from the purported illicit love of Melisende, Queen of Jerusalem (1105—1161) and a gallant Gallic knight from coastal Palestine. With the English lacking a great man on a white horse, like France's Charlemagne, these events and rumors galvanized for the English in song, plot, and story, similarly to how the Hebrews transmogrified an exodus of others into their imagined Exodus. The English found in Arthur a mythic harbinger that led its nationalism to what became an empire upon which the "sun would never set." This grand folly ended with the whimper of Margaret Thatcher's Falkland Island dispute. This is both the emblematic and the hopeful in that Merry Old England, while not nearly as extensive as in the days of Empire, now exists in a relatively peaceful state of civilization. Perhaps this is no evolutionary accident, as, when Empires fade, real *civilization* can arise.

The rhizomorphs of narrative and history exhibit how human minds grapple with the existential flux that threatens certitudes with ambiguities of contradictory realities. Mind and community fix in literary language melodic forms that structure not only *belle letters* but ancillary codes of culture, from those of politics, to diet, and to dress—even facial fashion: whether to grow a beard or not, a question that divided crusaders from those in the Holy Land as well as bearded Parisians conquering clean shaven Cathars a century later. That is the micro scale view of acculturation, in an individual's time. The larger view has a broader sweep, in and out of time.

Europeans emerging out of a state of disorder and chaos from the Dark Ages progressed from the 7th Century Synod of Whitby, where nascent thoughts of monks grappled to agree mathematically on a date for the annual celebration of Resurrection and of Easter. Then, three centuries later, around the year 1000, when the world failed to comply with some Biblical Armageddon, emerging intellectuals monastically engendered inquiries to challenge or question or clarify the logic of Trans-substantiation. Did the Eucharist celebrate the physical eating of God, a thesis eliciting the Berengaian controversy that proliferated in subsequent heresies?

Recognizing the futility of intra-Christian bloodletting, the Pope at Clermont in 1095 found a means to stop European fratricide with a plan of crusade against those occupying the Holy Land, which made Christianity during most of the First Millennium CE bound to worship an allo-centric geography, which during the next millennium Rome would resume. The center of Christianity is Jerusalem, but it is one occupied by Muslims. The effective plan was to band together Norman, Italian, Hungarian, Toulousain, and Castilian knights united in the First Crusade to win back the religion's center in a conquest of the infidels and heretics, by occupying the Holy Land. Before Urban's synod, there were no texts documenting a King Arthur. Suddenly, after the year 1100, the stay-at-homes learned about their Christian sons and brothers and fathers, whose religion featured the Eucharist, and they learned of the soldiers of Christ eating the enemy.

The shock of recognition must have been akin to a chosen people in the 1930s being eradicated in a final solution provided by a nation deemed the most intellectual in history, the land of Goethe, Bach, Heisenberg, Einstein, and the von Humboldts. We have lived through two centuries this shock that Smolo Sand illuminates in his discourse on *From Holy Land to Homeland*.[53] Shocks of recognition lead to curious manifestations in differing cultural codes from food taboos or favorite foods all the way to dress and to fashion for beards, as noted. European-sewn, form fitting clothing as opposed to near Eastern-draping testify to delineation of iron clad armor defining body parts with the clean-shaven faces to be distinguished from "goat-faced Saracens," as cited by crusaders; one *different* from the other.

European cannibalistic acts in the Levant in the early 1100s became fixed in art, in song, commemorated in novel genres to al Andalusian rhythm, with new musical instruments.[54] It is plausible that the notoriety of this had something to do with Cathar apostasy. These fixings of psychological trauma ingested contradictions, and the horror of a moment in medieval time came into the fantastical, the yarn, the national epic. It is ironic that Arthur's invented feats accommodated and assimilated the paradox of the Eucharist and what the followers of Christ did in violating the ultimate taboo, cannibalism. From the three witnesses of the cannibalism at Ma'arra, with possibly more in Antioch, historians back home first ameliorated the abomination in a logic that the conquering army was starving; thus, the horror is hopefully lessened by biological need. There was rumored an Arab precedent that the warriors to display cannibalism to frighten the enemy, for the Umayyads, when first landing in the Iberian peninsula, boiled the flesh of slain Visigoths to frighten those resisting.[55] But the possible rumor of Tariq feasting on European flesh in 711 compares unfavorably with the wider accounts of clerics who witnessed the Crusaders' abominations and reported them to Pope Pascall II (1055—1118). The common immorality in all of these instances stems from human's inability to ethically intervene, to operate in manual moral mode, over-riding our base instincts and drives with a higher principle. This principle must be the prized by the best of differing peoples, all contributing to a higher civilization of common culture, if we are to have peace.

Cannibalism occurs in desperate struggles (e.g. the true "Donner Party" in 19th Century California and the *Alive* stories in the Andes), and it occurs with exhilarations for the cause (e.g. the Crusades). In *Travels in the Congo*, Gide documents cannibalism in pre-World War I when Tuareg warriors in fierce combat ingested the enemy's heart to gain his vigor and strength.[56] While teaching in China in the early 1990s, Gage learned that he and his wife likely were teaching among cannibals, for Nanning, sixty miles north of the Vietnam border, some years earlier, was the scene of cannibalism. This cannibalism was not triggered by hunger but by competitive displays among rival gangs of the Red Guard youths to confirm their dedication to Mao.[57] From the Leviathan to Greek gigantomachy, cultural transformations project to the enemy a monstrous size and one with cannibal potential. Swift exploited this primal fear for literary irony in his ironic "Modest Proposal."

Cannibalism and human sacrifice fly in the face of Jewish, Christian, and Muslim protocol. In Maalula, Syria, in the mountainous Jabal to the north of Damascus, a Christian community speaking the language of Jesus takes communion before an altar of the female saint Thecla. The altar narrows at center to a lip, a feature erased in subsequent table altars, which forms the lip to function as a channel for escaping sheep or heifer blood. Pagan Greeks had participated in ritual sacrifice publicly, a practice after Jesus that was brought indoors like with the Hellenized Jews. Insular sacrificial performances may document progress toward civilization for an embarrassing human historical reality. Clearly, all people must eat and consequently defecate. God or gods only ingest via olfactory means with a little bit of help from mortals who pitch spices upon burning entrails. This human dilemma hasn't gone away with the popularity of poultry and meat in Safeway styrofoam boats to disguise the horror of raw meat of the sources from the prying eyes of the young and un-initiated of the species. Posted on the wall of a fashionable meat-centric restaurant in Ashland, Oregon, diners read, "If God didn't want us to eat meat, he should have made animals as vegetables." A neighbor in Humboldt County slaughtered a young daughter's pet calf, then informed her after dinner the source of the meal. Even contemporary humans haven't an adequate handle on accommodating and assimilating their harsh primal realities, with no way out unless we grab the moral, rational controls and fly by manual-override control.

We have done so occasionally: Heng's work convincingly provides a methodology for how the Medieval mind wrestled with the horror of cannibalism. Seeing is not only believing but potentially understanding; reporting out is potentially moving forward if others agree that the reported abomination should cease through democratization of ethics.

Heng documents how the horror of crusader cannibalism progressed from eyewitness accounts of what had been happening, to Papal reports in epistle genre of what happened, all the way to authors discoursing upon what is known commonly by a European audience on what happens to the ultimate cultural negotiation in narrative of what ought to or ought not to happen.[58] How might a stay-at-home European at the dawn of the 11th Century rationalize their cousins' cannibalism in the Levant? Why did God's instruments who departed to fight the heathens and regain Holy Jerusalem violate this taboo? How could Christian Anglo-Normans eat Arabs? Consider the recent "Shock and Awe" in the wake of the horror of 9/11: publics differentiate the good guys and bad guys to avoid investigating deeply. Then, painted aristocrats with henchmen a-horse, princes and a few Kings riding stallions into battle, looked down upon their soldier riffraff, on foot, earth-bound subalterns, a class at home capable of furthering feudal society with the labor necessary for those who pray, and the aristocrats who never work, the serf/slave who was designated in Medieval diction as "villein." So, abroad in battle, like Japanese soldiers after the fall of Nanking, these, some Zen-weaned, might do horrors, but with time the horrors haunted, especially when reflected upon on return home. Here is where literature, the shaping of language comes in, and can provide a conscience.

In brief, Professor Heng documents how the cannibalism of Ma'arra al Numen became cultural memory in story and joke. The records *sans* motive was recorded and reported. Then the record was projected upon the underclass or explained as "satisfying hunger." Then, decades later, the allusion to cannibalism was deleted. Paralleling these historical reportages, the fictive episodes of Arthur, an avatar of Charlemagne were created, all the while assimilating the deeds by attributing horrendous acts to the Other. Then appears the historical Richard the Lionhearted (1157—1199), a thug fraternity boy refashioned as national icon. A poet and native speaker of Languedoc, the language of ballads, Richard was also a ruthless and skilled warrior who came close to regaining Jerusalem for Christianity. On returning home, he was imprisoned in Austria while his feckless brother ruled egregiously. When released, Richard returned to his half of France and lore spawned of his bravado. After his death, his fame animated into cartoon, in which the King ate Saracens, though he never did in fact. This returning knight-errant augurs a Charlemagne, a real life Arthur, which the island nation so greatly needed. This is heteroglossia voiced in texts, certainly.

This kind of cultural negotiating is occurring as of this writing. Note Bradley Manning's whistle blowing how Americans in helicopters massacre non-combatants in Iraq or how graduates of our colleges and universities launch drones to target enemy like video gamers in insular America and cause collaboratively the unfortunate deaths of innocents a world away. We use familiar diction like "collateral damages" and "acceptable loses," which again conceal for us in order to refuse to face absolute horrors, ones equal to or surpassing archaic cannibalism. The ancient Hyksos' chariot and loom have both advanced and faded, but mankind seems much the same, intent still on killing first lest we be killed. Utilitarianism may be flawed, but it is a brave attempt to do better and should be applauded in our rational optimism for a better future. We can improve. . . If "the greatest good for the greatest number" is a starting premise. . . Then, the premise that all cultures may contribute to the good in turn warrants another premise that all cultures' highest moral contributions should be heard. A conclusion is that all must be welcome at the ethical party held on mutual higher ground.

There are analogues to the literary and cultural accommodation and assimilation of the Eucharist challenge. During the Dark Ages, travel to the Holy Land was impractical, for no matter how pious you were, those you met could as likely be a slaver as a merchant willing to guide you overland or by ship to the *Outremer* the Levant. The Children's Crusade is thus only a withering vestige of Dark Age barter. Our European languages echo that, during the Dark Ages, a hundred miles beyond the Mediterranean littoral, were sources of human chattels. From the fall of Rome until the year 1000, the "Slavs" of northern and eastern Europe were just that: slaves. Europe had been a source of slaves just as Africa would become from the Enlightenment when English, Dutch, and other Protestant entrepreneurs plumbed sub-Saharan Africa. Just as we are unconscious of the habitual memory that when we hear "California," there dwells a meaning "the furnace of the Caliph." So, the tourist departing Venice's Piazza St. Marco is equally unaware of the habitual memory when she hears "Rive degli Schiavoni," and she is unconscious of the meaning that the waterway to the left of the Doges Palace is where you head to get you a slave, one of the ethnos, "Slav."

Another aspect of how history becomes ritualized in myth that extenuates into continuities, shared across culture, concerns the Apostle James. In the Dark Ages, a Christian in Europe was even more isolated from the religion's epicenter, Jerusalem. Not only were there hostile Muslims and brigands in Palestine but also European roads became inaccessible to travel, essentially vanished from lack of use or posed where stretches did exist, with a total lack of safety. From the time of Constantine, Christian pilgrimage had been an important aspect of devotion to the faith. Homebound Europe likely looked with a kind of envy upon those Muslims, who fulfilled one of their five commitments to Islam by visiting even more remote Mecca.

When in the 9th Century, the body of the Apostle James was located, an alternative site to Jerusalem for Christians was in Santander, Spain. Gradually, pilgrimage south from Northern Europe led in four paths out of the Dark Ages to regenerate nascent capitalism. The martyr James, historically fine and gentle, gave rise out of time to James, the Muslim killer, "Matamoros," with another host of narratives inspiring zeal to rustic northerners to conquer a very rich and prosperous al Andalusia.[59] This distortion, like so many others, was driven by dreams of economic empire, not true history.

Figural transformations echo Aurebach's *Mimesis,* the pivotal text of the scholar refugee of the Nazi death camps who resided in neutral Istanbul to write his masterpiece. Heng uses such a transformation to explain how black became white via narratology. Today, the average citizen of the US or Europe, when asked about the Opium Wars in China, supposes that England and European interests, with some American help, entered the 20th Century affair to stop the spread of opium addiction. But, in fact, China wasn't Colombia; Britain was. Then, the West fought the Empress herself when her government attempted to stop the drug's spread as a commodity. Opium was the single commodity the West used to reverse its unbalanced payments when all silver currency found its graveyard in the Middle Kingdom. Story here wrestles with history, and history wrestles with story. Authentic history of civilization must advance beyond the politics of race and simplistic interests expressed in terms of good and bad guys. Our very survival may depend on that nexus of moving forward out of the muck and mire of legend and history, following the original Exodus to where it truly has already led, a tipping point in the reality of history.

Perhaps an answer lies in the shared past, also from the East. Nicholas Roerich asked, regarding warfare, "Is the heart of Asia beating, or has it been suffocated by the sands?"[60] In the 18th Century a Mongolian community of Khamariin Khiid, renowned for producing harmonious art, for decades enjoyed peace when a crime occurred, the stabbing murder of a Chinese, a dispute among the camps escalated beyond reason to limbic blood lust. Danzan Ravjaa, Khamariin Khiid's leader and a tantric yogi, called immediately for all his supporters to bring a knife from their households as an offering of allegiance to his law. They did more than put away knives: they made an iconic and artistic symbol of peace out of their metal instruments of violence, a lesson to us all, eastern, western, ancient, or modern. The overwhelming response of Khamariin Khiid resulted in over 10,000 knives collected. Ravjaa ordered his metal-smiths to craft an "exquisite statue" of the earlier 8th Century.

Lama Padmasambhava, the progenitor of the Nyingma genetic line, is known for peaceful co-existence. Sculptors and metal-smiths fashioned a statue, slightly less than a meter, based on lotus from the melted down 10,000 knives cast into the peace icon.[61] "The Statue of the 10,000 Knives" worked as nimble moral thinking as there was no additional violence during the remainder of Ravjaa's life and rule, and the statue is still extant today, housed in the noted museum.[62] In fact, the art made from potential violence seems to have engendered other acts of manual-override thinking and pacifism.

Another Danzan Ravjaa (1803—1856) chose martyrdom, despite his considerable popularity and earned favor of the Chinese Emperor. For years, Ravjaa's hundreds of popular songs and poems were celebrated with the East, though some had been critical of the Chinese occupying Mongolia. The Chinese occupiers sent Raviaa a seductive girl with a gift of poisoned vodka. The narratology has it that Raviaa apparently intuited that the drink was poisoned, told the girl that his life was complete, and drank the poison anyway; he then sat down to await death and to "write a long final lament on the dissolute state of the world."[63] His death in 1856 marks the first non-natural death since the decades-before murder. We, too, need to put away our knives.

With Ravjaa gone, like Socrates, writing his own "Apology" or defense, Khamariin Khiid's residents displayed even more nimble thinking, perhaps inspired by the statue with its "exceptionally intense expression and all the details suggesting suppression of evil from the demon head upon which the figure sits, to the outstretched right hand holding a *vajra* in the gesture of annihilation of all obstacles to good."[64] When the occupying Manchus eradicated all of the non-religious vestiges of Ravjaa's legacy, his followers took advantage of Manchu law that made it a capital offense to desecrate a tomb. Cleverly, mummifying Ravjaa's body and gathering some 1,500 crates full of his art, writings and possessions, his disciples placed all in one of Khamariin's temples to Ravjaa, thus protecting them all from attack. In this life, it pays to be clever, to be nimble, to put the camera on manual operation that we do not shoot first and ask questions later, that we think about the laughter of our grandchildren. Ravjaa's great, great, great grandchildren laugh today, and his legacy, more importantly his legacy of peace-building, endure today because of that laughter and delight.

Nimble human thinking should spread worldwide like a contagion for good, like the statue forged of melted knives. In the 21st Century, an eastern Gobi Parliament member, Sharavdorj, commissioned a new crown for the Statue of the 10,000 Knives, and the Dusn Lama, Khamarin Khiid's abbot, along with all in attendance wearing the traditional scarves of five colors, welcomed the peace symbol at the Danzan Ravjaa Museum.[65]

Acknowledging continuities of ritual, of morphing myths, of how social contexts reveal historical bases, whether of the function of the Roman *pharmakon*, God-eating Dionysians, appropriation of exoduses to height nationalistic zeal to illuminate common ground of religious and secular thinking promise dialogue, respect for all, and furthering of humans interacting with earth for the eventual enjoyment of our grandchildren. These exemplify "art in the sand" as manual override of human moral thinking. May we melt our nuclear arms once and for all, sometime soon, before it is too late. We scribes believe in the power of the human mind inventing and reinventing itself, mapping its own future, cognizant of the retrospective past with unflinching objectivity.

At the midpoint of existence of all earth-bound life, humankind must, to save this living legacy longer before entropy finalizes our narrative, *must* attend deeply to the exodus and immigration song we have been singing. Please sing with us, adding your own unique voice, the human chorus of civilization, that we might come further out of past darkness into future light. Amen.

Resources

Timeline

3000-2250 BCE	Old Kingdom.
2250-2050	First Intermediate Period.
2050-1990	Middle Kingdom.
1937-1757	12th dynasty: a period when Canaanites linked from Mari to Kythera, inland and islands between Thera and Peloponnese
1750	Hammurabi dies.
1675-1554	Second Intermediate Period: Commencing 13th, 14th, 15th, 16th, and 17th dynasties. This medley of local Egyptian and Hyksos rulers lacked centralized hierarchy as in the rule of Old, Middle, and New Kingdoms. Hyksos, under Salitis, liege lords over Egyptian Thebes. Pharaoh Kamose died fighting Hyksos, preceded by their exodus.
1575-1080	New Kingdom, commencing with Kamose's brother and successor Ahmoses, who pursues Canaanite overlords.
1539/1295	Hyksos Exodus, followed by waves traveling and emigrating east, north and to Aegean, known as Danaans, Cadmeans, then in 800 BCE referred to as Phoenicians.
1520 to 1492	Reign of the vengeful Thutmosis I.
1500	Thera: Volcanic eruption.

1479-1458	Hatshepsut, whose stele maintained rancor against the vile foreigners, whom we may assume are still being sought.
1352-1334	Amenhotep IV/Akhenaten, with Nefertiti, violated Ma'at. Monotheism, anticipating Hebrews' later monotheism: worshiped sun disk. At first maintained father's decoration, pharaoh-offering like a cartoon strip, yet with novel representation. Soon built a vast city, Al Amarna, purged the old Gods and abolished festivals, but died after 17 years and left a nation in chaos; expunged his intellectual, political, cultural transformation of natural philosophy that celebrated sun to invest his monomania. During this period, descendants of Hyksos might well have seen vulnerability and sought to return. Armarna letters indicate that buffer Egyptian states, created after the Hyksos, were without support and failing.
1334-1333	Tutankhamen's brief rule.
1313	Hellenistic citing from the Parian Chronicle citing Cadmus, the earliest date of the list of Greek chronology. However, Muhly (1970) puts Cadmus, as we do, some three hundred years earlier. The Calendar, broken in half, with one in British Museum, other in Paros, where Gage was Director of Aegean School of Classical Studies in 1987. Like early native American chronicling, a year records most awesome event, such as 2007 "Katrina," 2001 "Twin Towers," etc. For a modern example, consider *Chronicle for Iron and Steel* that cites 1881 the invention of the Jones' Hot Metal Mixer, or the Cradle of Civilization.

1305	Ulu Burum: Sinking of doomed Canaanite ship, excavated by George Bass, 1984.
1279-1213	Ramesses II "The Great," whose imperial armies in 1258 matched Hittites at the Battle of Kadesh in the Levant.
1350-586	De-facto Hebrew claims in Egypt arise. The first of the two ancient eras spanned from, and encompassed the periods of the Judges, the United Monarchy, and the Divided Monarchy of the Kingdoms of Israel and Judah, ending with the destruction of the First Temple. The second era was the period of the Hasmonean Kingdom spanning from 140 to 37.
1275	Kadesh, Hittites and Egypt draw in battle.
1184	Troy, as cited by Herodotus. However, destruction of palimpsest VIh (1255) figures to be Homer's Troy, two decades after Kadesh.
1180	Ugarit falls to Sea Peoples. Chaos nearly equaling time when Hyksos immigrated to Aegean from Nile. Ulu Burum treasure includes Nefertiti cartouche.
1250-1000	Sea People Invasions. History goes opaque, except that Joe Shaw linked continuity at Kommos, except for 85 years. Effect upon Egypt coincides with their giving up protecting tombs.
1100-1000	Iron Age city names shift from patronymic to tribal names. Iron, domesticated camels the "sh" icon of fast movement, yhw, apiru.
1000	Years of David; possible date for orally expressed Psalms.

943-922	Shoshenq I, the first intertextual link to validate anything in *Bible* of external historical fact: 1 Kings 14:26 Rehoboam post-Solomon.
900	Compiling of Oral Tradition back only to psalms with Canaanite/Hyksos traces. Lay source. From pastoral tradition. Oldest Elohist source. Elohim, plural of El, is always used. Canaanite heritage.
700	Yahweh source. Likely oral sources written down.
670	Assyrian invasion and near decade occupation. Likely when Hebrew scribes plagiarized as Noah story the Flood narrative text of a millennium earlier. 5?/ (History Extra Podcast "The Babylonian Noah," 13 Feb. 2014). Subsequently, in Misr, Egyptian priests with hereditary bureaucracy but foreign kings and mercenary armies will rule much in the future.
626	Jeremiah talked much about Egypt but never mentions Moses. He was writing in 7th Century when Jewish colony at Elephantine had settled as mercenaries since 9th C. Yet, no extant text from these soldiers. 4 / (Shmolo Sand citing PhD dissertation in Hebrew).
600	Joseph story. Joseph is most certainly a novella and not history: a Horatio Alger narrative of a local boy making good in the big city; its very crafted plot differs from biography. As biography, it would provide a historical link binding Jacob and his son Eber or Hebrew, the eponymy. The story for us is important because it is set in Egypt. In terms of literary standards, it is a rounded out story, not a sketchy myth. Unlike myth, the unity and plot

symmetry reveal but a single author. Though God is alluded to, the proper noun is absent. Unlike much biblical text, brother is used as the height of filial relations, not proper nouns of biography. Joseph stands out along the chain of text for a lack of exhortations, global struggles and destroying cities. It is a story with a protagonist and not of God's chosen leaders. As epigones of Israel, the characters of the story all go to Egypt, but elsewhere in the *Bible* they marry Canaanites. The setting doesn't need to be Egypt: it could as likely be Bozakoy. Three names could link to Egypt, but Pharaoh's father is Hebrew, not Egyptian. Titles are Egyptian but of Persian origin, which ironically dates the usage of the phrase and perhaps also the story to 600 BCE (Knowledge of Zodiac). Sardis coins or Aegina in Greek are about same date.

587-536	Babylon Exile.
550	Deuteronomist Source. Likely oral sources written down. Myth map of Israel borders Euphrates. / Havrelock
525-405	Persian invasion and occupation of Egypt during the 27th Dynast.
500-400	Priestly source. Likely oral sources written down.
484-425	Herodotus' travels to Levant and Egypt.
495-390	Hebrew Elephantine mercenaries stationed on island by Persians.
354	Second Persian invasion and occupation until 332.

332	Macedonian Invasion by Alexander and Occupation until the death of Cleopatra.
**********	Birth of Jesus **********
67 CE	Titus destroys Jerusalem, expels Jews.
100	Synagogue composed canon at Jaffa with translation in Greek. Oral texts in the anthology called the *Bible* but set often elsewhere, whether written or oral. Daniel clearly Hellenistic.
90-150	A Greek from Sardis. Pausanias writes of travels during reigns of Hadrian-Marcus Aurelius.
632	Death of Mohammed.
800s	Jews of Spain compose Hebrew Grammar following Arab codification of Arabic.
1440s	Gutenberg Press publishes *Bible*.

Appendix A
Uluburun late Bronze Age Shipwreck now in replica at Bodrum Museum of Underwater Archaeology

In the summer of 2002, Professor Gage discussed with Dr. Cermel Pulak the importance of the ingots of tin at the lab of the Navel Museum in Bodrum, Turkey. This small fingernail sample is the earliest evidence of the element thus found. From what source? Afghanistan? Cornwall, England? Either way, this element is needed to smelt with copper to yield bronze and testifies to how mobile and far traveling were 2nd Millennium entrepreneurs.

Over the years, the 14th Century BCE, artifacts of the sunken ship had spread over a large area; their origins indicate Syria, but included material from Greece, Cyprus, and Egypt. The fact that the cargo and materials of the ship came from an arc beginning in Northern Africa, the Levant, and Sicily advances evidence of a thriving commercial route used at least two hundred years earlier by migrating Hyksos.

The cargo of the doomed ship included more than a dozen pieces of both Canaanite and Egyptian jewelry, including gold from el Amarna, identifying the reign of Akhenaten. One cartouche had inscribed Nephrite's name, an indication likely of her husband's death. Other key items that evidence the extent of commerce during the period of the Hyksos exodus include ingots of copper, Canaanite jars, shards of other Canaanite amphorae from the 18th Dynasty, the earliest known ingots of glass, ebony from deep Africa, hippopotamus teeth, ostrich shells, and ivory not unlike the material found in Cadmus' palace in Thebes. Also found was a hinged wooden book within which wax was embedded for text or token, recalling the missive that illiterate Bellerophon carrying his own death warrant, as cited in Homer's *Iliad*.

Appendix B
The Code of Hammurabi; Gilgamesh, the Ancient Genesis of The Flood Story and Heteroglossia of the story of Noah and his Ark

Easter 1984 just outside Ain Devar in the duckbill of Eastern Syria, Professor Gage stood on the banks of the Tigris River, looking east toward Nineveh, beyond in Iraq. His host called to his attention Jabal Judi, a mountain in the far distance, "That is the mountain where Noah began sailing—he landed north at Ararat" The "Flood Tablet," discovered in the 19th Century, was found at Nineveh, a source of the Hebrew story of Noah. Gage's Fulbright predecessor in Aleppo, John Maier, had just co-authored *The Gilgamesh*, with Gage's former teacher John Gardner, the novelist killed the year before in a motorcycle accident (1984). The germ of our book was seeded that day on the Tigris banks. Within two years, Gage was in the Western Asiatic Department of the British Museum holding in his hand this 2nd Millennium BCE, palm-sized clay Muscle Face, Humbaba, Gilgamesh's antagonist.

A dozen years after Darwin had published the *Origin of Species*, George Smith of the Museum, perhaps at the very desk Gage had been assigned, experienced a shock of recognition. He read cuneiform on clay, nearly the size of the clay Humbaba, and recognized the Noah tale embedded in the Gilgamesh epic. Maier and Gardner translated Sin-Leqi-Unninn's version, a thousand years older than Smith's 6th Century BCE text.

From Sin-Leqi-Unninni's version, to Smith's text and down to Roman times, many more versions had been composed, of which several have been excavated between the century separating Smith and Maier/Gardner. Most translations include a deity, aiming to purge evil earth, who instructed a principal to assemble creatures, or "two-by-two aboard a rectilinear barge," "an acre was its whole floor space; ten dozen cubits the height of each wall; the dozen cubits its deck, square on each side" (Maier & Gardner, 1984, Tablet XI, Column ii). After the Great Flood, these protagonists send out birds to signal safe harbor, which ushers in another kind of second-coming for all species. Darwin's and Smith's findings surfaced questions about Hebrew authors appropriating much old myth/recollections.

Appendix C
Bibliography and Bernal's Ancient Model

Astour, Michael, *Hellenosemitica*, (Hague: Brill, 1967).
The Other Bible, ed Willis Barnstone, (New York: Harper, Row, 1984).
Bass George and Uluburun http://www.google.com/search?client=safari&rls=en&q=George+Bass+and+Ulu+baran&ie=UTF-8&oe=UTF-8#hl=en&client=safari&rls=en&sa=X&ei=5DuTTsL5EoPTiAKe36HNCA&ved=0CBkQBSgA&q=George+Bass+and+Ulu+baram&spell=1&bav=on.2,or.r_gc.r_pw.,cf.osb&fp=d7120621056a0a3&biw=1012&bih=670 6/24/2013.
Beltz, Walter. *God and the Gods: Myths of the Bible,* (London, UK: Penguin, 1983).
Bernal, Martin, *Black Athena Writes Back: Martin Bernal Responds to his Critics,* (Durham, NC: Duke U Pr, 2001).
Bernal, Martin, *Cadmeon* Letters, (Winona Lake, IN: Eisenbrsuns, 1990).
Bernal, Martin, *Black Athena*, (London, UK: Free Association Books, 1987).
Lefkowitz, Mary R. and Guy MacLean Rogers, *Black Athena Revisited,* (Chapel Hill, NC: U of NC Pr, 1996).
Bietak, Manfred, *Avaris: the Capitol of the Hyksos: Recent Excavations at Tell el:Daba*, (London, UK: British Museum, 1996).
Biligmayer, Hans Christian, *Cadmos,* Unpublished PhD Dissertation, UCSB, 1976.
Curtius, Adrian. *Ugarit: Ras* Shamra, (Grand Rapids, MI: Wm B Eerdmans Publishing, 1985).
Gordon, Cyrus H., *The Common Background of Greek and Hebrew Civilizations*, (New York, N.Y.: Norton, 1965).
Morris, Sarah, *Daodalus and the Origins of Greek Art,* (Princeton, NJ: Princeton Univ. Press, 1992).
Niemeier, W.D. "Minoan Artisans Traveling Overseas" 7,7 1991, 188-201.
Redford, Donald B., *Egypt, Canaan, and the Israel in Ancient Times,* (Princeton, NJ: Princeton U Pr, 1992).

Notes

Chapter One

1 Robinson Jeffers, *The Collected Poems of Robinson Jeffers*, (Palo Alto, CA: Stanford University Press, 2001).

2 Tom Gage, *American Prometheus: Captain Bill Jones: The Steel Genius who Made Andrew Carnegie*, (Cupertino, CA: iBooks, 2012).

3 Tiffany J. Smith, "From Trickster to Heroic Savior: Jake Sully's Journey in Avatar." www.americanpopularculture.com/film.htm. 224. (Smith, 2013).

4 Scott Pally, "March Arabs," *60-min Iraq's Marshlands,* 2009, http://www.cbsnews.com/news/iraqs-marshlands-resurrecting-eden-24-07-2011/ Accessed May 3, 2012.

5 Maxine Hong Kingston, *Tripmaster Monkey*, (New York, NY: Vintage, 1990).

6 Wu Chengen, *Monkey: Folk Novel of China*, tr Arthur Waley, (NY: Grove Press; Reissue edition, 2007).

7 Liu, Xinru. *Ancient India and Ancient China: Trade and Religious Exchanges AD 1-600*, (Delhi: Oxford U. Press, 1988). Also see Hsüan-tsang, Ta-T'ang Hsi-yü, Buddhist Records of the Western World, *Internet Archive.* https://archive.org/details/siyukibuddhistre01hsuoft 9 September 2009.

8 Theodore Gastor, *Thespis: Ritual, Myth and Drama in the Ancient Near East*, (New York, NY: Henry Schuman, 1950).

9 Adrian Curtis, *Ugarit: Ras Shamra*, (Grand Rapids, MI: Eerdmans, 1985).

10 Frank Moore Cross, *Canaanite Myth and Hebrew Epic: Essays in the History of the Religion of Israel,* (Boston, MA: Harvard U Pr, 1973).

11 Eric A. Havelock, *The Muse Learns to White: Reflections on Orality and Literacy from Antiquity to the Present*, (New Haven, CN: Yale U Pr, 1986).

12 Cyrus H. Gordon, *The Common Background of Greek and Hebrew Civilizations*, (New York, NY: W. W. Norton, 1962). Also see Cyrus H. Gordon *The Ancient Near East*, (New York: W. W. Norton,1958) and Cyrus H. Gordon, *Forgotten Scripts: Their Ongoing Discovery and Decipherment,* (New York, NY: Dorset, 1968).

13 Donald B. Redford, *Egypt, Canaan, and Israel in Ancient Times,* (Princeton, NJ: University of Princeton Pr, 1992). Also see James G. Frazer, *Folklore in the Old Testament,* (New York, NY: Hart, 1975).

14 Flavius Josephus, author of *Against Apion* and the *Antiquity of the Jews*.

15 Patrick Geary, "Medieval Matters: Modern European Nationalism and the Fight to Control the Past," Commonwealth Club of California, www.commonwealthclub.org/events/archive/podcast/patrick-geary-modern-european-nationalism-and-fight-control-past, 5/17/14).

16 Smolo Sand, *The Invention of the Land of Israel: from Holy Land to Homeland*, (London, UK: Verso, 2012), also see Smolo Sand, *The Invention of the Jewish People*, (London, UK: Verso, 2009).

17 Christopher Krebs, *A Most Dangerous Book: Tacitus' Germania from Rome to the Third Reich*, (New York, NY: Norton, 2011).

18 Albert Camus, *The Rebel*, (New York NY: Vintage, 1958), 4.

19 Melvin Bragg, "Le Morte d'Arthur *In Our Time*," *In Our Time*, 10 Jan. 2013, BBC http://www.bbc.co.uk/podcasts/series/iot/all Accessed March 2, 2013.

20 Ibn Munqidh, Usamah, *An Arab-Syrian Gentleman and Warrior in the Period of the Crusades: Memoirs of Ibn Munqidh, Usamah*, tr Philip K. Hitti, (London, UK: I. B. Tauris & Co Ltd, 1987).

21 James B. Pritchard, *The Ancient Near East: an Anthology of Texts and Pictures*. Vol 1 & 2, (Princeton, NJ: Princeton University Press, 1958).

22 Donald B. Redford, *Egypt, Canaan, and Israel in Ancient Times*, (Princeton, NJ: University of Princeton Pr, 1992), 315 ft 18, 378.

23 Donald B. Redford, "The Hyksos in History and Tradition." *Orientalia*. Vol 39, 1-52, (1970: 10, ft 4).

24 Donald B. Redford, *Egypt, Canaan, and Israel in Ancient Times*, (Princeton, NJ: University of Princeton Pr, 1992). Also see James G. Frazer, *Folklore in the Old Testament*, (New York, NY: Hart, 1975), 304-5.

25 1 Kings, Chap 6.

26 Richard Jude Thompson,"The Deuteronomicstic Covenant and Neo-Assyrian Imperial Ideology: a Study of the Deuteronomistic History in Its Historical Contexts." PhD diss, (Harvard University, 2011), 114-157.

27 Joseph Mélèze Modrzejewski, *The Jews of Egypt: From Rameses II to Emperor Hadrian*, (Princeton, NJ: Princeton U Pr, 1995), 6.

28 Donald B. Redford, *Egypt, Canaan, and Israel in Ancient Times*, (Princeton, NJ: University of Princeton Pr, 1992), 270.

29 Melvin Bragg "In Our Time," BBC http://www.bbc.co.uk/programmes/profiles/1nKPV5F8v9NKHLM7zRhG6yh/melvyn-bragg.

30 I Kings 8:1-21.

31 George Rawlinson, *Phoenicia*, (Salem, MS: Ayre, 1889, reprint 1972), 98.

32 "How Ukrainian Women Saved the Samaritans of Mount Gerizim." (2013) *The Guardian*, (http://www.guardian.co.uk/world/2013/feb/11/ukrainian-women-samaritans-mount-gerizim). Accessed 14 July 2013.

33 1 Kings 9:15-14.

34 1Kings 6, but of even greater grandeur was Solomon's own Palace.

35 1 Kings 7:1-12.

36 1 Kings 9:15-22.

37 1 Kings 11:14-44.

38 1 Kings 9:26-28; 10:11-12; 22.

39 1 Kings 9:26-28, 10:11-12.

40 1 Kings 9:10.

41 1 Kings 9:15-22.

42 Donald B. Redford, *Egypt, Canaan, and Israel in Ancient Times,* (Princeton, NJ: University of Princeton Pr, 1992), 313.

43 Geddes. MacGregor, *The Bible in the Making,* (Washington DC: University Pr, 1959.

44 Genesis 37-50.

45 Donald B. Redford, *Egypt, Canaan, and Israel in Ancient Times,* (Princeton, NJ: University of Princeton Pr, 1992), 236.

46 Michael C. Astour, *Hellenosemitica: An Ethnic and Cultural Study in West Semitic Impact on Mycenaean Greece,* (Leiden, The Netherlands: E. J. Brill, 1967.), 931. Also see Martin. Bernal, *Black Athena: the Afroasiatic Roots of Classical Civilization. Vol. II: The Archaeological and Documentary Evidence,* (New Brunswick, NJ: Rutgers University Press, Bernal), 426-27.

47 Robert Aubreton, Uploaded 2012. *Anthologie grecque* 49-50. 1973, https://sites.google.com/site/hellenisticbibliography/epigram Accessed 4 December 2013.

48 Donald B. Redford, *Egypt, Canaan, and Israel in Ancient Times,* (Princeton, NJ: University of Princeton Pr, 1992), 383.

49 Herodotus, *The Histories,* tr Aubrey de Selincourt, (Baltimore, MD: Penguin, 1965)145, 159-60.

50 Richard Jude. Thompson,"The Deuteronomicstic Covenant and Neo-Assyrian Imperial Ideology: a Study of the Deuteronomistic History in Its Historical Contexts." PhD diss, (Harvard University, 2011).

51 Theodore Gastor, *Thespis: Ritual, Myth and Drama in the Ancient Near East,* (New York, NY: Henry Schuman, 1950). Also see Cyrus H. Gordon *The Ancient Near East,* (New York: W. W. Norton, 1958) and Cyrus H. Gordon, *The Common Background of Greek and Hebrew Civilizations,* (New York, NY: W. W. Norton, 1962). Gordon, 1959; also see 1962.

52 Wim van Binsbergen. August 6, 2010, http://ethnicity.bravepages.com/topicalities/topicali.htm Accessed 4/12/14. 2010, Diagram 4.

53 Neil MacGregor, "Rhind Mathematical Papyrus," *A History of the World in 100 Objects,* (London, UK: Penguin, 2012), 88193. Also see "Rhind Mathematical Papyrus," The British Museum. 2/9/10. http://www.britishmuseum.org/explore/highlights/highlight_objects/aes/r/rhind_mathematical_papyrus.aspx Accessed 4,15/13. Also see John Van Seters, *The Hyksos,* (New Haven, CN: Yale University Pr, 1966.), 154.

54 "Plato's View on the Importance of Mathematics," March 14, 2005. http://faculty.kfupm.edu.sa/MATH/irasasi/PlatosView.pdf Access 7/16/14.

55 Herodotus, *The Histories*, tr Aubrey de Selincourt, (Baltimore, MD: Penguin, 1965), XVII.I.III.

56 Sigmund Freud, *Moses and Monotheism*, tr Katherine Jones, (New York, NY: Vintage, 1939).

57 Walter Beltz, *God and the Gods: Myths of the Bible*, (London, UK: Penguin, 1983), 41-88.

59 John Van Seters, *The Hyksos*, (New Haven, CN: Yale University Pr, 1966), 73.

60 "Uluburun Shipwreck," updated 21 November 2013, http://en.wikipedia.org/wiki/Uluburun_shipwreck Accessed December 1, 2013.

61 George Bass, "A Bronze Age Shipwreck at Uluburun (Kash): 1984 Campaign" *American Journal of Archaeology*, (90/3 July 1986): 59, 269–296.

62 Wim Van Binsbergen, *Alternative Models of Intercontinental Interaction towards the Earliest Cretan Script. Black Athena: Ten Years After*, (Groningen, the Netherlands: Talanta, 1997).

63 John Van Seters, *The Hyksos*, (New Haven, CN: Yale University Pr, 1966), 121-126.

64 Martin Bernal, *Black Athena: the Afroasiatic Roots of Classical Civilization. Vol. II: The Archaeological and Documentary Evidence*, (New Brunswick, NJ: Rutgers U Pr, 1991), 502-04.

65 Martin Bernal, *Black Athena: the Afroasiatic Roots of Classical Civilization. Vol. III: The Linguistic Evidence*, (New Brunswick, NJ: Rutgers U Pr, 2006), 538.

66 Plato, "Menexenus," *The Dialogues*, tr Benjamin Jowett, Vol. 2. (New York, NY: Random House, 1892), 775-790.

67 John Van Seters, *The Hyksos*, (New Haven, CN: Yale University Pr, 1966), 174.

68 Ibid, 175.

69 Martin Bernal, *Cadmean Letters: The Transmission of the Alphabet to the Aegean and Further West before 1400 BCE*, (Winona Lake, WI: Eisenbrauns, 1990), 67.

70 Martin Bernal, *Black Athena: the Afroasiatic Roots of Classical Civilization. Vol. II: The Archaeological and Documentary Evidence*, (New Brunswick, NJ: Rutgers U Pr, 1991), 320-358.

71 Berard, Jean. "Hyksos et la Legende d'Io Recherches sur la période premycenienne," *Syria*, tr by Robert Rasmussen, Paris, FR: Institut Francais du Proche-Orient. https://www.Hyksos%20et%20la%20Legende%20d'Io%20Recherches%20sur%20la%20période%20premycenienne.Berard69/ Accessed 12 October 2012.

Chapter Two

1 Herodotus, *The Histories*, tr Aubrey de Selincourt, 49 (Baltimore, MD: Penguin, 1965), 120.

2 George Barton, *The Royal Inscriptions of Sumer and Akkad*, (New Haven, CT: Yale U Pr, 1929), 61, 63, 65.

Rick Steves' "Europe. APT http://www.aptonline.org/catalog.nsf/vLinkTitle/RICK+STEVES+EUROPE+VIII.

3 Samuel Noah Kramer, *Inanna: Queen of Heaven and Earth: Her Stories and Hymns from Sumer*, (New York, NY: Harper, 1983).

4 Ibid, 115-173.

5 Pierre Amiet, *L'Art d'A gadé au musée du Louvre*, (Paris, Fr :Ed de la Réunion des musées nationaux, 1976) 29-32.

6 Nahum 3:7, 19.

7 "Hammurabi's Code of Laws," tr L. W. King, in *Exploring Ancient World Cultures, Readings from the Ancient Near East*, (Evansville, IN: University of Evansville, 1997).

8 Ibid.

9 Ibid.

10 David Sperling, "The Original Torah: The Political Intent of the *Bible's* Writers." *Reappraisals in Jewish Social and Intellectual History*, (New York: New York U Pr, 1998), xiv, 184.

11 Aristotle, *Nichomachean Ethics*, (Chicago, IL: U of Chi Pr, 2011).

12 Percy Bysshe Shelley, "Ozymandius," in *Six Centuries of Great Poetry*, eds Robert Penn Warren & Albert Erskine (New York, NY: Dell, 1965), 378).

13 "Sargon Inscriptions, " ed James Pritchard, *The Ancient Near East, Volume 1 An Anthology of Texts and Pictures*, (Princeton, NJ: the U of Princeton Pr, 1969), 195.

14 Rick Steves' "Europe. APT http://www.aptonline.org/catalog.nsf/vLinkTitle/RICK+STEVES+EUROPE+VIII 15 2 Kings 17:1-6.

15 Ibid.

16 Isaiah 10:6.

17 1 Kings 5:9.

18 Rick Steves, et al, *Rick Steves' Paris 2013*, (Avalon Travel, Perseus Books Group, 2013), 151.

19 "May This Never Happen Again." The "Bux/Mont Coalition for Peace Action" and "Hibakusha Stories" Groups, featuring Clifton Truman Daniel, Harry Truman's grandson; Setsuko Thurlow, a Hiroshima factory worker; and Yasuaki Yamashita, Nagasaki survivor Bucks County Community College: Oct. 16, 2012.

20 "Building Pharaoh's Chariots" Nova (2013) http://www.pbs.org/wgbh/nova/ancient/pharaoh-chariot.html.

21 Caryl Emerson, "Irreverent Bakhtin and the Imperturbable Classics," in *Arethusa*, 26.2 Spring 1993, (Baltimore, MD: The Johns Hopkins U Pr, 1993), 123-140.

22 Norman Davies, *Vanished Kingdoms: The Rise and fall of States and Nations*, (New York, NY: Viking, 2011).

23 Donald B. Redford, *Egypt, Canaan, and Israel in Ancient Times*, (Princeton, NJ: University of Princeton Pr, 1992).

24 Michael C. Astour, *Hellenosemitica: An Ethnic and Cultural Study in West Semitic Impact on Mycenaean Greece*, (Leiden, The Netherlands: E. J. Brill, 1967).

180   BIBLICAL TIME OUT OF MIND

25 Ruth B. Edwards, *Kadmos the Phoenician: a Study in Greek Legends and the Mycenean Age*, (Amsterdam, The Netherlands: Adolf M. Hakkert, 1979), 167.

26 George Bass, "Campaign American," *Journal of Archaeology*, July, 1986. 90/3, 269-296.

27 G.F. Bass, "Bronze Age Shipwreck Reveals Splendors of the Bronze Age," *National Geographic Magazine* 172.6, 1986, 693-733.

28 Nicholas Chr. Stampolidis and Antonios Kkotsomas, "Phoencians in Crete," in *Greece from the Mycenaean palaces to the Aga of Homer*, eds S Deger-Jalkotzy and I.S. Lemons, (Edinburgh, UK: Academia.edu, 2006), 337-369. *Academica.edu:* https://www.academia.edu/1013298/_Phoenicians_in_Crete_co-authored_by_Stampolidis_N.C._In_Ancient_Greece_from_the_Mycenaean_palaces_to_the_Age_of_Homer_Deger-Jalkotzy_S._and_Lemos_I.S._eds_Edinburgh_2006_337-360 Accessed 7 August 2014.

29 Geraldine Heng, *Empire of Magic: Medieval Romance and the Politics of Cultural Fantasy*, (New York, NY: Columbia U Pr, 2003).

30 Graywacke. 25 March 2007 *http://commons.wikimedia.org/wiki/File:MenkauraAndQueen_MuseumOfFineArtsBoston.png* Accessed January 7, 2013.

31 File: MenkauraAndQueen MuseumOfFineArtsBorston.png, http://commons.wikimedia.org/wiki/File:MenkauraAndQueen_MuseumOfFineArtsBoston.png Accessed January 7, 2013.

Chapter Three

1 Pausanius, *Guide to Greece*, Book IX:2 (New York, NY: Penguin, 1979), 317.

2 Lynn Truss, *Eats, Shoots, & Leaves*, (New York, NY: Gotham, 2004).

3 Harry Hook, "The Last of His Tribe," River City Productions HBO http://www.copyright-encyclopedia.com/the-last-of-his-tribe-by-hbo-films-inc-and-angelic/ Accessed May 4 1992), Uploaded 2013.

4 Robinson Jeffers, *The Collected Poems of Robinson Jeffers*, (Palo Alto, CA: Stanford University Press, 2001).

5 Hebrew language, 5 November 2014, (http://en.wikipedia.org/wiki/Hebrew_language), Accessed 5 August 2013.

6 Mehri Niknam, in Melvin Bragg's, "Muslim Spain," *In Our Time: BBC*, 21 September 2002. In Our Time. http://www.bbc.co.uk/programmes/p0054811 Accessed 5 March 2012.

7 Richard Jude. Thompson, "The Deuteronomicstic Covenant and Neo-Assyrian Imperial Ideology: a Study of the Deuteronomistic History in Its Historical Contexts." Diss. (Harvard University, 2011), 317-326.

8 Ibid, iii.

9 Robert Graves, "Europa and Cadmus," in *The Greek Myths*, Vol. 1, 58.6-58.g, (New York, NY: Penguin, 1979), 194-200.

10 Fyodor Dostoevsky, *The Brothers Karamazov*, tr & ed by David McDuff, Part II, Book V, Chapter V, (London, UK: Penguin, 2003).

11 *Leviticus, Numbers* and *Samuel, cited in* James B. Pritchard, ed *Ancient Near Eastern Texts*

Relating to the Old Testament, tr Theophile J. Meek, (Princeton, NJ: Princeton University Press, 1955), pp. 166-7, 170-7. Language modernized by Wayne Ackerson.

12 "Secrets of the Lost Empires II: Pharaoh's Obelisks," History Channel: February 27, 2013.

13 "Goshen," *Jewish Encyclopedia*, 2011. www.jewishencyclopedia.com/articles/6819-goshen 2 24 Accessed 3 June 2013.

14 Daniel C. Snell, *Life in the Ancient Near East*, (New Haven: U of Yale Pr, 1997), 63.

15 Manfred Bietak, *Amaris: the Capitol of the Hyksos. Recent Excavations at Tell el Daba.* (London, UK: British Museum, 1996).

16 Ibid, Snell, 78.

17 Sigmund Freud, *Moses and Monotheism*, tr Katherine Jones, (New York, NY: Vintage, 1939).

18 Donald Redford, *Egypt, Canaan, and Israel in Ancient Times*, (Princeton, NJ: University of Princeton Press, 1992), 73. Also quite pertinent here is that Redford corroborates Snell's dating and geography.

19 Ibid, 275-80. Hyksos presence documented by the Rind Papyrus of the 33rd year of Apophis.

20 John Van Seters, *The Hyksos*, (New Haven, CN: Yale University Pr, 1966), 154.

21 Berard, Jean. "Hyksos et la Legende d'Io Recherches sur la période premycenienne," *Syria*, tr by Robert Rasmussen. Paris, FR: Institut Francais du Proche-Orient.https://www.Hyksos%20 et%20la%20Legende%20d'Io%20Recherches%20sur%20la%20période%20premycenienne. Berard69/ Accessed 12 October 2012.

22 John Van Seters, *The Hyksos*, (New Haven, CN: Yale University Pr, 1966), 72.

23 Joseph Mélèze Modrzejewski, The Jews of Egypt: From Rameses II to Emperor Hadrian, (Princeton, NJ: Princeton U Pr, 1995).

24 Daniel C. Snell, *Life in the Ancient Near East*, (New Haven: U of Yale Pr, 1997), 68.

25 O.R. Gurney, *The Hittites*, (London, UK: Penguin, 1964), 63.

26 Ancient History Encyclopedia, 2011) http://www.ancient.eu.com/aleppo/ Accessed 10 November 2013.

27 Bill Hotchkiss, *Climb to the High Country*, (New York, NY: W.W. Norton, 1978).

28 Lawrence Kim, "Orality, Folktales, and the Cross-cultural Transmission of Texts" in *The Romance between Greece and the East*, eds Tim Whitmarsh and Stuart Thomson, (Cambridge, UK: Cambridge U Pr, 2013), 300-320. Also see Carl A. Rubino, "Opening up the Classical Past: Bakhtin, Aristotle, Literature, and Life," in *Arethusa*, 26.2 Spring, 1993. (Baltimore, MD: The Johns Hopkins U Pr, 1993), 141-158.

29 http://en.wikipedia.org/wiki/Imhotep Accessed 14 May 2009.

30 Ibid, Kim.

31 http://www.maravot.com/Work%20notes%20on%20the%20Pyrgi%20Gold%20Tablets. pdf Accessed 4 March, 2009.

32 Karen Ni Mheallaigh, "Lost in Translation: the Phoenician *Journal* of Dictys of Crete," in *The Romance between Greece and the East*, eds Tim Whitmarsh and Stuart Thomson, (Cambridge, UK: Cambridge U Pr, 2013), 196-210.

33 Ibid, 196-97.

34 Emily Kneebone, "Josephus' Esther and Diaspora Judaism," in *The Romance between Greece and the East*, eds Tim Whitmarsh and Stuart Thomson, (Cambridge, UK: Cambridge U Pr, 2013), 165-182.

35 *Bakhtin and Ancient Studies: Dialogues and Dialogics*. 26/2 (The Johns Hopkins U Pr, Spring 1993). See particularly Caryl Emerson, "Irreverent Bakhtin and the Imperturbable Classics," 123—140; Carl A. Rubino, "Opening up the Classical Past: Bakhtin, Aristotle, Literature, and Life," 141-158; and Nancy Felson-Rubin, "Bakhtinian Alterity, Homeric Rapport," 159-172.

36 Ibid, Kneebone, 166.

37 Ibid.

38 Ibid, 173.

39 Josephus, *In the Antiquities*, 1.14 Also see 1.26, http://www.biblestudytools.com/history/flavius-josephus/antiquities-jews/preface/chapter-1.html.

40 Ibid, Kneebone, 196.

41 Richard Morris, *Time's Anvil: England, Archaeology, and the Imagination*, (London, UK: Weidenfeld & Nicolson, 2012).

42 Ibid, Josephus *In the Antiquities*, Books 1 and 2, respectively.

43 Ibid.

44 Eric H. Cline, *1177 B.C.: The Year Civilization Collapsed (Turning Points in ancientHistory)*, (Princeton, NJ: Princeton U Pr, 2014).

45 John Dillery, "Manetho," in *The Romance between Greece and the East*, eds Tim Whitmarsh and Stuart Thomson, (Cambridge, UK: Cambridge U Pr, 2013). Also see in same anthology, Emily Kneebone, "Josephus' Esther and Diaspora Judaism."

46 Ibid.

47 The Project Gutenberg EBook of Against Apion, by Flavius Josephus.

Chapter Four

1 Sanchuniathon, http://en.wikipedia.org/wiki/Sanchuniathon from the writings of Philo of Byblos: Eusebius 1.10.40 Accessed 4 April 2013. Archaeology: Troy and Heinrich Schliemann. See also from Sarah P Morris, *Daidalos and the Origins of Greek Art*. Princeton, NJ: University of Princeton Pr, 1992), opening page.

2 The Golden Age is the first Age of Man in Greek mythology—in some ways comparable to the Garden of Eden from Genesis. See *Wikipedia* for more.

3 Aeschylus. *Seven Against Thebes,* tr Philip Vellacott, (London, UK: Penguin, 1961).

4 Sophocles, *Oedipus the King*, tr David Grene, (Chicago, IL: The University of Chicago Press, 1954).

5 Sophocles *Oedipus the King; Antigone,* and *Oedipus at Colonus,* tr David Grene, (Chicago, IL: The University of Chicago Press, 1954).

6 Euripides, *The Phoenician Woman*, tr Elizabeth Wyckoff and Euripides, *The Phoenician Women*, (Chicago, IL: The U of Chicago Pr, 1959).

7 Euripides, *The Bacchae,* tr William Arrowsmith, (Chicago, IL: The U of Chicago Pr, 1959).

8 Robert Graves, *The White Goddess*, (New York, NY: Farrar, Strauss, & Giroux, 1948).

9 Pausanias, *Guide to Greece, Volume 2,* tr Levi, Peter. (London, UK: Penguin, 1971), 449. Also see Book X, 17).

10 Herodotus, *The Histories*, tr Aubrey de Selincourt, (Baltimore, MD: Penguin, 1965), 331.

11 Parian Calendar 2013, (http://en.m.wikipedia.org/wiki/Parian_Chronicle Accessed 5 May 2004.Also see Bernal, 1990, 124.

12 Katie Demakopoulou and Dora Konsola, "*Archaeological Museum of Thebes*," tr Helen Zigada, (Athens, Greece: General Direction of Antiquities & Restoration,1981), PL 21.

13 Wolfgang Schiering, *Die Werkstatt Des Pheidias in Olympia: Zweiter Teil : Werkstattfunde (Olympische Forschungen),* (Berlin, GR: Walter de Gruyter, 1991).

14 Manfred Bietak, *Amaris: the Capitol of the Hyksos,* Recent Excavations at Tell el Daba, (London, UK: British Museum, 1996), PLs III—VIIID; also see Niemeier 1996, Vol 7. 7, 188—201.

15 Katie Demakopoulou and Dora Konsola, *Archaeological Museum of Thebes,* tr Helen Zigada, (Athens, Greece: General Direction of Antiquities & Restoration,1981), 51.

16 Ibid, PL 25.

17 Ibid, 52-6.

18 Ibid.

19 Ibid.

20 Ibid, 52.

21 Edith Porada, *Ancient Art in Seals: Essays*, eds Pierre Amiet, Nimet Özgüç, and John Boardman, (Princeton, NJ: Princeton U Pr, 1980), Introduction.

22 Ibid.

23 Pausanias, *Guide to Greece: Volume 1*, tr Peter Levi, (London, UK: Penguin, 1971), 124 and Pausanias, *Guide to Greece: Volume 11*, 384.

24 Robert Graves, *The White Goddess*, (New York, NY: Farrar, Strauss, & Giroux, 1948), 70a.

25 Ibid 70d.

26 Euripides, David Grene, tr *Hippolytus*, (Chicago, IL: U of Chicago Pr , 1961).

27 Robert Graves, "Europa and Cadmus," in *The Greek Myths, Vol. 1,* (New York, NY: Penguin, 1969), 58.6-58.g.

28 Ibid, Demakopoulou, 52-3, PL 23.

29 Ibid, Peroda, 1979.

184 BIBLICAL TIME OUT OF MIND

30 "Chariot," Wikipedia 8 November 2014 http://en.wikipedia.org/wiki/Chariot Jan. 21, 2013.

31 "The Greek Age" 2003. http://www.salimbeti.com/micenei/chariots.htm, April 3, 2013, conclusion Accessed 4 October.

32 Ibid, Redford, 1992, 96, 236.

33 Ibid, Demakoulou, 1981, 82-3.

34 Ibid, Redford, 1992, 136.

35 http://religion-by-kyle.blogspot.com. "The Greek Golden Age and the Great Peloponnesian War." Jan, 2013.

36 Homer, *Odyssey*, tr Bernard Knox, Book XI, (New York, NY: Penguin, 2006), 260-80.

37 Nicholaos Platon, "Oriental Seals from the Palace of Cadmus: Unique Discoveries in Boeotian Thebes," *London Illustrated News,* 28 Nov 1964. Also see Dakouri-Hild, Anastasia. 2001. The British School at Athens. Vol. 96. "The House of Kadmos in Mycenaean Thebes Reconsidered: Architecture Chronology, and Context." http://www.jstor.org/discover/10.23 07/30073274?uid=3739560&uid=2134&uid=377255061&uid=2&uid=70&uid=3&uid=3 77255051&uid=3739256&uid=60&purchase-type=article&accessType=none&sid=211031 22254081&showMyJstorPss=false&seq=47&showAccess=false Accessed December 10, 2011.

38 Plato, "Menexenus" *Dialogues of Plato*, tr B. Jowett, Vol. II, 245-246 (New York, NY: Random, 1892), 784.

39 Pausanias, *Guide to Greece: Volume 1*, tr Peter Levi, (London, UK: Penguin, 1971), 124. Also see Levi 1071, Vol. I, 448-9.

40 Ibid, Demakoulou, 22-6.

41 Ibid, 26-7.

42 Pausanias, *Guide to Greece: Volume 11*, tr Peter Levi, (London, UK: Penguin, 1971), 75-99.

43 Ruth B. Edwards, *Kadmos the Phoeniician: a Study in Greek Legends and the Mycenean Age*, (Amsterdam, The Netherlands: Adolf M. Hakkert, 1979), 167.

44 Michael C. Astour, *Hellenosemitica: An Ethnic and Cultural Study in West Semitic Impact on Mycenaean Greece*, (Leiden, The Netherlands: E. J. Brill, 1967).

45 Herodotus. *The Histories*, tr Aubrey de Selincourt, Book II (Baltimore, MD: Penguin, 1965), 43-47.

46 "Thebes in Egypt Thebes in Greece," Dec. 20 13.http://forums.civfanatics.com/archive/index.php/t-25281.html 1 December 2013). Uploaded 21 January, 2014.

47 George Rawlinson, *Phoenicia*, (Salem, MS: Ayre, 1889, reprint 1972), 98.

48 Martin Bernal, *Cadmean Letters: The Transmission of the Alphabet to the Aegean and Further West before 1400 BC*, (Winona Lake, WI: Eisenbrauns, 1990), 53.

49 Ibid, 53-64; also see Chart 2, 124.

50 Ibid, Bernal 1990, IX-XIII.

51 John Chadwick, *Reading the Past: Linear B and Related Scripts*, (Berkeley, CA: U of California Pr/British Museum,1987).

52 Israel Finkelstein and Neil Asher Silberman. Uploaded 2008. "The Bible Unearthed," The History Channel version. www.historychannel.com. 26 March 2009. 85 mins. "France 5" Four-Part Series. 120 mins. Accessed April 5, 2013.

53 Frank Moore Cross, *Canaanite Myth and Hebrew Epic: Essays in the History of the Religion of Israel*, (Boston, MA: Harvard U Pr, 1973), 112-144.

54 Ibid, Redford, 1992, 315, 378, 383.

55 Ibid, 136, 315.

56 Sarah P Morris, *Daidalos and the Origins of Greek Art*, (Princeton, NJ: University of Princeton Pr, 1992), 136.

57 Mihail Bakhtin, *The Dialogic Imagination*, ed Michael Holquist; tr Caryl Emerson and Michael Holquist, (Austin, TX: U of Texas Pr, 1981).

58 "Archaeology: Troy and Heinrich Schliemann," Section 4 para 4, 2013 http://www.usu.edu/markdamen/1320Hist&Civ/chapters/04TROY.htm Accessed 9 December 2011.

59 Wim van Binsbergen, *Alternative Models of Intercontinental Interaction towards the Earliest Cretan Script, Black Athena: Ten Years After*, (Groningen, the Netherlands: Talanta, 1997).

60 Ibid, Bernal, 1990.

61 Wim van Binsbergen, *Black Athena Comes of Age*, (Münster, GR: Transaction Publishers. 2011), 3.

62 Ibid, Bernal, 1990.

63 Jean Berard, "Hyksos et la Legende d'Io Recherches sur la période premycenienne," *Syria*, tr by Robert Rasmussen. Paris, FR: Institut Francais du Proche-Orient..https://www.Hyksos%20et%20la%20Legende%20d'Io%20Recherches%20sur%20la%20période%20premycenienne.Berard69/ Accessed 12 October 2012.

64 Ibid.

65 Ibid, Morris, 1992.

66 Ibid, Astour 1967.

67 Johannes Haubold, "Berossus" in *The Romance between Greece and the East*, eds Tim Whitmarsh and Stuart Thomson, (Cambridge, UK: Cambridge U Pr, 2013), 105-116.

68 Earl Miner "That Literature is a Kind of Knowledge." 1976. *Critical Inquiry*, 487-502. 2/3; also see Josephe Bogen, 1977; Leonard Shlain, *Art versus Physics: Parallel Visions in Space, Time & Light*, (New York, NY: Wm. Morrow, 1991); Shlain, *The Goddess versus the alphabet: the Conflict between Word and Image*, (New York, NY: Penguin1998); Shlain, *Sex, Time, and Power*. (New York, NY: Viking, 2003), and Shlain, *Leonardo's Brain*, pending.

69 Ibid, Berard, 1952.

70 Ibid.

71 Smolo. Sand, *The Invention of the Land of Israel: from Holy Land to Homeland*. (London, UK: Verso, 2012), also see Smolo Sand, *The Invention of the Jewish People*, (London, UK: Verso, 2009).

72 "Passover Letter," from *Aramaic Papyri of the Fifth Century*, tr & ed by A. Crowley, (Oxford, UK: Oxford U Pr, 1923), 44-45. See also Bezalel Porten et al, "May the Gods Seek the Welfare of My Brothers," in *The Elephantine papyri in English: Three Millennia of Cross-Cultural Continuity and Change*, ed by D. N. Freedman, (New York, NY: Doubleday, 1996), 125-26.

73 Bezalel Porten, 1999. Review of "The Original Torah: The Political Intent of the Bible's Writers" by S. David Sperling, *Reappraisals in Jewish Social and Intellectual History. Hebrew Studies* 40, 292-96. "May the gods seek the welfare of my brothers" (Cowley 1923 [2005]:44-45; Porten et al, 1996:125-26).

Chapter Five

1 Herodotus. *The Histories, IV: 254-255*, tr Aubrey de Selincourt, 49 (Baltimore, MD: Penguin, 1965).

2 Theodore Gastor, *Thespis: Ritual, Myth and Drama in the Ancient Near East*, (New York, NY: Henry Schuman. 1950), 154, ft XIV.

3 Israel Finkelstein and Neil Asher Silberman, *The Bible Unearthed: Archaeologicaly's New Vision of Ancient Israel and the Origin of its Sacred Texts*, (New York, NY: Simon & Schuster, 2001). Also see Attwell and Ragobert, "The Bible Unearthed," History Channel 26 March 2009. http://www.amara.org/bg/videos/qyW3jUwc6YsO/info/the-bible-unearthed-history-channel-version-2009/ Accessed 8/28/12.

4 Ibid.

5 Ibid.

6 Yuval Peleg. *Biblical Archeology Review*, Emergent Press, vlmn. IIc: 2014.

7 Ibid.

8 Ibid, Friedman.

9 Smolo. Sand, *The Invention of the Land of Israel: from Holy Land to Homeland*, (London, UK: Verso, 2012), also see Smolo Sand, *The Invention of the Jewish People*, (London, UK: Verso, 2009). Also see Bezalel Porten, "Passover Letter," from *Aramaic Papyri of the Fifth Century*. ed & tr by A. Crowley, (Oxford, UK: Oxford U Pr, 1923), 44-45; the 1999. Review of "The Original Torah: The Political Intent of the Bible's Writers" by S. David Sperling, *Reappraisals in Jewish Social and Intellectual History. Hebrew Studies* 40, 292-96. "May the gods seek the welfare of my brothers" (Cowley 1923 [2005]:44-45; Porten et al. 1996:125-26).

10 Moore, Megan Bishop and Brad E. Kelle, *Biblical History and Israel's Past: The Changing Study of the Bible and History*, (Grand Rapids, MI: Wm B Eerdmans Publishing, 2011), 33.

11 Ian Provan and Kenneth Kitchen cited in Keith Whitelam's *The Invention of Ancient Israel: The Silencing of Palestinian History*. (London, UK: Routledge, 2013), 185.

12 Moore, Megan Bishop and Brad E. Kelle, *Biblical History and Israel's Past: The Changing Study of the Bible and History*, (Grand Rapids, MI: Wm B Eerdmans Publishing, 2011), 34.

13 Thomas L. Thompson, *The Historicity of the Patriarchal Narratives: The Quest for the Historical Abraham*, (Harrisburg, PA: Trinity Press International); John Van Seters, *Abraham in History and Tradition*, (New Haven, CT: Yale U Pr).

14 Moore, Megan Bishop and Brad E. Kelle, *Biblical History and Israel's Past: The Changing Study of the Bible and History*, (Grand Rapids, MI: Wm B Eerdmans Publishing, 2011), 18-20.

15 Robert Coote and Keith Whitlam, *The Emergence of Early Israel in Historical Perspective*, (Sheffield, UK: Almond Pr, 1987).

16 Moore, Megan Bishop and Brad E. Kelle, *Biblical History and Israel's Past: The Changing Study of the Bible and History*, (Wm B Eerdmans Publishing, 2011), 27-33.

17 Biblical Minimalism http://en.wikipedia.org/wiki/Biblical_Minimalism Accessed 5 May 2013.

18 Moore, Megan Bishop and Brad E. Kelle, *Biblical History and Israel's Past: The Changing Study of the Bible and History*, (Grand Rapids, MI: Wm B Eerdmans Publishing, 2011), 34-35.

19 N. P. Lemche, *The Israelites in History and Tradition*, (Sheffield, UK: JSOT Pr, 1998), 165–166.

20 Moore, Megan Bishop and Brad E. Kelle, *Biblical History and Israel's Past: The Changing Study of the Bible and History*, (Grand Rapids, MI: Wm B Eerdmans Publishing, 2011), 36.

21 Philip R. Davies, *In Search of Ancient Israel*, (Sheffield, UK: JSOT Pr, 1992).

22 Ibid.

23 Keith Whitelam, *"The Invention of Ancient Israel: The Silencing of Palestinian History*, (London, UK: Routledge, 1997).

24 Moore, Megan Bishop and Brad E. Kelle, *Biblical History and Israel's Past: The Changing Study of the Bible and History*, (Grand Rapids, MI: Wm B Eerdmans Publishing, 2011), 37.

25 Thomas L. Thompson, *The Mythic Past The Historicity: Biblical Archaeology and the Myth of Israel*, (New York, NY: Basic Books, 1999).

26 William Dever, *What Did The Biblical Writers Know and When Did They Know It?*, (Grand Rapids, MI: Wm B Eerdmans Publishing, 2001).

27 Kenneth Kitchen, *On the Reliability of the Old Testament*, (Grand Rapids, MI: Wm B Eerdmans Publishing, 2003).

28 Hurvitz, Avi, Bible Apologetics bibleapologetics.wordpress.com/tag/ "Apologetics, Bible archaeology, Bible historicity, Old Testament," 2009.

29 Moore, Megan Bishop and Brad E. Kelle, *Biblical History and Israel's Past: The Changing Study of the Bible and History*, (Grand Rapids, MI: Wm B Eerdmans Publishing, 2011), 38.

30 Moore, Megan Bishop and Brad E. Kelle, *Biblical History and Israel's Past: The Changing Study of the Bible and History*, (Grand Rapids, MI: Wm B Eerdmans Publishing, 2011), 39, 291.

31 Lester Grabbe, *Ancient Israel: What Do We Know and How Do We Know It?*, (Edinburgh, UK: T & T Clark, 2007).

32 Victor Matthews, *Studying the Ancient Israelites: A Guide to Sources and Methods*, (Chicago, IL: Baker Academic, 2007).

33 Hans Barstad, *History and the Hebrew Bible*, (Tübingen, GR: Mohr Siebeck, 2008).

34 K.L. Knoll, *Canaan and Israel in Antiquity*, (London, UK: Continuum, 2001).

35 Mario Liverani, *Israel's History and the History of Israel*, (Ithaca, NY: Cornell U Pr, Equinox Pr, 2005).

36 Moore, Megan Bishop and Brad E. Kelle, *Biblical History and Israel's Past: The Changing Study of the Bible and History,* (Grand Rapids, MI: Wm B Eerdmans Publishing, 2011), 39, 291.

37 Sarah P Morris, *Daidalos and the Origins of Greek Art,* (Princeton, NJ: University of Princeton Pr, 1992), 136.

38 Pindar, *The Olympian and Pythian Odes,* tr Basil Gildersleeve, (New York, NY: Persius, 1885), 4:11.

39 *Ibid*, Morris, 102.

40 John Steinbeck, *The Acts of King Arthur,* (New York, NY: Ballantine, 1976), 425.

41 Alexander Murray, *Reason and Society in the Middle Ages*, (Oxford, UK: Clarendon Pr, 1978), 148.

42 Ibid, Shlain, 1998.

43 Deborah Tarn Steiner, *The Tyrant's Writ: Myths and Images of Writing in Ancient Greece*, (Princeton, NJ: Princeton U Pr, 1994).

44 Berard, Jean. "Hyksos et la Legende d'Io Recherches sur la période premycenienne," *Syria*, tr by Robert Rasmussen. Paris, FR: Institut Francais du Proche-Orient. https://www.Hyksos%20et%20la%20Legende%20d'Io%20Recherches%20sur%20la%20période%20premycenienne.Berard69/ Accessed 12 October 2012.

45 Neil MacGregor, *A History of the World in 100 Objects*, (London, UK: Penguin, 2012), 88-93.

46 Otfried Müller *Comparative Philology*, Leipzig, 71, vol. I (Kekulé, *Das Leben Friedrich Gottlieb Welckers* 1828), 137.

47 Genesis 29:1; Judges 6: 3, 33; 7:12; 8:10; and Job 1:3.

48 Michael Wood, *In Search of the Trojan War,* (New York, NY: New American Library, 1985).

49 Otfried Müller *Comparative Philology*, Leipzig, 71, vol. I (Kekulé, *Das Leben Friedrich Gottlieb Welckers* 1828), 77-168.

50 Ibid, vol. I, 77.

51 Genesis, xxv. 15.

52 Genesis, xv. 19.

53 S. E. Lokovidis, *Mycenae-Epidaurus,* (Athens, GR: Ekdotike Athenson,1982), 49.

54 Ibid, Lokovidis, 1979, 14.

55 Katie Demakopoulou and Dora Konsola *"Archaeological Museum of Thebes,"* Translated by Helen Zigada. (Athens, Greece: General Direction of Antiquities & Restoration, 1981), 11.

56 Luis Buneul, *Land Without Bread,* movie in French, 1933.

57 DNA tests reveal Prince William's Indian ancestry http://www.cnn.com/2013/06/14/world/europe/britain-prince-william-india).

58 Richard Jude. Thompson,"The Deuteronomicstic Covenant and Neo-Assyrian Imperial Ideology: a Study of the Deuteronomistic History in Its Historical Contexts." PhD diss. (Harvard University, 2011).

59 Mehri Niknam, in Melvin Bragg's, "Muslim Spain." *In Our Time: BBC,* 21 September 2002. In Our Time. http://www.bbc.co.uk/programmes/p0054811 Accessed 5 March 2012.

60 Matthew 5-7.

61 Martin Bohl. Facebook: (June 3, 2013).

Chapter Six

1 Herodotus. *The Histories,* tr Aubrey de Selincourt, 49, (Baltimore, MD: Penguin, 1965), 122.

2 Walter Beltz, *God and the Gods: Myths of the Bible,* (New York, NY: Penguin, 1983), 3.

3 Manfred Bietak, *Amaris: the Capitol of the Hyksos,* Recent Excavations at Tell el Daba, (London, UK: British Museum, 1996), 41.

4 Jon-Christian Billigmeier, "Kadmos and the Possibility of a Semite Presence in Helladic Greece," PhD diss., (University of California at Santa Barbara, 1976), 89.

5 Manfred Bietak, *Avaris: the Capitol of the Hyksos,* Recent Excavations at Tell el: Daba, (London, UK: British Museum, 1996).

6 Ibid, 30.

7 Ibid, 31.

8 Sarah Morris, "The Legacy of *Black Athena,*" in *Black Athena Revisited,* eds Mary Lefkowitz and Cuy MacLean Rogers. (Chapel Hill, NC: U of N. Carolina Pr, 1996), 171.

9 Donald Redford, *Egypt, Canaan, and Israel in Ancient Times,* (Princeton, NJ: University of Princeton Press, 1992) 299.

10 Martin Bernal, *Black Athena: The Afroasiatic Roots of Classical Civilization. Vol. I: The Fabrication of Ancient Greece 1785–1994,* (London, UK: Free Association Books, 1987. Also see Martin Bernal, *Black Athena: The Afroasiatic Roots of Classical Civilization Vol. II: The Archaeological and Documentary Evidence,* (Durham, NC: Duke University Press, 1991); Martin Bernal, *Black Athena: The Afroasiatic Roots of Classical Civilization Vol. III: The Linguistic Evidence,* (New Brunswick, NJ: Rutgers University Press, 2006).

11 Smolo. Sand, *The Invention of the Land of Israel: from Holy Land to Homeland,* (London, UK: Verso, 2012), 81-89. For further investigation, see Patrick Geary, *The Myth of Nations: the Medieval Origins of Modern Europe,* (Princeton, NJ: University of Princeton Press, 2002).

12 Ibid, Morris.

13 Deborah Holland, *Venice and the East,* (New Haven, CN: Yale University Pr, 2000), 51-3.

14 Patrick Geary, *The Myth of Nations: the Medieval Origins of Modern Europe,* (Princeton, NJ: University of Princeton Press, 2002).

15 Michael C. Astour, *Hellenosemitica: An Ethnic and Cultural Study in West Semitic Impact on Mycenaean Greece*, (Leiden, The Netherlands: E. J. Brill, 1967, 2002).

16 Ibid, Geary, 2002.

17 Ibid, Astour, endnote 149, 391.

18 James P. Boyd, *Bible Dictionary*, 1995, http://www.amazon.com/Large-Dictionary-Concordance-Bibical-Reference/dp/B000BJOYCA. Ottenheimer Publishers 1958), 137. Accessed June 5, 2012.

19 Ibid, Billigmeier, 99.

20 Gen. 29:1; Judges 6: 3, 33; 7:12; 8:10; Job 1:3. Orthography: there is no "C" in Attic Greek; the "C" only appears in demonic or Byzantine Greek. No Greek letter other than "K" transliterates the Phoenician/Hebraic "qu."

21 Ibid, Billigmeier.

22 Parian Calendar (http://en.m.wikipedia.org/wiki/Parian_Chronicle. Also see Bernal, 1990, 124.

23 Martin Bernal, *Cadmean Letters: The Transmission of the Alphabet to the Aegean and Further West before 1400 B.C.*, (Winona Lake, WI: Eisenbrauns, 1990), 124.

24 "The Alphabet" Bragg In Our Time. BBC http://www.bbc.co.uk/programmes/p0054950.

25 Ibid, Billigmeier.

26 Ibid, Astour, 220-224.

27 Ibid, Astour, 142.

28 Ibid, Astour, 144.

29 Theodore Gastor, *Thespis: Ritual, Myth and Drama in the Ancient Near East*, (New York, NY: Henry Schuman. 1950), 231.

30 Ibid.

31 Adrian Curtius, *Ugarit: Ras Shamra*, (Grand Rapids, MI: Eerdmans, 1985), 47.

32 Ibid, 116.

33 Ibid, 118-121.

34 Ibid, Bernal, 1990, 128.

35 Ibid, Curius, 108.

36 Ibid, *Ugarit:* 109. Also see Ugarit Library www.logos.com/product/5765/Ugarit-library.

37 Ibid, (110). [104.3b + 65.11].

38 Ibid, Beltz, 22.

39 Ibid, Curius, 116.

40 Ibid, Astour, 128-138.

41 Ibid, Billigmeier, 99.

42 Leonard Shlain, *Sex, Time, and Power: How Women's Sexuality Shaped Human Evolution,* (New York, NY: Viking, 2003).

43 Sarah Morris, "The Legacy of *Black Athena,*" in *Black Athena Revisited,* eds Mary Lefkowitz and Cuy MacLean Rogers. (Chapel Hill, NC: U of N. Carolina Pr, 1996), 93. Gr. Chousor/ Kothar + Hephaestus/Hassis Ptah).

44 Michael Wood, *In Search of the Trojan War,* (NewYork, NY: New American Library, 1985).

45 Ibid, 175-79.

46 Jon-Christian Billigmeirer,. "Kadmos and the Possibility of a Semite Presence in Helladic Greece." PhD diss., (University of California at Santa Barbara, 1976), 93.

47 Ibid, 94.

48 T.S. Eliot, "East Coker V.", *Collected Poems,* (New York, NY: Harcourt Brace& Company, 1945), line 20.

49 Randall S. Barton 2013. "Triumph of Gilgamesh," *Reed Alumni Magazine,* Vol. 53. June, 2013, 5.

50 Ibid.

51 John Gardner, and John Maier, *Gilgamesh: Translated from the Sin-Leqi-Unninni Version,* with the assistance of Richard A. Henshaw, (New York, NY: Knopf, 1984).

52 Ibid.

53 Ibid, Tablet XI, Column ii, 233-34.

Chapter Seven

1 Plato, "Menexenus" *Dialogues of Plato,* tr B. Jowett, Vol. II, 245-246 (New York, NY: Random, 1892), 784.

2 Joel R. Primack & Nancy Ellen Abrams, *View from the Center of the Universe: Discovering Our Extraordinary Place in the Cosmos,* (New York, NY: Riverhead Books - Penguin, 2006),133-141, 156-166.

3 Matt Ridley, *The Rational Optimist,* (New York, NY: HarperCollins, 2010), 349-360.

4 "May This Never Happen Again." The "Bux/Mont Coalition for Peace Action" and "Hibakusha Stories" Groups, featuring Clifton Truman Daniel, Harry Truman's grandson; Setsuko Thurlow, a Hiroshima factory worker; and Yasuaki Yamashita, Nagasaki survivor Bucks County Community College: Oct. 16, 2012.

5 "45-Years of Asian American Studies, 2007: *www.aasc.ucla.edu/cab/200708230009.html*" 11/28/13).

6 Personal interview with Dave Middleton: Redding, CA, 7 May 2013.

7 Joseph O'Neill, *The Blood-Dark Track: A Family History,* (London, UK: Granta, 2001), 308-09.

8 Richard Bulliet, *A Case for an Islamic-Christian Civilization,* (New York, NY: Columbia U Pr, 2004), 45.

9 Patrick Geary, *The Myth of Nations: the Medieval Origins of Modern Europe,* (Princeton, NJ: University of Princeton Press, 2002).

10 Matthew Derrick, "Containing the Umma?: Islam and the Territorial Question. *Interdisciplinary Journal of Research on Religion*, (Waco, TX: Baylor U, 2013).

11 Smolo. Sand, *The Invention of the Land of Israel: from Holy Land to Homeland*, (London, UK: Verso, 2012), 63.

12 Ibid, 177-253.

13 *Song of Songs* 2.4-9.

14 "The Red Heifer" The Temple Institute, 1991-2013: www.templeinstitute.org/red_heifer/original_ashes.htm.

15 Ibid, Sand, 2012, 27.

16 Ibid, 55.

17 Terry Eagleton, *Reason, Faith, and Revolution: Reflections on the God Debate*, (New Haven, CN: Yale U Pr, 2009).

18 Ibid.

19 John Raines "Gulen Charter Schools Truth," http://gulenchartertruth.blogspot.com/2011/04/gulen-inspired-schools-promote-learning.html.

20 Tamin Ansary, *Destiny Disrupted: A History of the World Through Islamic Eyes*, (San Francisco, CA: Public Affairs, 2010).

21 Geddes. MacGregor, *The Bible in the Making*, (Washington DC: University Pr, 1959).

22 Amin Maalouf, *The Crusades through Arab Eyes*, (London, UK: al Saqi, 1984), 37-55.

23 Stephen O'Shea, *The Prefect Heresy: The Revolutionary Life and Death of the Medieval Cathars*, (London, UK: Walker, 2000).

24 Maria Rosa Menocal, *The Arabic Role in Medieval Literary History*, (Philadelphia, PA: U of Penn Pr, 1987), 48. Also see Menocal, *The Ornament of the World: How Muslims, Jews, and Chistians Created a Culture of Tolerance in Medieval Spain*, (Boston, MA: Little, Brown, & Co, 2002), 178-81. Also see Asin Palacio, Miguel, *Islam in the Divine Comedy*, tr Harold Sunderland, as pertaining to Abul ala al-Maarri (New York, NY: E. P. Dutton & Co, 1926), 33-3 & 248-256.

25 Asin Palacio, Miguel, *Islam in the Divine Comedy*, tr Harold Sunderland, (New York, NY: E. P. Dutton & Co, 1926), 55-71 & 55-67 as pertaining to Abul ala al Maarri (d. 1058 CE), and 44-54, to Al Arabi (d.1240).

26 "Israili-Palestinian Conflict: Pros and Cons (Chart III). http://israelpalestinian.procon.org/view.resource.php?resourceID=000636

27 Ibid, Sand, 2012. For further analysis read Edward Said, *Culture and Imperialism*, (New York, NY:Vintage, 1994).

28 Wade Faith, (2009: back cover blurb There must be a deliberative peace-making "basis for a rich dialogue between biology, social science and religious history."

29 (Ibid 1).[24] This rational discussion needs to be purposeful in discovering, Campbell, Herodotus, and Saint Thomas Aquinas-like, the real connections between evolutionary psychology, genetics and anthropology to reach an essential "turning point, and advancement, in the science-religion debate."

30 Bill Hotchkiss, "Climb to the High Country," (New York, NY: W.W. Norton, 1978), 12.

31 Joshua Greene, *Moral Tribes,* (New York, NY: Penguin Press, 2013), back cover.

32 Carrie Brown, "Listening to the Majestic Silence of Visual Art," 2013, *www.GlimmerTrain.com* 22 12/13 issue.

33 Ibid, Greene.

34 Ibid.

35 Ibid.

36 Ibid, 204.

37 Ibid, 206.

38 Marina Warner, *Six Myths: Managing Monsters,* The Reith Lectures 1994, (London, UK: Vintage), 6-10; also see Duarte Mimosa-Ruiz, "Medea" in *Companion to Literary Myths, Heroes, and Archetypes,* ed Pierre Brunel, (London, UK: Routledge, 1992), 769-778.

39 A Dream of Passion. Directed by Jules Dassin. http://en.wikipedia.org/wiki/A_Dream_of_Passion.

40 Rachael Havrelock in *River Jordan: the Mythology of a Dividing Line,* (Chicago, IL: the U of Chicago, 2011).

41 Ibid, 8-12.

42 Ibid, 17-40.

43 Richard Jude. Thompson,"The Deuteronomicstic Covenant and Neo-Assyrian Imperial Ideology: a Study of the Deuteronomistic History in Its Historical Contexts." PhD diss. (Harvard University, 2011), 114-157.

44 Ibid, Beltz, 24.

45 Ibid, Havrelock, 20, 23, 31.

46 Ibid, Beltz, 25.

47 Ibid, Havrelock, 277.

48 Ibid, Havrelock, 275-90.

49 Ibid, Havrelock, 284.

50 Lennon, John and Paul McCartney. "The Beatles" "We Can Work It Out/Day Tripper," 45 single, two sides. Capital Records:1965).

51 Ibid, Maalouf, 1984, 37-55.

52 Geraldine Heng, *Empire of Magic: Medieval Romance and the Politics of Cultural Fantasy,* (New York, NY: Columbia U. Pr, 2003), 17.

53 Smolo. Sand, *The Invention of the Land of Israel: from Holy Land to Homeland,* (London, UK: Verso, 2012).

54 Maria Rosa Menocal, *Shards of Love: Exile and the Origins of the Lyric,* (Durham, NC: Duke U Pr, 1994). Also see Maria Rosa Menocal, *The Arabic Role in Medieval Literary History,* (Philadelphia, PA: U of Penn Pr, 1987), 48. Also see Menocal, *The Ornament of the World: How Muslims, Jews, and Chistians Created a Culture of Tolerance in Medieval Spain,* (Boston, MA: Little, Brown, & Co, 2002), 178-81.

55 Chris Lowney, *A Vanished World: Medieval Spain's Golden Age of Enlightenment*, (New York, NY: Free Pr, 2005), 29-42.

56 Andre Gide, *Travels in the Congo*, (New York, NY: HarperCollins, 2000).

57 Lui Binyan, "An Unnatural Disaster," tr Perry Link, *New York Review of Books*, 8 April 1993, http://www.nybooks.com/articles/archives/1993/apr/08/an-unnatural-disaster/.

58 James Moffett, *Teaching the Universe of Discourse*, (Montclair, VT: Heinneman, 1968).

59 Ibid, Lowney, 43-54.

60 Norbu 2008: "Treasures of the Sand—The Legacy of Danzan Ravjaa" www.tibetan.museum.society.org.

61 Ibid.

62 Norbu "Treasures of the Sand—The Legacy of Danzan Ravjaa" 2008: www.tibetan.museum.society.org.

63 Ibid, Norbu.

64 Ibid.

65 Ibid.

Acknowledgements

We want to especially thank Professor Matthew Derrick, of the Department of Geography, Humboldt State University, for his maps that designate by fonts those 2nd Millennium cities, peoples, and nations from 1st Millennium BCE. We also deeply appreciate for his translations Dr Bob Rasmussen, of the Biology at Humboldt State University. Many thanks to Dr Patricia Engle for her deep teachings about Time concepts, on cross-cultural communication, for her peace-making tip on the melted knives in "Treasures of the Sand—The Legacy of Danzan Ravjaa," and for her ongoing Bucks County Peace Center volunteerism.

Index

Al-
Al-Andalusia, 59, 92, 111, 118, 161

A

Aeschylus, 17, 24, 30, 32, 51, 68, 78, 84, 87, 104, 115, 119, 123, 135
Alphabet, 9, 17, 20, 23-25, 32, 37, 39, 51-54, 56, 66-67, 69, 72-75, 77-82, 84, 86-87, 94, 103-104, 106-108, 113-115, 119-122, 124-126, 129-130, 135, 143, 167, 172, 178, 180-181, 183-184, 190
Archaeological proof, 17, 21, 23, 27, 31, 38, 52-54, 56, 60, 72-80, 82-83, 89, 104-105, 109, 114, 119-120, 124, 129-130, 166, 172, 182-184, 188
Aurebach, Erich, 161
Avignon, 47

B

Baal, 9, 36-38, 62, 66, 88, 96, 109, 123, 125-126, 128, 138, 169, 171-172, 174, 179, 181, 183, 189, 191
Barstad, Hans, 102, 188
Bakhtin, Mikhail, 19-20, 24, 30, 44, 46, 51-53, 57, 62-63, 65-66, 68, 70-71, 80, 90, 99, 112, 115, 122, 130, 150, 159, 173
Berard, Jean, 62, 71, 83-87, 89, 105-106, 109, 123, 178, 181, 185, 188
Bernal, Martin, 30, 37, 39-40, 63, 66, 79, 81-82, 86, 116-117, 119-120, 123; 139, 174, 177-178, 183-185, 189-191
Bible (Holy Bible), 3, 6-7, 17-18, 20-22, 24-25, 28-30, 32-36, 39-40, 46, 49-50, 52-53, 55-56, 58, 60-61, 64, 67-72, 75, 80-81, 84, 87-94, 97-104, 106-108, 113, 115-116, 119-120, 122, 124-126, 129, 131-133, 136, 147, 150-156, 169-171, 174, 177-180, 184-190, 192, 204
Bible Maps, 32-33, 84, 94, 97, 129, 151-154, 170, 180, 184
Biblical myths, 19-21, 29-32, 34, 37-38, 41, 48, 50, 53-56, 60, 67, 70-71, 73, 78, 81, 84, 87-88, 92-93, 95, 98-99, 106-107, 109, 114-115, 118, 121-122, 124, 128, 131-132, 136-137, 145-146, 150, 156, 161, 163, 166, 169, 172-173, 179

C

Cadmean Letters, 39, 73, 82, 120, 124, 178, 184, 190
Cadmean Thebes in Boeotia, 119
Cadmus, 17, 20, 23-25, 32, 37, 51-54, 69, 73, 75, 77-82, 84, 86-87, 94, 103-104, 106-108, 113-115, 119-122, 124-126, 129-130, 135, 143, 167, 172, 180, 183-184
Campbell, Joseph, 19, 21, 43, 48, 62, 87, 124, 131-132, 134, 146, 192
Cathars, 144, 155-156, 158, 160
Code of Hammurabi, 42, 44-45, 60, 166, 173, 179
Commandments, 17, 20-21, 23-32, 35-39, 44, 46, 50-53, 56-64, 67-68, 70, 76, 78, 82-84, 87-88, 91, 94-95, 97-99, 102-105, 107-109, 111, 113, 115-116, 121-126, 128, 130-132, 137, 141, 145, 151, 153, 168-171, 173-175, 177, 180, 185-186, 188, 190
Commedia, 44, 65-66, 143, 145, 147, 171
Crusades, 118, 157, 176, 192
Cult of Continuity, 9-10, 17, 23, 31, 63-69, 143, 149, 156, 160, 163, 176
Cylinder seals, 54, 74-76, 105-106, 120, 183-184

D

Danaus, 17, 24, 27, 32, 34, 51, 68, 78, 84, 87, 94, 99, 104, 106, 109, 115, 119, 122-123, 151, 135, 66, 203
Darwin, Charles, 32, 35, 132, 135, 148, 173
Davies, Philip, 52, 98-101, 179, 187
Debt to grandchildren, 34, 135-136, 138, 140, 142, 151, 162-163
Descartes, 25
Dhimmi, 143
Dinah, 20-21, 27-28, 30-31, 34-36, 39, 44-45, 53, 55, 59, 62-64, 67, 69-71, 81, 84,

87-90, 92-95, 107-108, 110, 112, 114-115, 118, 121-122, 124, 129, 151-154, 156, 167
Dostoyevsky, Fyodor, 60

E

Early Jewish cities, 9, 15, 28, 30, 48, 53, 58, 61, 66, 77, 84, 92, 94-97, 101, 109, 136, 141, 144-145, 147, 151-153, 155-156, 159-161, 171
Earth life, 47-48, 135-136, 163, 191, 194
Egypt, 9, 13, 19-21, 23, 25, 27-28, 30-31, 35-40, 42, 44, 50-55, 58, 61-63, 68-71, 73-79, 81-89, 92, 94, 104-107, 109-110, 113-115, 118-119, 121-123, 128-129, 147, 152, 168-170, 172, 174-177, 179, 181, 184, 189
Eshcol, Levi, 140, 146
Emperor Charlemagne, 22, 24-25, 55, 92, 104, 117, 155-157, 159, 175-176, 188
Esther, 6, 19-20, 30, 34, 111, 170, 193
Exodus, 19-21, 29-32, 34, 37-38, 41, 48, 50, 53-56, 60, 67, 70-71, 73, 78, 81, 84, 87-88, 92-93, 95, 99, 106-107, 109, 114-115, 118, 121-122, 124, 128, 136-137, 145-146, 150, 156, 161, 163, 166, 172
Ezra, Nehemiah, 84, 97, 151-154

F

Female, 34, 62, 73, 75, 83-87, 94, 109, 110, 115, 119, 123, 151, 178, 181, 183, 185, 188
Finkelstein, Israel, 93, 119, 185-186
Freud, Sigmund, 20-21, 29-35, 37-38, 45, 49, 53-55, 62, 67, 70-71, 87-89, 91, 93, 95, 106-107, 114-115, 122, 128, 135, 140, 152, 167-169, 178, 181

G

Gardner, John, 49, 115, 130-132, 173, 191
Gastor, Theodore, 9, 20-21, 25-27, 29, 31-32, 35-38, 53, 59, 62, 66-67, 75-76, 78, 81, 84, 87, 93-94, 99, 103-104, 106-109, 113-115, 121-126, 128, 141, 152-153, 168, 174-177, 179, 181, 186, 188-190
Geary, Patrick, 23, 119, 176, 189-191
Genesis, 21, 24, 34, 38-39, 52, 56, 82, 94, 98-99, 115, 121, 123, 148, 152-153, 173, 177, 182, 188
Geniza, 88

Genre Theory, 7, 23-24, 38, 46, 63, 69, 84-86, 91, 121, 139, 145, 150-151, 155, 159, 161-162
Gordon, Cyrus, 20-21, 27, 28, 30, 32, 32, 34-36, 38-40, 44-45, 50, 53, 55, 59, 62-64, 67, 69-71, 73, 81-82, 84-85, 87-90, 92-95, 103-104, 106-108, 110, 112-115, 118, 120-122, 124, 129, 151-154, 156, 166-167, 170
Grammar, 17, 20-21, 23-28, 30, 32, 35, 39, 44, 46, 50-53, 56-64, 67-68, 70, 82, 87-88, 91, 94-95, 97-99, 102-103, 107-109, 111, 115-116, 122-124, 126, 130-132, 137, 141, 145, 151, 153, 168-171, 173-175, 177, 180, 185-186, 188
Greek dramatists, 17, 24, 29-30, 58, 72, 75-76, 88, 115, 123, 150, 155, 182-183
Greene, Joshua, 46, 134, 137, 148, 155, 193

H

Havrelock, Rachael, 34, 53, 61, 72, 87, 93-95, 114, 118, 150-152, 154, 170, 193
Heng, Geraldine, 155, 180, 193
Herodotus, 9, 31, 33-34, 44, 69, 73, 77, 84-86, 116, 120, 124, 171, 183-184
Hiroshima, Japan, 50, 136, 138-139, 147, 179, 191
Historical validity, 61, 87-88, 169
History, 19-23, 25, 28, 30, 32, 35, 37-39, 42-45, 51-52, 54, 58, 63-64, 73, 75, 78, 80-81, 84-86, 88-89, 97, 101-102, 106, 109, 111, 114-117, 119-120, 122, 124-125, 130-132, 136, 139, 147, 150-153, 155, 160, 167, 169-170, 173, 175, 177, 183, 185-187, 189-191
Hittites, 27, 29, 35, 51, 76, 113, 115, 118, 121, 129, 168, 181
Homer, 20, 37, 123, 151, 172, 184
Hotchkiss, Bill, 63, 147. 181, 193
Hussein, Saddam, 19, 41-42, 47, 49, 74, 90, 131, 147, 159, 173, 175
Hyksos, Canaanites, 7, 19-27, 29-32, 34, 36-42, 45, 48, 50-58, 61-64, 66-84, 86-90, 92-94, 97, 101, 103-111, 113-120, 122-124, 128-130, 132-133, 136-137, 142, 150-156, 160, 166-169, 172, 174, 176-178, 181, 183, 185, 188-189

I

Institutional memory, 6, 24, 30-31, 38,

198 BIBLICAL TIME OUT OF MIND

51-52, 56, 59-61, 63, 71, 77-79, 84-85, 87, 92-93, 96-97, 114-116, 118-122, 125, 129, 132-133, 140, 143, 148, 150, 155, 159-160, 203
Israel and Judea, 20, 28, 35, 51, 80, 89, 91, 102, 116, 122, 153, 175-176, 181, 187

J

Jeffers, Robinson, 18, 21-22, 34, 40, 44-48, 50, 57-58, 79, 134-135, 137-138, 175, 180
Jerusalem, 9, 15, 20, 28, 30, 35, 41, 43, 47-48, 51, 60, 65-66, 79-80, 88-89, 91, 95-96, 102, 116, 122, 130, 136-137, 139-141, 143-147, 153, 168, 175-176, 181, 187, 192
Jesus, 112, 116, 142
Jewish boundaries, 41-42, 53, 61, 93-95, 121, 140, 151-152, 154, 170
Jewish monotheism, 93
Josephus, 21, 31, 36, 63-71, 150, 175, 182
Joshua, 106-108, 121-122, 148, 152, 193

K

King Arthur, 24, 104, 155-156, 188
King David, 20, 28-30, 34-36, 46, 53, 71, 89, 99, 153-154, 168, 179-180, 182-183, 186
King Josiah, 29, 33, 37, 45, 47-48, 60-61, 64, 81, 92, 95-97, 109, 124, 126, 128, 133, 135, 137, 141, 143, 149, 151-152, 159, 161-162, 171-172, 192, 203
King Solomon, 9, 26-30, 41, 43, 47-48, 53, 60, 65-66, 71, 79, 81, 87-89, 91, 95-96, 110, 126, 130, 136-137, 139-141, 143-147, 153-154, 168, 177, 192
Krebs, Christopher B., 23, 176, 189, 191
Kylix, 17, 32, 37-38, 41, 53, 78, 94, 103, 106-107, 115, 120-123, 125, 129, 143, 180, 183

L

Leviathan, 9, 19-21, 27, 29, 34-35, 38, 43, 47-48, 55, 59-60, 65-68, 70-73, 75, 77, 79, 81, 84, 91-93, 95-96, 104, 107, 114-115, 123-128, 142, 145, 153, 155-156, 158-159, 170, 174, 178, 189, 192

M

Maier, John, 49, 115, 130-132, 173, 191

Memory, 21, 32, 46, 56, 59-61, 63, 68, 77-79, 84, 90, 92-93, 96-97, 99, 101, 113-116, 118-122, 125, 129, 133, 146, 148, 150-151, 153, 160, 163, 179, 186, 192
Memory theory, 21-22, 30, 32, 38, 46, 56, 59, 61, 63, 68, 71, 77-79, 84-85, 87, 90, 92-93, 96-97, 99, 101, 113-116, 118-122, 125, 129, 133, 140, 146, 148, 150-151, 153, 159-160, 163, 179, 186, 191-192, 203
Merneptah stele, 20-21, 23, 27-31, 34-36, 39, 44-46, 53, 55, 59, 62-64, 67-71, 81, 84, 87-90, 92-95, 107-108, 110-112, 114-115, 118, 121-122, 124, 129, 132, 140, 144-146, 151-154, 156, 158, 167-168, 171, 175-176, 181, 192-193
Metallurgy, 6, 18, 37-38, 51, 62, 92, 95, 101, 104, 157, 167-168, 172, 175, 201
Mheallaigh, Karen Ni, 21, 31, 36, 63-71, 150, 175, 181-182
Minoan art, 73, 76, 174
Morris, Sarah, 17, 20, 23-25, 32, 37, 51-54, 69, 73, 75, 77-82, 84, 86-87, 94, 103-104, 106-108, 113-115, 117, 119-122, 124-126, 128-130, 135, 143, 167, 172, 174, 180, 182-185, 188-189, 191
Moses, 9, 13, 19-21, 23, 25, 27-28, 30-31, 34-40, 42, 44, 50-55, 58, 61-63, 68-71, 73-79, 81-89, 92-95, 104-107, 109-110, 113-115, 118-119, 121-123, 128-129, 147, 151-152, 154, 168-170, 172, 174-177, 179, 181, 184, 189, 193
Muslims in Europe, 17, 24, 38, 52, 60, 92, 116, 118-119, 145, 161, 171, 180, 189, 192-194

N

Names, 35, 78, 80, 85, 104, 119, 122
Nationalism, 25, 39, 63, 111, 119, 134, 141-142, 155-156, 176

P

Parian Chronicle, 20, 25, 38, 54, 59, 64, 73, 78, 99-100, 102, 120, 167, 171, 183, 190
Peace, 6, 22, 26, 37, 40, 42-43, 46, 50, 52, 56-57, 63, 68, 71, 90, 92, 95, 103, 112-117, 123, 125, 133, 135-136, 138, 141-143, 147, 151, 154, 157, 161-163, 179, 191, 195, 200, 202, 204
Perry, Milman, 20, 57, 63-65, 71, 81, 93,

99, 175, 181, 194, 202-204
Phineas, 37, 53, 78, 80-81, 103, 106-107, 121-123
Phoenix, 17, 29, 32, 37-38, 41, 53, 78, 83, 86, 94, 103, 105-107, 113, 115, 120-123, 125, 129, 143, 176, 180, 183-184
Polytheism, 30
Porten, Bezalel, 39, 88, 186
Pyrgi Tablets, 9-10, 17, 20, 23, 31, 38, 63-69, 75, 81, 93, 114, 123-126, 143, 156, 160, 176

Q
Quran (Holy Quran), 116

R
Race, 23, 31, 38, 53, 64, 76, 84, 86, 101, 103, 109, 142, 152, 176, 178, 184, 191
Rehoboam, 61, 87-88, 169
Religious fundamentalism, 19, 21, 23-24, 28, 39, 59, 61, 64, 67-70, 83, 86, 88-89, 91-97, 100-103, 107, 110-111, 116-117, 119, 121, 125-126, 136-137, 139-141, 143-145, 147, 151-153, 155, 157-161, 169, 174, 176, 179-181, 185-186, 189
Rhind Math Papyrus, 7, 19-27, 29-32, 34, 36-42, 45, 48, 50-58, 61-64, 66-67, 69-84, 86-90, 92-94, 97, 101, 103-111, 113-115, 117-120, 122-124, 128-130, 133, 136-137, 142, 150, 154, 160, 166-169, 172, 174, 176-178, 181, 183, 185, 188-189

S
Sand, Smolo, 23, 39, 97, 140, 157, 176, 185-186, 189, 192-193
Sargon II, 36, 42, 44, 47-49, 59, 100, 131-132, 152, 173, 179
Script, 17, 42, 67, 74, 108, 122, 124, 132, 173
Sea Peoples, 9, 13, 19-21, 23, 25-32, 35-40, 42, 44, 50-55, 58-59, 61-63, 66-71, 73-79, 81-89, 92, 94, 103-107, 109-110, 113-115, 118-119, 121-126, 128-129, 147, 152, 168-170, 172, 174-177, 179, 181-182, 184-185, 189-190
Shelley, Percy Bysshe, 42, 46-48, 179
Silberman, Neil Asher, 93, 185-186
Sperling, David, 46, 89, 91, 97-99, 103, 179, 186-187

syllogism, 133

T
Thasos, 17, 32, 37-38, 41, 53, 78, 94, 103, 106-107, 115, 120-123, 125, 143, 180, 183
Thebes, Egypt, 17, 23, 31, 38, 52-54, 56, 60, 72-80, 82, 104, 109, 114, 119-120, 124, 129-130, 166, 172, 182-184, 188
Thebes, Greece, 17, 23, 31, 38, 52-56, 60, 72-80, 82, 104, 109, 113-114, 119-120, 124, 129-130, 166, 172, 182-184, 188
Theory of the Commons, 71, 112, 125, 129, 141-142, 144, 146, 148, 163, 180, 200
Thompson, Richard Jude, 30, 91, 95-96, 121, 152
Time Out of Mind, 3, 6-7, 18, 24, 34, 43, 45, 47, 57, 111, 119, 125, 133, 135, 150, 204

U
Ulu Burun wreck, 37, 54, 168, 174, 178, 180
Utilitarianism, 149-150, 160

W
Weaponry, 29-30, 39, 48, 50, 53, 62, 75-76, 92, 108-109, 114, 128, 136, 156, 179, 184

Y
Yahweh, 20, 28, 33-35, 38, 51, 62, 80, 88-89, 91, 93, 95-96, 102, 108, 115-116, 121-122, 125-126, 147, 153, 169, 175-176, 181, 187

Authors

Tom Gage
A life-long peace activist, Gage's first year at Berkeley led to the initiative "Place a Freedom Fighter in Greek Houses." In 1958, this resulted in many Hungarian student refugees, quarantined at New Jersey's Camp Kilmer, resuming studies when adopted by fraternities and sororities. Subsequently, he participated in Robert Pincus' "Turn Toward Peace Nuclear Disarmament" and participated in the earliest Anti-Viet Nam protest before his 1961 graduation.

The academic year of 1958–59, Gage stopped out of Berkeley to sojourn half way around the world, initially inspired to join a kibbutz in the decade-old state of Israel but after entry realized the incongruity of media portrayal and reality. He has served as dean and director of academic programs abroad, including the Aegean School of Classical Studies. Since 2010, he has chaired the Youth Platform, an international writing contest for high school students, sponsored by Houston's Gülen Institute. Derived from his Berkeley PhD dissertation, this project has brought more than a hundred student winners, with chaperones, among the thousands of competing authors to an award assembly in Congress, with tours of historical sites and universities around Washington, DC.

In 1983-84 Gage was Senior Fulbright Scholar in American Studies at Syria's Aleppo University. He is also a charter member on the board of directors of the Consultants for Global Programs, a California NEO in its second decade of international programs. He has run in-service training of writing teachers in Athens, Istanbul, and Nanning, China. In Athens in 1984, teachers attended from schools from Morocco to Bangladesh. Since the 1960s, he has been a member of the sixty-four-year-old Fall Asilomar English Conference, where he chaired the 2006 "Inhabiting and Expanding the Common Ground," featuring several Arab and Turkish presenters. In 2015, he chaired "James Moffett, Educational Prophet: Education for Global Dialogue, Wide Awakeness and Service to Life"; this conference, held at Estes Park, Colorado, was the annual national gathering of the Assembly for Expanded Perspectives on Learning of the National Council of Teachers of English. He lives with his wife in rural Northern California where they raise champion Irish Setters.

Other Books
by Tom Gage

Gülen's Dialogue on Education: a Caravanserai of Ideas (Cune Press, Seattle, WA: 2014).
American Prometheus: Captain Bill Jones, the Steel Genius who Made Andrew Carnegie (Apple iBook, 2012).

James A. Freeman
Born in Montreal, Canada, and a graduate of Shasta College, Reed College, and Humboldt State University, James A. Freeman is a transplanted northern Californian, who, for thirty-three years, has taught English at Bucks County Community College in Newtown, Pa.

Extensively published in composition theory and in critical thinking, he has since 1981 attended many professional conferences, often presenting on student engagement. Also a veteran creative writer and an editor, Freeman is the author of twenty books, including a new textbook: *English Composition II, Best Practices: American Literature and Culture Theme,* (2015 BVT Publishers). Freeman's fiction titles include the children's book *Lady* and *Sierra's Storage Shed Summer,* (2014 bn.com, amazon.com); the story collection *Irish Wake Illustrated: Celebrating Life While Still Living It,* (2014 amazon.com, bn.com and googlebooks.com); the historical novel *Ishi's Journey,* (Naturegraph 2006, 1992); the novel *Parade of Days* (2005 Xlibris); and the novel *Never the Same River Twice,* (1995 with Phyllis Agins—Charles B. McFadden Co).

An advocate of peace since his days of hiding under elementary school desks during early 1960's fallout drills, Jim lives in Langhorne, Pa with his family, traveling as often as he can to see his parents and his three siblings, near their northern California mountains and rivers. Jim would like to note, however, that the mid-Atlantic is his home, his adopted *patria*, and that he deeply appreciates both American coasts and the heartland in between. He is likewise a proponent of world travel, having lived in Japan for three years in the 1960's, and is a firm believer in the universal and uniting power of human empathy and of talk story.

Writing of James Freeman's *Ishi's Journey* as his "Editor's Pick" in Jan, 2006, the *Philadelphia Inquirer's* Books Editor, Frank Wilson, captured Freeman's writing grace and style best: "This is a wise and wonderful book . . . If *Ishi* does not occasionally make you smile and more often move you to tears, then you may be in need of a heart transplant."

Other Books
James A. Freeman
English Composition II, Best Practices: American Literature and Culture Theme. (BTV Editions, 2015 Redding, CA).
Lady and Sierra's Storage Shed Summer (Sept., 2014, America Star Books, www.amazon.com, www.bn.com).
Irish Wake Illustrated: Celebrating Life While Still Living It (Oct. 2014, America Star Books, www.amazon.com, www.bn.com).
Temporary Roses Dipped in Liquid Gold (Poetry, Finishing Line Press 2013).
Irish Wake: In Loving Memory of Us All (short stories, Publish America 2011).
Liars' Tales of True Love (spin-off of the previous novel below, Publish America 2007, amazon.com, bn.com).
Parade of Days (novel, Xlibris, 2005, amazon.com, bn.com).
Ishi's Journey from the Center to the Edge of the World (faction novel, reissued 2006, Naturegraph Publishers, 1992, bn.com, amazon.com).
Never the Same River Twice (novel with Phyllis Carol Agins, Charles B. McFadden Co, 1995, bn.com, amazon.com).
Sins of the Father, Sins of the Son (stories and poems, Northwoods Press, 1997).
Death Threats, Short and Long (stories, Northwoods Press, 1994).
The Rising Cost of Getting By, Editor (anthology of poems and short stories, Northwoods Press, 1989).
Broken Things, Fixed Things (poems, Dan River Press, 1988).
Hidden Agenda (stories and poems, Conservatory of American Letters, 1987).
Fever Dreams (stories and poems, Adams Press, 1985).
Glyphs of Tehama (novella, Garall Press 1985).

Tom Gage   **James A. Freeman**

Tom Gage is an emeritus professor from Humboldt State University who hitch-hiked through Damascus, Syria in 1959 and returned in 1983 to teach at Aleppo University on a Fullbright scholarship. His specialty is the study of higher education and his wide-ranging intellectual interests have brought him back to the Middle East many times.

James A. Freeman is a professor of Language & Literature based in Newtown, Pa. He is a prolific writer, editor, and an expert on composition theory. He is featured as James Andrew Freeman in www.contemporary authors.com.

Both men count themselves as peace advocates. *Biblical Time Out of Mind* is a scholarly romp that brings the verve of two academic outsiders to the dusty field of Biblical scholarship and Near Eastern history and emerges with a compelling argument for peace.

Comment on Other Books by the Authors
If [*Ishi's Journey* by James A. Freeman] doesn't occassionally make you smile and move you to tears, then you may be in need of a heart transplant. This is a wise and wonderful book."
—*Philadelphia Inquirer*

Gulen's Dialogue on Education by Tom Gage is a sweeping work that recalls the achievements of the West's great educational thinkers.
—Dr Paul M. Rogers (George Mason University)

www.cunepress.info/btom

www.ingramcontent.com/pod-product-compliance
Lightning Source LLC
Chambersburg PA
CBHW070535170426
43200CB00011B/2434